Arlott and Trueman on Cricket

'I tell you it will never catch on'

Arlott and Trueman
on Cricket

Edited by Gilbert Phelps

British Broadcasting Corporation

This book accompanies the BBC Further Education
Television programmes, **Arlott and Trueman
on Cricket,** first shown on BBC2 at 7.05 pm
on Mondays, starting on 11 April 1977 and repeated on BBC1 at 10.00 am on the following
Saturdays.

Series produced by Gordon Croton

Published to accompany a series of programmes
prepared in consultation with the BBC Further
Education Advisory Council.

This book is set in Monotype Old Style
Printed and bound in Great Britain by
Morrison & Gibb Ltd, London and Edinburgh

Cover photograph and photographs on pages
9 and 201 by Peter Pugh Cooke

© John Arlott, Fred Trueman, Gilbert Phelps
and the British Broadcasting Corporation 1977
First published 1977
Published by the British Broadcasting Corporation
35 Marylebone High Street, London W1M 4AA

ISBN 0 563 16115 9

Contents

John Arlott

Joined the BBC in 1945 as a talks and poetry producer and began regular cricket commentaries in 1946. Has broadcast during every Test series in England since then and on MCC tours abroad. Cricket correspondent of *The Guardian*. Author of more than thirty cricket books as well as books of verse and other topics.

Fred Trueman

Yorkshire and England. Played first class cricket for twenty years—far beyond the fast bowler's normal allotted span—and became the first man in the history of cricket to take 300 wickets in Test Matches. Noted for pungent turn of phrase as BBC radio commentator and cricket journalist.

Gilbert Phelps

Novelist, literary critic, historian and at one time a BBC producer. He is a life-long follower of cricket—especially of the fortunes of his home county, Gloucestershire—and has been an avid reader of the literature of the game for as long as he can remember.

David Frith

Has edited *The Cricketer* since 1972. Author and editor of several books including biographies of A. E. Stoddart and Archie Jackson, a history of fast bowling (*The Fast Men*), and *England versus Australia: A Pictorial History of the Test Matches Since 1877*.

Introduction

Devotees of cricket aren't likely to demand any explanation for the appearance of yet another book about the game. They are prepared to devour almost anything that's written on the subject. For them, familiar facts, figures and performances are no more of a deterrent than meeting old friends, or hearing the refrain of some age-old ballad. Even the inevitable omissions—great games which *ought* to have been mentioned, cricketing areas which *should* have been covered, great players who *ought* to have been featured—will be meaningful to them. Disappointment or indignation will themselves stir memory and imagination, bridging the gaps and peopling the voids. In any case, a glimpse of the names of John Arlott and Freddie Trueman on the dust-jacket will provide all the assurances they need that they can count on stimulus, expertise, first-hand experience and considered reflection.

But even a largely captive audience won't object if such a book has some specific aim, especially if one of them is to capture—or, rather, captivate—those who are new to the game or who need convincing that it's worth thinking about. For instance this book sets out to relate cricket to its historical and social contexts, and to give to the old cliché that cricket isn't only a game but also an institution more substance than it sometimes receives. This is the exploration that John Arlott undertakes in his opening contribution, and it would be difficult to envisage anybody better qualified for it, in knowledge or understanding, or in breadth of imaginative response.

It is a commonplace of criticism that the abstract and the concrete must co-exist and intermingle. John Arlott himself, of course, writes from a vast body of experience; but if there isn't much that he doesn't know about cricket in all its social and atmospheric implications, neither is there much about its practicalities and techniques that can have escaped Freddie Trueman. With his remarkable powers of recall, moreover, he can re-create in detail all the games in which he has ever played. To read his contribution is not only to absorb the relevant facts and figures, but also to hear and see the crowds and the players, to feel sun and turf, ball and finger, sweat and muscle, and the whole personality of the man. He provides something of the living context to John Arlott's reflections and assessments. The old word for the creative writer was 'makar' or 'maker': in a sense, though, it is a term which is equally applicable to John Arlott, the poet of the game in prose and verse, and to Freddie Trueman, the greatest 'maker' of fast bowling in our and perhaps any other time. They are parts of the same proposition, complementing each other.

The anthology, too, aims at complements and balances, as well as at contrasts and simple entertainment. From the early decades of the eighteenth century onwards, some of the finest creative minds have been fascinated by the game, while in other cases its excitements have called out hitherto unsuspected powers of evocation. There is in consequence a pretty extensive literature of cricket, in poetry as well as in prose, and plenty of examples will be found here. But the passages haven't always been chosen exclusively for their literary merits. Some of them are there, of course, simply because they are funny or intriguing or provocative. But although the anthology doesn't pretend to approach anywhere near a comprehensive historical survey, the items are arranged in roughly chronological order, and they do seek to illustrate some of the major changes in the game, from the points of view of both participants and spectators—changes in organization and techniques as well as in attitude and response. At the same time, the anthology attempts, too, to preserve a just balance between the lyrical and the down-to-earth, the serious and the light-hearted, the theoretical and the strictly practical.

Something more must be said about the omissions. They are un-avoidable in any anthology, which must, after all, be controlled to some extent by personal choice, as well as by the limitations of space. Ideally, for example, there should be separate sections about the growth of the game in the West Indies, New Zealand, South Africa and other parts of the world. Ideally, too, a far greater number of cricketing personalities would have been represented. No one is likely to quarrel with those names that have been included, but every reader will regret the absence of his own particular heroes. But for an anthology to attempt a complete gallery of cricketing notabilities would obviously be impossible and it seemed best to be guided entirely by the content and general appropriate-ness of the passage itself. Needless to say, none of the omissions implies any lack of appreciation or respect.

At any rate, it can perhaps be claimed that this book will contain something of interest, for every type of reader, about cricket past and present. At the same time, although cricket, like the golden days that—in theory—provide its natural setting, is a game peculiarly susceptible to reminiscence and nostalgia, this is not a backward-looking book. The most important of all its aims is to present cricket as a game—or institution—full of toughness and vitality. It is, therefore, particularly appropriate that John Arlott's closing section should be devoted to its future.

If it comes to that, a static or over-indulgent approach is the last thing that producer Gordon Croton, who brought this present team together, would tolerate, either in this book or in the television series to which it is an accompaniment.

Gilbert Phelps

Cricket: a facet of English life

John Arlott

Chapter 1
Cricket in proportion

Cricket is a game of many facets. If it is not all things to all men, at least it is different things to different men. According to their outlook they may see it as violent or pastoral, profound or shallow, romantic or pragmatic, graceful or harsh, dramatic or soporific, compelling or boring. There can be no doubt, however, that it commands extremely deep loyalties from people of completely different character.

They, in their enthusiasm, hardly question it. It has, for instance, rarely been examined from a sociological standpoint, yet its actual play and its impact on its enthusiastic followers are far less important than its effect on those for whom it has been a livelihood. It should be said that, after the formative stages of the game, this book is concerned primarily with first-class cricket and its English setting.

'What do they know of cricket who only cricket know?' That question was, at last, and pertinently, posed by C. L. R. James in *Beyond a Boundary*, a key book not only in cricket but in all sporting literature. Far more significant than the game's scores and results are its effect on the life in which it is set, and its infallible reflection of that life.

Some have seen the high wall of Lord's ground, symbolically, as cutting off cricket from the outside world. It is true, too, that some of its most passionate devotees give it less than its due importance in thinking it can be cut off from the greater realities, treated as a separate, almost cloistered, activity. 'Keep politics out of sport' was the cry during the contention about the 1970 South African tour. The fact is that sport is part of life; and life, whether cricketers or other people wish it or not, is regulated by politics; and no sport runs deeper into life than cricket. Therefore it cannot be fairly evaluated—nor even understood—unless it is seen in its relation to the world outside the walls; not only that part of the world which is concerned with cricket and cricket values, but that part of it which—often unrecognized, or its existence disbelieved, by the zealots—is utterly indifferent to cricket.

Cricket is in many ways unique. Yet to seek superlatives for it is to underestimate its innately human quality. Perhaps other games are older, more profound, more popular, more diverse, more skilful. Arguments on those lines would be fruitless even if they were conclusive, which they cannot be.

It is in so many ways a game of figures—after all, figures decide its outcome—that there exists an Association of Cricket Statisticians, whose interest lies in the arithmetic of the game. Others, equally devoted, but irked by the false critical significance sometimes attributed to figures, profess to abominate them and to consider that style is all. That essential difference of opinion indicates the multiplicity of attitudes towards the game. They exist in such width and variety because cricket is more closely woven into the social fabric of the countries which have adopted it than any other game. A single example is enough to demonstrate the point. England, probably the most class-conscious, and multi-classed society in the modern world, for long—even after the commencement of Test matches—accepted as the peak of its season the match between amateurs and professionals known as Gentlemen *versus* Players. Nowhere else except in Philadelphia was such a fixture even considered and here it went out with the acceptance of the welfare state and (relative) equality of opportunity; though the primary cause of its rejection was the economic circumstances which made it impossible for the formerly privileged classes to participate in a six-day-a-week game without payment.

A man may play billiards or snooker with his face permanently in shadow; nothing in his performance will indicate in the slightest his nationality, class or age. A footballer or a baseball player may behave completely out of character on the instructions of a manager or coach. See Australian, English, Indian or West Indian cricketers in action, however, and—regardless of their caps or colour—within minutes they will identify themselves by their method, manner or attitude. Which is a way of saying that most games are skin-deep; but cricket goes to the bone.

It would be more than mildly interesting to know for certain the true origin of cricket for, again, without seeking the ultimate, cricket has always been a rapidly—even strikingly—evolving game. Since its earliest known form it has changed—developed is a better word—virtually as much as it possibly could while remaining essentially itself. If it is now a highly skilled, even sophisticated, pursuit, its essentials are the spontaneous reactions of a young human. Bowling is simply aiming at a target, as happens in baseball, stoolball, bat-and-trap, archery. Batting is the defence of the target as in stoolball, bat-and-trap, or goalkeeping in hockey or football; plus the striking of the missile to score as in baseball, knur-and-spell or golf. Many ball games obviously had identical or similar origins in one country, or different countries, simply because they represent different forms of the same primitive play-urges in the young.

For centuries, in most countries, play was regarded as the province of children. Indeed, the great majority of people all over the world were (and in many regions still are) compelled to devote their entire time to producing food or to earning a wage solely in order to keep themselves alive. Although there were fifty-eight saints' days in the sixteenth-century English calendar, the law gave the lords of that primarily agricultural community power to over-ride them when they required work of their labourers. For the labourers themselves, a single bad harvest meant privation and perhaps death: they could not spare working time for games. Even in mid-nineteenth-century England, men's wages in agriculture and some industries were not sufficient to maintain a family; and many unemployed farm labourers and city-dwellers starved, or had to go into the workhouses to avoid that fate. The same applied almost everywhere. The land-owning upper classes had time to spare for amusements but theirs, except for a few of the martial exercises of chivalry, were not team games. They were concerned with riding and hunting. Indeed, Joseph Strutt began his *Sports and Pastimes of the People of England* (1801) with a section of 'Rural Exercises Practised by Persons of Rank' (specifically hunting, hawking, fowling, fishing and horse racing). Cricket fell among 'Rural Exercises Generally Practised'. Strutt deals with it in the chapter on ball games, after tennis, hand-ball, fives, balloon ball, stool ball, hurling, football, camp ball, golf, cambuc, bandy ball, stow ball, pall-mall, ring-ball and club-ball; and affords it no greater attention; indeed, less than trap ball, tennis or football. He writes, however, 'Cricket of late years is become exceedingly fashionable, being much countenanced by the nobility and gentlemen of fortune, who frequently join in the diversion.'

Nevertheless, his placing is salutary for those who take cricket too seriously; which is a constant danger for all who talk or write about it.

Although it lies outside any chronological shape for this account, it is relevant to leap forward to the historic Old Trafford Test of 1902, which must stand among the greatest cricket matches ever played. Although it was interrupted by rain, twenty wickets fell, 767 runs were scored, and it reached a quite Homeric finish within three days. Australia won the toss and batted on a sluggish, wet wicket, Trumper scored a century before lunch. When afternoon sun made the pitch difficult, their last nine wickets went down for 24 runs. In the same conditions England collapsed to 44 for five before Braund and Jackson saved them with a stand which continued into the second day and Australia led by only 37. On a still awkward surface, Lockwood, Tate and Rhodes bowled them out for 86, which would have been significantly less if Fred Tate had not dropped Darling, their top scorer, leaving England 124 to win. After that error as Fred Tate, last man in, walked to the wicket with England wanting eight to win, rain held up his innings for a tense three-quarters-of-an-hour. He made four and then was bowled. Australia had won the Test by three runs and taken the rubber with it. Some time after the match the only two players remaining in the England dressing-room were Len Braund and Fred Tate, who were going to travel down to London together on the way to their county matches starting next morning. Tate, as Braund later related, was so bitterly distressed at his 'failure' that he wept. This was his only Test match—'I shall never play for England again,' he said, 'I have let them down.' Braund was always a cheerful creature. 'Never mind, Fred,' he said, 'go upstairs and get your money—it's only a game.' If, at that historic moment, it was only a game, it is only a game now. The thought is welcome. In its matches and scores cricket is, indeed, only a game—like darts or marbles, except that it is played on a larger stage. It is a more serious matter in its impact on the lives of the men involved, especially those who make their living from it. So, as we shall see, it has been through its recorded history. Yet it has suffered more from being taken too seriously than too lightly. As a final perspective, we may turn to a piece of dialogue in R. T. Johnston's *Century of a Lifetime*—

'But this is no ordinary cricket match. He is playing for England.'

'I don't care if he's playing for Tottenham Hotspur. He's not playing tennis with me and that's all I care about.'

Chapter 2
Taking shape

No evidence has ever been adduced to indicate where or how cricket began. Indeed, it must have been a gradual evolution among children who also played such similar games as stoolball, bat-and-trap, stob-ball, cat-and-dog and what was loosely termed club-ball, which was perhaps a generic term for all of them. The likeliest hypothesis is that it took shape as the sport of shepherd boys on the downland of south-east England. There the sheep-cropped grass was short enough to allow the earliest bowling to be—as it was—simply trundled all along the ground. If the entrance gate to the hurdle sheepfold was the bowler's target, that would account for the term 'wicket' for it consisted of two forked uprights with a crossbar—called a 'bail'—laid across them; and the whole was called a wicket. If the ball was hit away with the shepherd's crook, that would explain the curved shape of the earliest known bats.

The ball could have been knotted or matted sheep's wool. Many years afterwards Ephraim Lockwood, a well-known Yorkshire player of the mid-nineteenth century, recalled that as a boy he played cricket at Lascelles Hall with a seat-board leg for a bat, and 'crewelled yarn balls'. The colour of the ball—red as far back as it is recorded—could be accounted for by the wool being matted together with the reddle or ochre used to mark the sheep.

Ante-dating concrete evidence of a game identifiable as cricket and known by that name, there are several possible, but not certain, pictorial or textual, references to it. By far the earliest occurs in an illuminated manuscript of Bede's *Life of St Cuthbert*, executed at Durham, authoritatively dated 1120–30, and now in the Bodleian. It illustrates the passage reading 'The boy St Cuthbert, too fond of playing games, was warned in a vision to be more serious'. The picture is of a young man wielding what looks like a hockey stick—not unlike an early cricket bat—with an orthodox left-hander's two-handed grip, right shoulder pointing down the line of the pitch; while another player is making, by twelfth-century standards, a convincing enough caught-and-bowled. The fact that the illustration is crowded with the figures of other young men tumbling and

The First Cricket Illustration? from Bede, Life of St Cuthbert.

playing at other games is simply in the tradition of medieval illumination. This is a completely isolated source; and the game may not be cricket; if it is not, however, it looks remarkably like it.

Wherever the name 'cricket' came from—and from the various theories 'cricce', Anglo-Saxon for a stick, is the generally accepted origin—it can be assumed that it was played before it was called cricket. Partly for that reason most cricket historians have thought it likely that an entry in the Wardrobe accounts of Edward I for 1300 refers to cricket. Translated from the Latin it runs 'To Master John de Leek, chaplain to Prince Edward, the King's son, for monies paid out himself or by the hands of others, for the said Prince playing at creag and other sports at Westminster on the 10th March, 100 shillings. And by the hand of his Chamberlain, Hugo, at Newenton in the month of March 20s. In all £6.'

No one has yet produced an alternative meaning for creag; neither, it seems, has the word been discovered in any other context. One faint hint lies in the fact that if, as seems likely, 'Newenton' is Newendon, in Kent, it is on the edge of the Weald where the game is generally thought to have taken shape. This whole attribution, however, awaits confirmation.

Cricket is first referred to by that name as being played in about 1550. In 1598, John Derrick, a county coroner for Surrey, was a witness in a court case about the ownership of a piece of former wasteland which had been enclosed and used as a timber yard. Derrick, who was then fifty-nine, deposed in testimony still preserved in the court records that 'being a scholar of the Free School of Guildford he and diverse of his fellowes did runne and play there at creckett and other plaies'. That testimony would refer to about 1550; and it probably is significant that cricket is the only one of the 'plaies' referred to by name. At about the same time, when the Reformation forced the Jesuit school, Stonyhurst, to leave England for St Omer, Rouen, they took their 'Stonyhurst Cricket' with them; and, when they returned at the time of the French Revolution, they brought it back virtually unchanged.

In the same year as John Derrick gave his evidence, Giovanni Florio, a tutor in the household of the Earl of Southampton, published an Italian–English dictionary in which he gave the meaning of 'sgrittare' as 'to make a noise like a cricket, to play cricket-a-wicket and be merry'. Cotgrave's French dictionary (1611) gives one of the meanings of 'crosse' as 'the crooked staff wherewith boys play at cricket'. When Oliver Cromwell went to London in 1617 at the age of eighteen he is said to have 'gained himself the name of royster' by playing 'football, cricket, cudgelling and wrestling'. At a hearing in the King's Bench in 1640, there was testimony that 'there was . . . about 30 years since a Cricketting between the Weald and Upland'.

So the game entered the seventeenth century shaped and named but still largely a children's game.

Quite rapidly, however, there are references to its being taken up by adults. At Boxgrove, near Chichester, in 1622 a Bill of Presentment was brought against six parishioners for 'playing at Kreket in evening prayer tyme on Sunday', and two churchwardens for aiding and abetting them. There are other instances, especially in Kent and notably at Maidstone, of people charged with playing cricket on the Sabbath. Both Jasper Vinall at West Hoathly in 1624 and Henry Brand of Selsey in 1647 were killed by blows on the head from a cricket ball.

In 1629, Henry Cuffin, a curate of Ruckinge near Romney Marsh, was proceeded against for 'playing At Cricketts in very unseemly fashion with boys and other very mean and base persons' on Sunday afternoons. He protested that, so far as being 'mean and base', they were 'persons of repute and fashion'. More significantly, at Coxheath in 1646, two young men, Samuel Filmer and Thomas Harlackenden, were good enough to beat four players from Maidstone in the first match on which wagering is reported. Their ability to win against such odds, and the fact that the form of players was sufficiently well-known to justify betting, indicates an appreciable standard of performance. Indeed, a court case over the non-payment of a bet provides the record of the match having taken place.

Cromwell's Commissioners forbade the playing of 'Krickett' in Ireland by an order of 1656 and ordered all 'sticks and balls' to be burnt by the common hangman. In England, though, the game was beginning to assume some economic significance. It was still generally a game for the young and the poorer classes. There are, though, records of publicans being rated for cricket grounds in a relationship that was to prove strong. The granting of licences for the sale of beer at matches indicates that crowds were beginning to attend them: and, indeed, in 1693 spectators at a match at Lewes were fined for riot and battery.

According to the journal of the Rev. Henry Teonge, naval chaplain on H.M.S. *Assistance*, in 1676 he and three other officers went ashore at Aleppo where with at least forty of the English, they did divert themselves with various sports including krickett'.

The Foreign Post for 7 July 1697, reported: 'The middle of last week a great match at Cricket was played in Sussex; they were eleven of a side, and they played for fifty guineas apiece.' Skills and playing performances had improved steadily over the century. By the end of the century, William Bedle was twenty years old. Born at Bromley and living later in Dartford, he was described at his death in 1768 as 'formerly the most expert cricket player in England'. That standing indicates that there had been an advance on the performance levels of the earlier Filmer and Harlackenden; already, definite comparative technical standards were recognized.

Seventeenth-century growth of the game had been healthy; though, if it is to be measured by press reports, its development was confined mainly to the south-east, Kent in particular, Sussex and London. Yet it would be a mistake to accept newspaper coverage as an authoritative guide. Papers were few; and they did not generally report sport, which simply was not considered a newsworthy subject. In the long period before there was any worthwhile reportage or appreciation, cricket matches were considered worthy of notice for reasons other than cricket, because the stakes played for were large, or where there was some unusual element about them—a match between women, or between cripples for instance—which would titillate newspaper readers in a world not yet orientated towards sport.

The evidence we have indicates that the growth of the game was strongest and most highly developed about Kent and this was soon to be handsomely demonstrated on the field. It must, though, already have taken firm hold in many other districts not mentioned in the press but which within a decade were recognized as strongholds of the game. Almost from the start of the eighteenth century there are indications of progress at many levels and in many directions.

Chapter 3
Georgian Cricket

Eighteenth-century England was still largely an agricultural country, its affairs controlled by the noble landowners whose great estates dominated the rural areas and, at closer quarters, by the squires and country gentry. Increasingly, however, fashionable London attracted the well-to-do to the world of the 'bucks', their newly established clubs, and the social set at the centre of which stood the Prince Regent. Especially in the cities, this was a reckless age, addicted to gambling—with consequent corruption—violence, drinking and general profligacy. Cricket, now an adult game, true to the character it has since maintained, reflected that life. The best of it was played under the aegis of aristocratic patrons, in the early part of the century generally on their private grounds, later increasingly in London. They wagered huge sums on it and formed and played in exclusive clubs —including M.C.C.

There were riots at matches involving, on one occasion, the use of looted firearms; duels were fought over it and some were killed. Cricketers, like boxers and jockeys of the time, were bribed to 'throw' matches. Importantly for cricket, though, patronage and payment brought about the establishment of a professional 'school' of technically informed players capable of teaching the game at a high level. Like all other activities, cricket was affected by the long session of wars—England knew no twenty-year period of peace in the entire century—and a projected visit to Paris by a team of English cricketers was prevented by the French Revolution.

Hitherto, most cricket had been a localized group pursuit: in the eighteenth century it resolved itself more and more into match-play. At the outset, in 1700, cricket was reported on Clapham Common—the term 'a Clapham Common player' persists, to the righteous displeasure of the cricketers who play there—while at Malling, a famous early cricket centre in Kent, 'a match at Cricket between eleven gentlemen of the West Part of Kent and those of Chatham for 11 guineas a man' was played in 1705. Kent *versus* Surrey at Dartford in 1709 is usually accepted as the first county match.

On a different plane of significance, in 1706, A. Baldwin, of Warwick
Lane, published *Musae Juveniles* by William Goldwin, a series of Latin
poems, one of which is titled

In Certamen Pilae.
Anglice, A Cricket-Match

It is a 95-line description of play which, by either of the rival nineteen-
twenties translations, accurately describes the game of cricket, then played,
as an unmistakable ancestor of the form in which we know it now. By
now the various versions of the game seem to have been generally recon-
ciled to a point where, as in many children's games today, there were no
major, but many local, variations from a generally understood basic set
of rules. Certainly Goldwin's players had curved bats, a leather ball, two
stumps and a bail, two umpires, two scorers, bowlers, and long stop;
batsmen were bowled out and caught. One, though, is 'hit wicket' after
slipping, which would conflict with the first printed Laws (1744). It is
significant, too, that Goldwin was an Etonian and a Cambridge graduate,
subsequently headmaster of Bristol Grammar School, and Vicar of St
Nicholas, Bristol. This is a final indication of the acceptance of cricket at
social, educational and adult levels virtually beyond challenge.

During the eighteenth century, the bat gradually evolved from the long,
heavy, curved relics of the crook—many of which were out of fashion
before they wore out—to the shouldered, straight shape we know today.
The progress was, no doubt, uneven and dependent on the development of
bowling in any area. The sweeping effect of the longer, curved bat
remained more effective against the ball rolled all along the ground than
the narrower straight bat which was so much better suited to the bounce
of 'length' bowling which was increasingly practised as the century
advanced. An important disadvantage of the curved bat was that it
could not be used by both right and left-handers because of its curve.
The ball was of leather tightly stretched round worsted and a hard core.
It was stated in 1811 that the firm of Duke was making cricket balls at
Penshurst in the sixteenth century.

Goldwin's poem twice refers specifically to 'the laws' but no printed
version of any Laws is known prior to the 'London' code of 1744.

Heavy bats (William Ward, scorer of the first double-century, used the
same four-pounder for forty years), indifferent pitches, lob bowling—
frequently of grubs—meant that scoring was often slow (Aylward batted
for nearly two days to make his 167 at Sevenoaks Vine in 1777). For much
of the century it seems that the main attraction to spectators was the
suspense about the outcome of their wagers.

In the late nineteen-forties, however, Dr H. F. Squire, of Henfield, the
historian of early Sussex cricket, discovered in the Duke of Richmond's
archives at Goodwood House the 'Articles of Agreement' drawn up for
two cricket matches, home and out, to be played in 1727 between the

teams of the second Duke of Richmond and a Mr A. Brodrick of Peper Harow in Surrey. Although they were never published—indeed their very existence was unknown until Dr Squire found them—they form, if not the first set of laws, the first written evidence of Laws having existed, for their purpose is less to codify than to clarify a code which existed, whether printed or not. Three items did not survive until the first published Laws. They are those calling for twelve players a side; wickets pitched twenty-three yards apart and, as confirmed by Goldwin's poem, to complete a run, the batsman had to 'touch the umpire's stick'.

So far as they apply to the conduct of play, the articles stipulate that—'A ball caught, the Striker is out'; 'when a ball is caught out, the Stroke counts nothing'; 'Catching out behind the wicket allowed'; 'it shall not be lawfull to fling down the wickets, & that no player shall be deemed out by any wicket put down unless with the ball in hand'. So far as discipline is concerned 'That there shall be one Umpire of each side; and that if any of the Gamesters speak or give their opinion, on any points of the Game, they are to be turned out and voided in the match this not to extend to the Duke of Richmond and Mr Brodrick. If any Doubt or Dispute arises on any of the aforementioned Articles, or whatever else is not settled therein, it shall be determined by the Duke of Richmond and Mr Brodrick on their Honours; by whom the Umpires are likewise to be determined on any difference between them.'

The Duke of Richmond was one of the first noblemen to plan and run a team, and it was of considerable stature. Just as Hambledon sometimes played as 'Sir Horace Mann's Side' or 'The Earl of Winchilsea's Side' so, in the first half of the eighteenth century, the village players of Slindon, near the Duke of Richmond's Goodwood estate in West Sussex, appeared as his team and, probably, at times, as Sussex. In a letter to the Duke of Newcastle in 1741, Richmond wrote of 'poor little Slindon against almost your whole county of Surrey' with a sly postscript 'We have beat Surrey almost in one innings'. Up to then they had lost only one of their last forty-three matches and, though London beat them in the following year, they did so 'only with the greatest difficulty'.

These matches were played hard, as the need for 'Articles of Agreement' shows. They were played for money, of course; and the Duke's regular matches against Sir William Gage's side were played, according to the document, for a hundred guineas a side. That, at least, was the overt bet which, spread over eleven men, amounted to about £9 each and thus evaded the law of 1711—in a clause not repealed until 1845—which forbade any game to be played for a stake of over £10. There may, too, have been some sharp practice, for the present-day morality of the game was inculcated by the Victorians. The Georgians went hard; a wager was a wager, and there was no mercy for 'gulls'. On one occasion in Surrey, the Duke of Richmond's team were attacked by the mob for arriving at the match too late to allow their opponents time to win.

Frederick Louis, Prince of Wales, and father of George III, became an enthusiastic patron and player of cricket. Largely as a reaction to the unpopularity of his parents, the Prince, a somewhat unprepossessing young man, had a considerable popular following and his interest enhanced the prestige of the game. He began to play in 1735 and two years afterwards, at Moulsey Hurst, he captained Surrey against the Duke of Marlborough's London team for £500 a side.

His favour, however, did not prevent *The Gentlemen's Magazine*, probably the most popular and certainly one of the most influential periodicals of the day, carrying in its issue for September 1743 an attack on 'Publick Cricket Matches'. 'Cricket is certainly a very innocent and wholesome exercise yet it may be absurd if either great or little people make it their business. It is grossly abused when it is made the subject of public advertisement to draw together great crowds of people who ought, all of them, to be somewhere else. Noblemen, gentlemen and clergymen have certainly a right to divert themselves in what manner they see fit, nor do I dispute their privilege of making butchers, cobblers or tinkers their companions. But I very much doubt whether they have any right to invite thousands of people to be spectators of their agility at the expense of their duty and honesty. The diversion of cricket may be proper in holiday time and in the country; but upon days when men ought to be busy, and in the neighbourhood of a great city, it is not only improper but mischievous to a high degree. It draws numbers of people away from their employment to the ruin of their families. It brings together crowds of apprentices and servants whose time is not their own. It propagates a spirit of idleness at a juncture when, with the utmost industry, our debts, taxes and decay of trade will scarce allow us to get bread. It is a most notorious breach of laws as it gives the most open encouragement to gaming'.

The diatribe had little effect. The next year admission charges at the Artillery Ground in Finsbury, where cricket had been played since at least 1725, were increased from twopence to sixpence, a considerable sum in those days for working people. It was done, presumably, to reduce the size of the crowds and to exclude the poorer—or perhaps rougher?—element from such occasions as Lord John Sackville's challenge match between Kent and All-England, which was attended by the Prince of Wales, the Dukes of Cumberland (the 'Butcher' of Culloden who raised teams to play for extremely high stakes), and Richmond, Admiral Vernon and 'many other persons of distinction'. It is the first match recorded in Haygarth's monumental work of reference, *Scores & Biographies*. All four innings were small and Kent won by one wicket.

The England team was captained by Richard Newland who made the two highest scores of the match and took eight wickets. He was an outstanding player for Slindon. Indeed, the club's eminence did not survive his departure to Chichester where he became a surgeon. He, in line of descent from William Bedle, was the outstanding player of his day. His two brothers, Adam and John, and Cuddy, the Slindon tailor, also played for England. So, too, did Waymark—once described as 'the father of cricket professionals'—and Dingate, both prominent Surrey players of the time, who were employed as cricketers by the Duke of Richmond. Once, when Waymark was ill, the Duke's match with Sir William Gage's side was postponed until he was fit to play. Kips was the most successful batsman for Kent in each innings.

The match was reported in the most substantial piece of writing about cricket until that date; three-hundred lines of verse:

Illustrated with the critical observations of Scriblerus Maximus
entitled *Cricket; an Heroic Poem*

by the actor James Love (James Dance). Dance was a friend of Boswell and, in fact, first suggested that he should write his *Journal*. The verse is dramatically couched and ends with Waymark, of all people, dropping the crucial catch—

> Or the lamented Youth too much relied
> On sure success and Fortune often tried;
> The erring ball, amazing to be told!
> Slipp'd through his outstretch'd hand and Mock'd his hold
> And now the Sons of Kent compleat the Game
> And firmly fix their everlasting Fame.

Cricket in the Artillery Ground by Francis Hayman

In the same year was issued the first known—'London'—version of the Laws—'The Game of Cricket, as settled by the CRICKET-CLUB in 1744, and play'd at the ARTILLERY-GROUND, LONDON.'

This code does not stipulate the number of players; by no means all matches could have been eleven-a-side since so many single-wicket games were played at this time. It does, though, call for a twenty-two yard pitch; a two stump wicket twenty-two inches high and six wide; with a popping crease three-feet-ten-inches in front of it. It specifies a four-ball over; defines a 'back-foot' no-ball, bowled, caught, stumped and run out; the last may now be 'by throw or with ball in hand'.

The President of the London Club was Frederick, Prince of Wales, who, in 1751, died from an 'abscess' caused by a blow from a cricket ball. The event was marked, as Horace Walpole recalled, by the street-ditty which ends

> 'But since 'tis only Fred
> Who was alive and is dead,
> There's no more to be said'

This was the century of the great clubs. In cricket, from the original rural or semi-rural stock rose Slindon, Dartford and Hambledon; from the emergent London club life of the wealthy, the London, White Conduit, Star and Garter, the Thursday, Montpelier, and, eventually, Marylebone.

Kent and Sussex had long been the most advanced, and the most frequently reported centres of the game. The Duke of Dorset, Master of the Horse and later Ambassador to Paris, was as enthusiastic a patron of the game as the Duke of Richmond; and employed several of the leading players of the day—like Miller, Minshull (Minchin) and Bowra—on his estate at Sevenoaks. After Slindon it was little surprise that a Kent club should rise to similar eminence, able to play London or the Rest of England, as Dartford or—to satisfy the widespread public county loyalty, and increase the gate—Kent. In fact, like Slindon in Sussex earlier and, later, Hambledon in Hampshire, Dartford had so long been a focal point for outstanding players within the county—many of whom seem to have come from Bromley—that its team was entitled to be called Kent.

Certainly they played both London and 'All-England' on even terms and with considerable credit. By the time players were named, after the seventeen-forties, the outstanding Dartford players were John Hodsoll, John Bell—once referred to as 'the most noted cricketer in England'— Lord John Sackville and John Frame.

In 1756 Dartford played Hambledon at the Artillery Ground. The result is not known but it must have been regarded as a match of considerable importance to have been taken away from either county to the chief London ground.

This is the first reference to a Hambledon team, or club, of any significance. The records of their matches, as of most cricket of that time, are incomplete; many of the important records were lost when Lord's pavilion was burnt down in 1825. The club was probably founded by the Rev. Charles Powlett (or Paulet), an illegitimate son of the third Duke of Bolton by the original Polly Peachum of Gay's *Beggar's Opera*, Lavinia Fenton (whom he married on the death of his first Duchess). 'Squire' Paulet became Curate of Itchen Abbas and was born and died in Hampshire. His usual co-backer was Philip Dehaney, a Bristol merchant; the two were at Westminster and Trinity College, Cambridge together.

It is difficult to explain quite why they should have picked on Hambledon. It is a pleasant village, but its eighteenth-century cricket grounds—first Broadhalfpenny and then Windmill Down—are remote from the village, bleak hills whose discomforts caused first the move from one to the other, and eventually the decision to abandon major play there in favour of London. The Bat and Ball Inn, at Broadhalfpenny, kept by their club captain, groundsman and occasional secretary, Richard Nyren, was little more than a cottage. On Windmill Down there were only marquees. It might have been thought that Petersfield or Alresford—the other major cricketing centres of the area—would have been more convenient. Hambledon it was, however, and it has been called 'The Cradle of Cricket', which is completely inaccurate. It was simply the village whose local club was the first in the history of cricket both to achieve major success, and to be adequately chronicled. Hambledon's period of eminence was 1772 to 1781 when, of 51 matches against England, they won 29. In the language of the period, a match was the subject of a wager while a game was not. Those between Hambledon and All-England were invariably played for 'a purse of 500 guineas'; and the side-bets might amount to towering sums. On basic stakes alone, F. S. Ashley-Cooper estimated that Hambledon won £22,497 and lost £10,030 on those games.

Years later (1832), in his old age, John Nyren, son of the Hambledon captain in its great days, and 'a sort of farmer's pony to my native club', contributed a series of feature articles about the Hambledon players to *The Examiner*. His amanuensis—to an extent never likely to be established —was Charles Cowden Clarke, author of *The Shakespeare Concordance*. Although these articles are padded out by almost as much again of instruction (to justify the title *The Young Cricketer's Tutor*) it still runs to little more than 25,000 words. The section of *The Young Cricketer's Tutor* called 'The Cricketers of My Time' remains the enduring classic of the game of cricket. Neither Clarke nor Nyren ever wrote anything else of comparable quality; but here the two talents fused into inspiration. It brings to life the country players of two hundred years ago more vividly than those of any other sports writing. One by one they cross the page: Brett 'delivering his ball fairly, high and very quickly, and with a force of a point blank shot': Richard Nyren 'the chosen General of all the matches, ordering and directing the whole . . . When Richard Nyren left Hambledon, the club broke up. The head and right arm were gone'. Tom Sueter—

'What a handful of steel-hearted soldiers are in an important pass, such was Tom in keeping the wicket'.

George Lear—'our best long-stop: so firm and steady was he that I have known him stand through a whole match against Brett's bowling, and not lose more than two runs. The ball seemed to go into him; and he was as sure of it as if he had been a sand-bank'. Lamborn—the first off-spinner— 'Egad! this new trick of his so bothered the Kent and Surrey men that they tumbled out one after another as if they had been picked off by a rifle corps.'

Tom and Harry Walker—'Never sure came two such unadulterated rustics into a civilized community. Tom's hard, ungain, scrag-of-mutton frame; wilted, apple-john face (he always looked twenty years older than he really was); with his long spider legs, he was the driest and most rigid limbed man I ever knew'. 'Silver Billy' Beldham—'The finest batter of his own, or perhaps of any age. He would get at the balls and hit them away in a gallant style; but when he could cut them at this point of his bat, he was in his glory; and, upon my life, their speed was as the speed of thought'. David Harris—'between any one and himself, comparison must fail. His bowling was the finest of all tests for a hitter. You were obliged to get in or it would be about your hands or the handle of your bat; and every player knows where its next place would be.'

John Small the elder—'His decision was as prompt as his eye was accurate in calculating a short run . . . a remarkably well made and well knit man of honest expression and as active as a hare'. Sometimes, too, the quality is epic—of a Hambledon v. England match—'I remember when upon one occasion Miller and Minshull, being in together had gained an uncommon number of runs, the backers of the Hambledon men, Dehaney and Paulet, began to quake, and edged off all their money, laying it pretty thickly on the England side. Of the Hambledon men, Small went in first, and continued until there were about five out, for very few runs, when Nyren went in to him; and then they began to show fight. The mettle of our true blood was roused into full action, and never did they exhibit to finer advantage. Nyren got 98, and Small 110 runs before they were parted. After the former was out (for Small, according to his custom, died a natural death) the backers came up to Nyren and said, "You will win the match, and we shall lose our money". The proud old yeoman turned short upon them, and, with that honest independence which gained him the esteem of all parties, told them to their heads that they were rightly served, and that he was glad of it. "Another time" (said he) "don't bet your money against such men as we are!" I forget how many runs the Hambledon men got, but, after this turn in affairs, the others stood no chance, and were easily beaten.'

It was virtually the earliest sports-writing and remains unexcelled in its kind. To present-day thought it seems strange that, though Dehaney and Paulet raised the Hambledon team and put up their original stake, they did not hesitate to bet against them if they thought they might lose: but they were men of the Regency.

Nyren ends by naming the most eminent players in the Hambledon Club when it was in its glory:

David Harris	Tom Walker
John Wells	Robert Robinson
Richard Purchase	Noah Mann
William Beldham	Tom Taylor
John Small junior	Thomas Scott
Harry Walker	

and the words—'No eleven in England could have had any chance with these men; and I think they might have beaten any two and twenty'. (In fact, in 1772 at Moulsey Hurst, they did beat twenty-two of England.)

Much of it is similarly evocative, even emotional—'Half the county would be present and all their hearts with us. Little Hambledon pitted against All-England was a proud thought for the Hampshire men'. Apart from the romantic aspect, however, it is plain from Nyren's analysis that, no doubt as part of a process begun earlier and elsewhere, the Hambledon cricketers were highly professional. Apart from their study of tactics and batting and bowling technique, playing on their hilltop grounds with the ground falling away so steeply and far, made them, of necessity, fine fieldsmen.

Some idea of the side may be gathered from the fact that when, in 1787, a wager match was played between the White Conduit Club (with six given men) and England at Lord's, seven of the England side and all six of the club's given men were Hambledon players. Even more convincingly, in England v. Hambledon on Windmill Down in 1787, four of the England side—including John Nyren—were of Hambledon.

The Hambledon uniform was elaborate—sky-blue coat with velvet collar and the letters 'C.C.' embossed on the buttons; gold-laced tricorn hats, white breeches, stockings and buckle shoes. When they went into the field, however, they exchanged their hats for dark velvet caps and, doffing their jackets, appeared, like the teams in James Love's poem 'In decent white most gracefully array'd'.

Scores and Biographies shows matches like 'Storrington with Wells and Beldham v. Sussex with the two Walkers and Small'. This, played at Storrington, was obviously a professional engagement for which, before the days of the railway, Wells and Beldham had to travel from Farnham; the Walkers from Hindhead, and Small from Petersfield. The score notes 'Betting started 5 to 4 on Sussex'—Storrington won.

There was, too, occasional sharp practice. Beldham recalled many years later 'Ring, one of our best hitters, was shabby enough to get his leg in the way and take advantage of the bowlers and when Tom Taylor did the same, the bowlers found themselves beaten, and the law was passed to make

leg-before-wicket Out'. He was referring to the amended—'Star & Garter'
—code of 1774. Three years before, 'Shock' White of Reigate went to the
crease with a bat wider than the wicket. There had also, obviously, been
instances of batsmen barging fieldsmen who were going for a catch.
Hence the new Laws limited the width of the bat to four-and-a-quarter
inches—indicating that by now most bats were straight—and the batsman who 'runs out of his ground to hinder a catch' was out. Indeed this
code was the basic version of today's; plus betting conditions.

The event which prompted the adoption of a third—middle—stump can
be dated more accurately than its actual introduction. The single wicket
match of 1775 was five of Hambledon, with White, *versus* five of Kent, with
Lumpy Stevens, at the Artillery Ground. John Small senior, then regarded
as almost unbowlable, went in last for Hambledon with 14 wanted to win,
and made them, despite the fact that 'Lumpy' three times bowled the ball
between the two stumps. Such evidence, seen by the leading patrons,
players and followers of the game, made it laughably obvious that a
middle stump had to be added. Its adoption, though, was by no means
uniform; it is known to have been used in one match in 1776; and for more
at the highest level in 1777, which is usually accepted as the year of its
general use. In some parts of the country, though, the two-stump wicket
survived for a few years more.

The question is often asked—'How fast was underarm bowling?' We
have the testimony of Beldham that Harris made the ball rise so steeply
that if the batsman did not move in to the ball it 'would grind his fingers
against the bat; many a time have I seen the blood drawn in this way
from a batter.' Brown of Brighton, a redoubtable single-wicket player
and probably the fastest of his time, is said to have bowled a ball which
beat bat, wicket, wicket-keeper, long stop, went through a defensively
held coat on the boundary and killed a dog on the other side.

Gambling was still a considerable attraction. Despite the possibility of
one of the 'great matches' being thrown, at least form was known. On the
other hand, a match between 'eleven women of Hampshire and eleven of
Surrey of all ages and sizes from 14 years old to upwards of 40 made
between two noblemen of the respective counties for five hundred guineas
aside' was equivalent to betting on flies crawling up a window-pane. *The
St James's Chronicle* in 1765 reported that a butcher lad 'being entrusted
with about £40 to buy cattle in Smithfield market, instead went to the
Artillery Ground and sported away the whole sum in betting upon the
Cricket players'.

General public interest, however, is demonstrated by *The Kentish
Express* report of an attendance between 15,000 and 20,000 for Hambledon
versus England at Bishopsbourne Paddock in 1772.

In mid-century the Earl of Sandwich used to raise a side of Old Etonians
to play England for £1,500 a side; and contemporary opinion had it that
'near £20,000 is depending'. It was patently stupid that the players who

went to London to play in such a match should be paid only five guineas if they won; three if they lost. The Green Man and Still in Oxford Street was the professionals' pub. As one old player told the Rev. James Pycroft in the following century, 'All the men whose names I had ever heard as foremost in the game, met together, drinking, card-playing, betting, and singing at The Green Man in Oxford Street—no man without his wine, I assure you; and such suppers as three guineas a game to lose and five to win could never pay for long.' Of course there was bribery; as Beldham said many years later. 'The temptation really was very great—too great by far for any poor man to be exposed to, who was no richer than ten shillings a week, let alone harvest time.'

Again it is Beldham speaking: 'In that Kent match—you can turn to it in your book (Bentley's scores), played July 28, 1807, on Penenden Heath—I and Lord Frederick had scored sixty-one, and thirty remained to win, and six of the best men in England went out for eleven runs. Well, sir, I lost some money by that match, and as seven of us were walking homewards to meet a coach, a gentleman who had backed the match drove by and said, "Jump up, my boys; we have all lost together. I need not mind if I hire a pair of horses extra next town, for I have lost money enough to pay for twenty pair or more." Well, thought I, as we rode along, you have rogues enough in your carriage now, sir, if the truth were told, I'll answer for it; and one of them let out the secret, some ten years after. But, sir, I can't help laughing when I tell you: once, there was a single-wicket match played at Lord's, and a man on each side was paid to lose—one was bowler and the other batsman—when the game came to a near point. I knew their politics, the rascals, and saw in a minute how things stood; and how I did laugh, to be sure! For seven balls together, one would not bowl straight, and the other would not hit; but at last a straight ball must come, and down went the wicket.'

These men with a few of their opponents—Minshull (properly Minchin), 'Lumpy' Stevens, John Boorman, John Frame, 'Shock' White, Joey Ring, and William Bowra—stood out clearly above the other professionals of their day and for twenty years virtually no great match was played without a dozen or more of them.

Although a few of the patrons sometimes took part in great matches they were not of comparable class as players; indeed only one amateur—or perhaps the term should be 'one of the gentry'—of the period could compete equally with the professionals. The Rev. Lord Frederick Beauclerk, son of the fifth Duke of St Albans and himself a Vicar of St Albans, played cricket of some standing for thirty-five years. He was a slow underarm bowler who made some pace off the pitch; a fine and extremely fast fieldsman; and, as a batsman, even Nyren ranked him second only to Beldham. He had a sound defence; was one of the first to follow the example of Beldham and Fennex in going out of his crease to the bowlers; and, apart from a dangerous tendency to cut at the straight ball, was a controlled attacking batsman. He could, and was, teased out by bowlers who tied him down or bowled wide to him when he would often lose his notoriously short temper and destroy himself. Handsome, strongly but wirily built, autocratic and generally unpopular, he habitually played in a tall beaver hat which he would dash on the ground when irked. He estimated, quite openly, that he made six hundred guineas a year from cricket; which did not prevent him, in 1826, from describing cricket—in a speech as President of M.C.C.—as a game 'unalloyed by love of lucre and mean jealousies'.

After Kent v. England in 1744 (which he incorrectly entered as 1746) Haygarth, in *Scores and Biographies* has no further score until 1772; then, until 1784, virtually every match involves Hambledon; and, until 1792, Hambledon—or Hampshire—are concerned in many fixtures. From 1790, however, as the Hambledon matches grew fewer, those of M.C.C. increased.

The Hambledon members (annual subscription £3) sometimes played— though they engaged the professionals for great matches—sometimes watched and sometimes compensated for lack of cricket. The club song had the line 'He's best who drinks most' and a minute book entry records 'A wet day; only three members present; nine bottles of wine'. Another runs 'An extra meeting to eat Venison and drink Bonhams and Fitzherberts claret'. Nothing in the minutes, though, is historically more important nor more intriguing than that for the meeting on 29 August 1796. It recorded 'Three members and twelve non-subscribers (including Mr Thos Pain, author of 'The Rights of Man') present. No business noted'. The presence of Henry Bonham, chairman of the club and a radical; and the unusual imbalance between three members and twelve non-subscribers adds to the interest and possibilities. It has never been elsewhere suggested that Tom Paine returned to England after 1792 when, having published the second part of *The Rights of Man*, he was warned that if he went home he would be a dead man. He managed to take ship from Dover only half an hour before the warrant for his arrest reached the quay. It is nowhere recorded that he returned to England in 1796, when he was certainly liable to arrest. He is known to have been in Paris in that year but it was believed that he feared even to sail for America from France for fear of British cruisers in the Channel. This piquant situation can hardly now be resolved. The next entry in the minute book of the Hambledon Cricket Club is the last. Dated 21 September 1796, it says, simply, 'No Gentlemen'.

M.C.C.—Marylebone Cricket Club—was founded in 1787, largely by members of the Je-ne-sais-quoi Club who used to play at White Conduit; and, at the start, its headquarters was Lord's first ground. Of Yorkshire farming stock, Thomas Lord came, by way of Norfolk, to London in about 1778 and became a fringe cricket professional. His chief talents lay in bowling—slow underarm—and fielding at point. He acted as a net bowler for the members of the White Conduit Club and regularly attended all matches at the Artillery Ground. It was there that the Earl of Winchilsea and the Honourable Colonel Lennox promised him support in starting a cricket ground. He opened it in 1787 on the site of the present Dorset Square and, in the same year, it became the headquarters of the newly founded M.C.C. When that ground was sold for building while Lord was haggling over a small increase in rent, he took his original turf and moved to a second half a mile to the north. When the Regent's Canal was cut through that (1814), he moved his turf north again to the present Lord's. M.C.C. went with him on each occasion and in 1825 a prominent member of the club, William Ward—a director of the Bank of England and later an M.P.—bought out Lord and transferred the property to M.C.C.'s nominee, J. H. Dark.

When Lord, a hard, mercenary and reactionary man, sold the lease he had amassed considerable capital. By strange irony he, who established the metropolitan ground which drew the great matches away from the country areas, especially Hambledon, bought a farm at West Meon and retired there, only a few miles from Hambledon. His tombstone, lately replaced by M.C.C., is in West Meon churchyard.

The early years of the new century were troubled; the wars with France and America and the sordid return of soldiers and sailors from the Napoleonic Wars made for a disorderly, often poverty-stricken and violent, shifting population. Cricket belonged in all English life and a press report of 1802 announced—'Colonel Greville had his pocket picked on Monday last at Lord's ground of cash to the amount of £30. The pickpockets were so daring on Monday evening in the vicinity of Lord's Cricket Ground that they actually took the umbrellas of men and women by force, and even their watches and purses, threatening to stab those who made resistance. They were in gangs of between twenty to thirty, and behaved in a manner the most audacious.'

Nevertheless, Thomas Lord's first, second and third grounds flourished, and, in 1799, for instance, quite apart from M.C.C. matches both the home and out fixtures of Surrey v. England were played there. Soon it was the centre of the English game and the scene of its deliberations and chief matches and has remained so ever since. The Marylebone club, too, grew in strength, power and membership. The amateur players began to flex their muscles and in 1806 the first Gentlemen (amateurs) *versus* Players (professionals) match took place on Lord's first ground. (The fixture was to endure long after it became an anachronism, until 1962. The amateur-professional distinction was never sharp enough to merit such a fixture outside England except in Philadelphia, where it was played regularly about the end of the nineteenth century.) It was won by the Gentlemen— with Beldham, Lambert and John Nyren as given men; and, with Lambert given, they also won the return when Lord Frederick Beauclerk was even more effective than Lambert as a batsman, though not as a bowler.

William Lambert was clearly the finest cricketer of the first quarter of the nineteenth century; outstanding as a near-round-arm spin bowler, forcing batsman—'he hit what no one else could meddle with', said Beldham—fieldsman (he had huge hands) and wicket-keeper. He was the first and, for fifty years, the only cricketer to score two centuries in a match. Once in a single wicket match against two of the best players of the day, Lord Frederick and Howard, Lambert's partner, Osbaldeston, could play only a few balls; and was not allowed to field; yet Lambert contrived to win, virtually single-handed.

In 1817 an argument broke out among a group of professionals at Lord's with a series of accusations and counter-accusations of 'selling' matches which accorded so well with the facts that the listening members could not fail to recognize their truth. Lambert was accused of 'throwing' the England v. Nottinghamshire match of that season (though it has been said that it was 'sold' on both sides) and was never allowed to appear at Lord's again, which meant that he fell completely out of major cricket.

About this period there were some gifted amateurs as well as Lord Frederick, in 'Squire' Osbaldeston ('Squire of where?' 'Why, of all England, of course') who never appeared for the Gentlemen because of Lord Frederick's hatred for him; the all-round athletes, E. H. Budd and Thomas Assheton Smith; and William Ward. Yet, except when they had professional given men or played sixteen (1825) or seventeen (1827) the Gentlemen were no match for the Players. Indeed, in the return of 1827, their seventeen were beaten by an innings.

The increasing dominance of batsmen prompted reaction from the bowler inevitable throughout cricket history. For some time a number of players, conscious of the limitations of underarm, had experimented with bowling to the height of the shoulder. Authority reacted severely by requiring the hand to be below the elbow at the moment of delivery. Tom Walker had bowled roundarm in the seventeen-eighties, and others had kept the idea in mind. One of them was John Willes, good enough cricketer to be in the Gentlemen's XI for their first match with the Players. He had bowled roundarm in a match between Twenty-three of Kent and Thirteen of England at Penenden Heath in 1807 with considerable effect. He practised the skill for fifteen years and persevered until, often, the crowd closed on the players and pulled up the stumps. He made his supreme gesture of confrontation at Lord's in 1822, when he opened the bowling for Kent against M.C.C. with a roundarm delivery which was promptly 'no-balled' by Noah Mann, namesake son of the Hambledon player. Thereupon Willes threw down the ball and with immense histrionic effect, strode off the ground, leapt on his horse and rode out of first-class cricket for ever.

He had, however, made his point. Two Sussex professionals, William Lillywhite—nicknamed in the rolling Victorian style the 'Nonpareil'—and James Broadbridge picked up roundarm where Willes put it down. They met bitter opposition from people whom roundarm supporters claimed could not play it. The opposition case was put by William Denison, the first cricket reporter, who describes the debate in his book

Sketches of the Players. He believed the 'new, throwing' bowling would put scientific defence at a discount and prove physically dangerous. He was supported by, among others, William Ward, who certainly could play it, Thomas Lord, and the now elderly John Nyren. The advocates of round-arm or 'March of Intellect' bowling, as they called it, believed that straight-arm was the antithesis of throwing, would adjust the balance with the bat, and that M.C.C. had taken a retrograde step in insisting that the hand should be below the elbow.

Five years after John Willes' dramatic exit, Sussex—who had succeeded Surrey as the major county power—were matched against All-England in three 'Experimental Matches' to try out the new bowling. In the first match, on the famous old ground at Darnall, Sheffield, England, batting first, lost their first five wickets for two runs. Lillywhite and Broadbridge took thirteen between them; and Sussex won by seven wickets. At Lord's where William Ward made top score in each innings of England (42 and 20), Sussex won by three wickets. Nine of the England players declared they would not play in the third fixture but when they withdrew the threat, four of them were not chosen. Over four-thousand people watched the first day of the match on the Royal Grounds at Brighton when, although Lillywhite and Broadbridge bowled out England for 27 in their first innings, Sussex were beaten, largely by G. T. Knight, (a kinsman of Jane Austen), a protagonist of roundarm, who bowled it for England.

In the following May, M.C.C., in a hollow compromise, amended the law to allow the bowling hand to be raised as high as the elbow. It was too late; Lillywhite and Broadbridge and, soon, everyone else who cared to do so, was bowling from shoulder height without objection from the umpires. So, although M.C.C. did not legalize the general practice until 1835, by the death of George IV in 1830, cricket had passed through a complete series of social, technical and moral revolutions. For thirty-four years to come— until the legalization of overarm bowling—the changes in cricket were to be of degree, development and extension.

Chapter 4
The professionals

The middle period of nineteenth-century cricket was dominated by the professionals. They were not only far and away superior to the amateurs of the day in performance. They could, and did, command the highest money and much of the power in the game. At this time, too, they virtually created their separate identity. The English professional cricketer is unique; essentially a craftsman, sometimes seeming almost to eschew the spectacular in his preoccupation with technical soundness. His influence, of course, has been profound, for it has been exerted, not only in first-class play, but at all levels—through the teaching of schoolboys, the coaching and example of the club professional, and in umpiring.

This phase has been given little attention; it lacks the romantic quality of Nyren's Hambledon, the international and often epic importance of subsequent Test matches, or the popular appeal of such individual players as W. G. Grace, Jack Hobbs or Don Bradman. Yet it was peopled by cricketers of skill and character, working out a destiny for their kind.

Victorian England was imperialistic, jingoistic, class-conscious, missionary-minded, patriotic, prosperous and poverty-stricken all within a single embrace. It produced its eminent Victorians, who were enterprising, materialistic and, on the surface at least, moralistic. Victorian cricket was a microcosm of that world. Touring teams were sent and welcomed; coaches went to many countries; a Test match won was a rightful glory. Gentlemen *v* Players became an institution; wealthy amateurs played side by side with professionals who were in want; the touring elevens spread the gospel of technically sound cricket all over the country; created a 'star' system and made considerable profits from the gates; W. G. Grace became a major nineteenth-century figure; matches and overseas tours made substantial profits; and Sir Henry Newbolt wrote *Vitae Lampada:*

> 'But his captain's hand on his shoulder smote—
> Play up, play up, and play the game.'

In the age of the Reform Bills, professional cricketers made a series of bids to control the game. At a time when many textile workers of the north were on piecework, the cricketers among them tended to adjust their hours to suit their game; so, by consistent practice, they built a generation of highly competent performers. With the opening up of the entire country by the railways, amateur and professional teams, for their different reasons, often travelled long distances to matches; and when the Factory Act of 1850 created the Saturday half-day, cricket became the chief spectator sport of England.

They even looked different from the cricketers of any other period, these players of the 'Elevens' who stumped the country like travelling actors, but on a higher level of importance. They were heroes on the provincial cricket grounds, with their beards and side whiskers, in their white 'All-England' shirts with the red spots, sporting all kinds of head-gear from a slouch cap or billycock to smart black topper; crested belt-buckles, baggy trousers and stout brown boots.

By the eighteen-forties, English cricket had reached a new high standard which was less of a peak than a plateau, for there were many outstanding players and, although Kent and Nottinghamshire were the leading counties, the talent was widely distributed. It was largely professional and increasingly technically minded.

The successful Kent team attracted large crowds from all parts of the county, and in 1842 the Canterbury 'Week' was first held, with stage per-formances by 'The Old Stagers' to entertain the visitors in the evening. The first matches were played on the Beverley Club's ground in Sturry Road but in 1847 the move was made to St Lawrence, where the Festival has flourished ever since.

The first major effect of the legalization of roundarm was exactly what its opponents had prophesied, and its advocates had denied. It enabled bowlers to bowl faster than they had ever done before. At first only a few were able to exploit the opportunity but on the rough pitches which abounded at the time, they were menacing indeed. It was fortunate for the health—perhaps, indeed, the very existence—of cricket that a generation of batsmen was on hand if not completely to master it, at least to stand up to it and maintain a balance between bat and ball.

This was the first true 'star' period in the sport and it may be well to list some of those who now gave the shaped game stability and solidity. The quotations are from Haygarth's *Scores and Biographies*:

Tom Adams, 'a fine and punishing hitter', was a tall opening batsman who played consistently over twenty seasons for Kent in their great period. Unusually among roundarm bowlers he delivered from over the wicket and was straight and accurate.

Thomas Box, the Sussex wicket-keeper, first played county cricket in 1825 when he was sixteen and had a first-class career of some thirty years. Haygarth described him as 'one of the best who ever assumed that important post'. He was at first an indifferent batsman but his cricketing middle age was outstanding—'His style of play was exceedingly fine and

William Clarke

his position erect and commanding'. He was one of several cricketers who kept a public house with an associated cricket ground—first the Hanover Arms and Ground in Lewes Road, Brighton; and later the Brunswick Cricket Ground and Hotel at Hove.

Julius Caesar—a not uncommon name about the Hampshire–Surrey borders—was a powerful batsman for Surrey, especially strong on the leg and in front of the wicket. He was a brilliant catcher at point and an occasional fast roundarm bowler.

As a batsman, William Caffyn, of Surrey, was 'mostly known for his splendid cut'. He bowled roundarm at medium pace, was a capable field anywhere, and accounted 'one of the most accomplished cricketers ever seen'. He was a coach at Winchester and, for a period, in Australia. His autobiography *Seventy-One Not Out* (1899) probably was 'ghosted' but is, nevertheless, a valuable source book for the cricket of his period.

William Clarke was one of the most remarkable and important characters in nineteenth-century cricket. In 1837 he married the widow who owned the Trent Bridge Inn at Nottingham and opened the meadow behind it as Trent Bridge cricket ground. A powerfully built, Nottingham bricklayer, he lost an eye playing fives when he was young; but became an outstanding slow bowler, useful batsman and extremely shrewd tactician. He bowled rather like Lambert, near-round-arm; his pace was slow and he broke from leg, but his outstanding gifts were his accuracy and his ability to detect, and play on, the weaknesses of opposing batsmen. He first appeared for Nottinghamshire at seventeen and played until 1856, when he died at the age of 57. Known as 'Old' Clarke, he was not chosen for the Players against the Gentlemen until he was forty-seven, but he continued to take part in those matches until he was fifty-five. In one period of seven years, from 1847 to 1853, when, certainly, he played many matches against odds and indifferent opponents, he averaged 340 wickets a season—in 1853, 476. He took a wicket with the last bowl he ever bowled.

James—Jemmy—Dean, of Sussex, known as 'The Ploughboy', was a short, stout man; a tireless fast roundarm bowler with awkward rise from the pitch. He developed into a sound batsman and Caffyn considered him the best long-stop of his time.

James Dearman was one of the leading Yorkshire players of the period. Short and stocky, he was a sound batsman, a fast roundarm bowler and a safe mid-wicket fieldsman. He was an accomplished single-wicket player but in 1838, when he issued a challenge to play any man in England, he was twice beaten by Alfred Mynn. He kept the inn and the old cricket ground at Darnall near Sheffield.

William Dorrinton, a tall, slim Kent batsman, was an inconsistent but highly entertaining strokemaker, who was at the peak of his career in 1845 and 1846. Originally a long-stop, when Wenman went into partial retirement, he became relief wicket-keeper for Kent. A tailor in Town Malling, he was a 'civil and obliging man' who was only thirty-nine when he died from a chill caught while playing for the All-England Eleven in wet weather.

Nicholas Wanostrocht, a schoolmaster of Belgian origin, played under the pseudonym—which he persuaded Haygarth to adopt in his *Scores*—of 'Nicholas Felix' to avoid affronting the parents of his pupils. He matured relatively late but played for Gentlemen *v* Players from 1831 to 1852. A short, well-built left-hand bat, he 'possessed the most brilliant cut (from the shoulder) ever seen . . . his drives and forward play were also very good'. He occasionally bowled slow left-arm lobs and was a fine field at point. He was an accomplished artist, whose lithographs of his con-temporaries—notably a group of the All-England XI—are some of the best of all cricket pictures. He wrote a pamphlet called *How to Play Clarke*, and *Felix on the Bat*, an instructional book which ran to three editions, one of which was illustrated by G. F. Watts, who had been a pupil at Felix's school. A mentally alert and witty man, he invented the Catapulta—a bowling machine—and tubular batting gloves.

Joseph Guy, of Nottinghamshire, was 'a fine upright and scientific batsman, very forward in style and could cut to the off and hit to leg in a brilliant manner'. He was among the three or four best batsmen of his time, at his best against the best bowling. He was immortalized in the comment 'Joe Guy, all ease and elegance, fit to play before the Queen in Her Majesty's parlour'. He was first a baker and then a publican.

William Hillyer, of the great Kent eleven, was a lively, medium to fast roundarm bowler. Sometimes described as 'the best of all bowlers', he had an easy action, varied his pace skilfully, commanded steep lift from the pitch, and cut the ball sharply from leg to off. He was a fine short slip but an indifferent batsman. He rented and let out shooting near Maidstone but, an extremely sick man with rheumatism—which ended his playing career—liver disease and consumption, he died at forty-seven.

William Lillywhite, slow roundarm, was called 'the Nonpareil bowler'. Infallibly accurate and straight, Haygarth said 'He was indeed like a piece of machinery, and in his old age wanted only a little oiling, when he would have been as effective as ever'. Short and stout—five-feet-four and eleven-and-a-half stones—there is no record of his cricket prior to 1822, when he was thirty. After that, however, he played regularly for over twenty seasons and bowled accurately in his own benefit match at Lord's when he was sixty-one. Originally a bricklayer from West Hampnett near Goodwood, he became landlord of The Royal Sovereign Inn and a cricket ground at Brighton.

Tom Lockyer, of Surrey, was usually regarded as the best of the three pre-eminent wicket-keepers of the period; Box and Wenman were the others. Tall, strong and long-armed, his great reach and extreme speed of reaction enabled him to make some remarkable leg-side catches and rapid stumpings. A hard hitter with a good eye, he batted valuably in the middle order; and was a talented roundarm fast bowler on the rare occasions when he could be spared from wicket-keeping, or was called on to break a stubborn stand. An immense trier and a shrewd reader of the game, he generally managed matches for both Surrey and the 'United' XI. Originally a bricklayer, he subsequently became landlord of the Prince Albert Inn at Croydon.

Thomas Marsden was one of the great Sheffield cricketers of the mid-nineteenth century. Left-handed, he was a 'hard slashing hitter' and fast underarm or medium roundarm as a bowler; a good field at mid-wicket; and a notable single-wicket player. At the age of twenty-two he played a remarkable innings of 227 for Sheffield against strong Nottinghamshire bowling. A brickmaker of about average height and strong build, he was seriously injured in a coach accident and died at thirty-eight.

Alfred Mynn was the most spectacular cricketer of his time and an outstanding all-rounder. Six-feet-one tall and weighing twenty stone, he bowled roundarm 'very fast and ripping'; was a terrific hitter; and with his huge hands, a superb slip field. Popular, good-humoured, immensely strong, he was a hop farmer, but a poor businessman and eventually went bankrupt. W. J. Prowse's obituary verses on him end with 'Lightly lie the turf upon thee, kind and manly Alfred Mynn'.

Fuller Pilch was, in Haygarth's considered judgment, 'the best batsman that has ever yet appeared . . . His style of batting was very commanding, extremely forward and he seemed to crush the best bowling by his long forward plunge before it had time to shoot, or rise, or do mischief by catches'. Originally a tailor in his native Norfolk, he was persuaded for £100 a year to settle in Kent and play for that county. In his early days he was a successful slow left-arm bowler and was always a safe field; but he was pre-eminent for his batting: even the incomplete records of his time credited him with the then unparalleled record of ten centuries in major matches. He was, too, noted for his skilful tactics. A quiet, ruminative man and a bachelor, he became a publican in Canterbury.

George Parr—'The Lion of the North'—succeeded Fuller Pilch as the best batsman in England. His defence was extremely sound but his fame was as a mighty leg-side hitter—the tree on the square-leg boundary at Trent Bridge was called 'Parr's tree' because he sent the ball there so often. Powerful, round-shouldered, with a slight limp, he bowled slow lobs; and was a terrific thrower from the deep field. Son of a farmer, he became secretary of the All-England XI in succession to William Clarke; and later, coach at Harrow School. Parr was extremely highly strung; honest, introvert, irascible; fearless against the most terrific bowling but nervous of thunderstorms and sea voyages. He was much addicted to gin-and-water. From the day he ceased playing he took no further interest at all in cricket.

Samuel Redgate, a Nottingham lace-maker, was one of the first truly fast roundarm bowlers. Haygarth emphasizes that he had 'a beautiful easy delivery and was unexceptionable as to fairness'. He proved particularly effective against, of all people, Fuller Pilch. In the second innings of Kent against England at Town Malling in 1839 he bowled a remarkable four-ball over. The first narrowly missed Stearman's stumps; the second bowled him;—and Redgate tossed back a glass of brandy; the third bowled Alfred Mynn; and Redgate took another glass of brandy; the last bowled Fuller Pilch—and Redgate took his third glass of brandy. That kind of pace does not last. According to Haygarth his bowling 'was very fast and ripping, with a good deal of "spin", but the last few years it was slow and feeble, owing to ill health'. He died at the age of forty.

Thomas Sewell, called 'Busy Tom' because of his quick, active, bustling —and sometimes destructively impatient—style of batting, played first for Surrey and then for Kent. He was an accurate underarm bowler who never attempted roundarm, and a safe fieldsman. As a young man he was a heavy scorer for the famous Mitcham club but did not come into the first-class game until he was thirty-three. He was a calico printer who later took over the Chequers Inn at Sevenoaks and subsequently became a respected umpire at Lord's and The Oval.

C. G. Taylor, an Etonian who played for Sussex, was the outstanding 'pure' amateur of the time; described by a contemporary versifier as 'Taylor, the most graceful of all'. Haygarth says he 'was one of the most finished and brilliant batsmen that has ever appeared; and was supposed to have a greater variety of hits than any other cricketer of his day'. Quick-witted, athletic and versatile—he was talented at billiards and tennis—he was a gifted slow roundarm bowler, sure field and a major power in the Gentlemen's XI until he retired from the game early, at the age of thirty.

Edward Wenman, of the great Kent eleven, played in the first-class game for over forty seasons from 1819. He was a splendid all-round wicket-keeper, who, in a period when most were content to deal with straight and off-side balls, was masterly down the leg side; skilful with either hand, and safe, even when standing up to the stumps to Alfred Mynn's tremendous pace. Worth his place in a team for his batting alone, he was primarily a back-foot player—he was, too, a capable match manager and shrewd in developing young players. By trade a carpenter and builder.

John Wisden, who came from Brighton and played for Sussex, was of quite remarkably slight physique—five-feet-four-and-a-half and seven stones—for a fast bowler. Yet for at least ten years he was in Haygarth's words 'very fast indeed and ripping'. In the great match in 1859, playing for the North (because he had taken over a ground at Leamington), he cleaned bowled all ten wickets of the South. 'Without exaggeration,' says Haygarth, he 'turned a yard from the off, delivering from the Pavilion end.' He and Frederick Lillywhite opened a 'cricketing and cigar depot' at 2 New Coventry Street, Leicester Square, but the partnership was dissolved and Wisden is remembered now chiefly for founding his *Cricketers' Almanack* which has appeared without a break since 1865. A straight and steady batsman and a capable slip, he was hardly bettered as an all-rounder or single-wicket player in his time.

Their trades and professions are given since they indicate a striking uniformity among these players. Virtually every one of them came from a craft demanding dexterity; and they show the tendency to take public houses which was common among nineteenth-century cricketers.

These were the cricketers who were to accept the opportunities of the time to establish cricket as a spectator sport throughout England. The coming of the railway meant that matches could be played all over the country more conveniently than ever before. The introduction of piece-work in the midland and northern textile industries gave many people greater freedom to play or watch than they had ever known, and largely accounted for the ending of southern domination of the game and for the rise of Nottingham, Sheffield and Manchester as centres.

I Zingari was the first of the amateur clubs to roam the country on social cricket tours. I Zingari—or 'I.Z.'—the name is Italian for 'The Gypsies'—played their first match in 1845, at and against, Newport Pagnell. Their object was to find *gentlemen* bowlers and for this reason they never engaged professionals. 'They have no ground, the entrance to the club is nothing, and the annual subscription may not exceed the entrance.'

> 'They pitch their tents where'er they please
> And always find a home.'

'The original members were selected from the Canterbury Amateur Dramatical Society but others were added in mysterious ways from various sources.'

There was, though, no obvious invitation to professionals to do the same. Yet the demand for 'grand matches' was strong and plain. The opening of The Oval in 1845—after members of the Montpelier Club had taken the lease and founded the Surrey County Club—reflected the increasing public interest in London; and it was echoed sharply in the north of the country.

Gentlemen *versus* Players was generally too one-sided to satisfy the demand. Even in 'The Barn Door Match' of 1837, otherwise known as 'Ward's Folly', since, at William Ward's insistence, the Players defended four-stump wickets three-feet high and a foot wide, the balance was not redressed; indeed, the Players won by an innings. So in the records of the years up to 1846, fixtures not only like North *versus* South, which was the major attraction, but Fast Bowlers v. Slow, A to K v. L to Z, M.C.C. v. West of England, Kent or Sussex or Hampshire v. England, the 'blood' matches like Bradford v. Rochdale, Sheffield v. Nottingham, Manchester v. Liverpool, Sheffield v. Bradford, Harewood, Otley and Dacre Banks, and a host of single wicket matches between likely and unlikely performers show the extent of the spectator demand for cricket entertainment.

'Old' Clarke perceived the opportunity and seized it. When he first opened the Trent Bridge ground in 1837, his introduction of an admission charge was extremely unpopular with a Nottingham public accustomed to watching matches free on the Forest. He was as mercenary as he was shrewd; as strong-willed as he was artful. He resolved on building a touring 'missionary' team of outstanding players who would stump the country playing local teams—fifteens, sixteens or even twenty-twos—or reinforced by professionals—of club players. He was a shrewd manager of a team, a sound judge of players, the best slow bowler in England and, valuably, he retained his zest for the game through to the end. 'I'll have this end, you have whichever you like' he would say to a fellow bowler; and, if counselled to make a change in the bowling, 'All right, I'll have the other end.' When J. H. Dark, the proprietor of Lord's Ground and an important cricket goods dealer, heard that Clarke had made a fixture in Newcastle he protested to him that the local players were not capable of making a game of it against professionals. 'Never you mind,' said Clarke, 'I shall play all over the country, too, and it will be good for cricket and for your trade, too.' 'Sure enough,' said Dark later, 'the increase of my bat and ball trade is witness to his long-sightedness.'

His scheme took time to establish. It was probably discussed during the M.C.C. v. The North match at Trent Bridge in 1845. In August 1846, he gathered fifteen capable players together in a match for his 'benefit' at Southwell which served as a trial run and gave them the opportunity to discuss his plans. Then, later in the month, he took his 'All-England Eleven' to play Twenty of Sheffield at Hyde Park, Sheffield. Parr, taken ill during the benefit match, was not able to play and the team was not so strong as it was to become: nevertheless it was the strongest that had ever been seen in Sheffield until then. It was Clarke, Dean, Dorrinton, Pilch, Mynn, Guy, Martingell, Sewell, Butler, Smith and Hillyer. The England players were bothered by the unaccustomed number of twenty opponents in the field against them. There was considerable local excitement when, despite innings of 33 by Dorrinton and 38 by Sewell, and the bowling of Hillyer (17 wickets) and Dean (14) the Twenty won by five wickets. For social reasons, and as 'front men' when local dignitaries came to the matches, Clarke always had one or two amateurs in his side. Now they were Alfred Mynn, the greatest crowd attraction in the game of the time, and V. S. C. Smith. Villiers Smith was a Wykehamist who made history by being the oldest 'schoolboy' to appear at Lord's. When he last appeared against Harrow and Eton for Winchester, in 1843, he was only a couple of months short of his twenty-second birthday. He was an attacking bat, particularly strong on the leg side; a fast underarm bowler and a fine field with a long, accurate throw. A fellow of New College, Oxford, he gave up public match-playing when he entered the Church.

Straight from Sheffield to Manchester, and next day the same Eleven met Eighteen of Manchester in another three-day match. Pilch made 62; Hillyer took 18 wickets, Dean 11; and the All-England Eleven won by an innings and 31 runs.

On, immediately, to Leeds and a fixture with Eighteen of Yorkshire on Woodhouse Moor. Here England, batting first, were reduced to 16 for five by the fast bowler, Ibbetson. The innings was salvaged by Smith (34) and Butler (34); and Hillyer, 21 wickets, and Dean 11, won the match by 69 runs. Ibbetson took altogether twelve wickets for 52 runs. 'His bowling was by some considered unfair' and after he had been no-balled nineteen times, the umpires were changed to enable him to continue. Such was the fundamentally non-competitive nature of these matches. Ibbetson played in four matches for Yorkshire but, although he took twelve wickets in them, the county did not persevere with him.

That was the end of the All-England Eleven's matches for 1846: but it was enough to prove to Clarke that it was a highly profitable operation; and that was his main concern. On the technical side, the players had to consider the problem of scoring runs against a field sixteen to twenty-two strong. On the other side of the coin, they had found out how valuably deadly Dean and, even more, Hillyer were against club players, particularly in destroying the tail.

Clarke had no doubts at all about 1848. He made fixtures as rapidly as he could: in all, sixteen. There were two together in succession in June; two at the beginning of August; then, after a week's 'rest', while the England v. Kent and Kent (with eight of his cadre) v. Sussex matches were played, All-England had twelve engagements to the 30 September. The single possible break was filled by a three-a-side single wicket match against Sheffield.

By 1849 Clarke was building to his optimum team. Parr and Box were generally available. He made 'Felix', a capable speech-maker and public relations man, 'President' of the Eleven; the other 'amateur' was Alfred Mynn.

Invariably, three or four out of Mynn, Lillywhite, Wisden, Dean, Hillyer and Clarke himself were to hand as bowlers. Incidentally, in the Gentlemen v Players match of 1847, at Lord's, Lillywhite, at fifty-five, took eleven wickets for 36 runs and Clarke, now forty-eight, nine for 54. From time to time, he also brought in Edmund Hinkly (otherwise Hinkley or Hinckley), a fast left-arm bowler who had proved very effective for Surrey against the Eleven. Hinkly had a short but extremely successful career and in his first match at Lord's—against England—he took six wickets in the first innings and all ten in the second. He constantly got out George Parr. All the sixteen matches of 1848 were against odds. At one point in the season someone else—whose name was not revealed—raised an 'England' eleven to play Twenty-two of Walsall, but it was a poor side by comparison even with Clarke's weakest. He maintained a high standard.

The 'official' England teams raised by Lord's and Kent for their matches were all but identical in personnel with Clarke's or perhaps a little weaker. By 1849 he regularly controlled a group of players from which any chosen team would have beaten any other eleven in England with the utmost ease.

Felix and Alfred Mynn, though in name amateurs, and who appeared regularly for the Gentlemen against Players, were paid by Clarke: and in summer, at least, they made a living from cricket. So far as can be ascertained, Clarke, who paid all expenses of travel and board, gave them £5 a match by contrast with the £4 for the recognized 'professionals'. Clarke lived apart from his team. Before play he would walk round the field assessing the opposition and would then return to the pavilion with 'I value them at so many runs', and he was more often right than wrong. During a match his lunch was a cigar and a glass of soda water; but he liked to dine—alone—off a goose and a bottle of claret.

He would never accept an All-England match engagement without a 'subscription' of £70 to cover him if rain prevented any play; plus the provision of meals and entertainment for his side. Tom Sherman later told Ashley-Cooper: 'Clarke must have made a deal of money out of the A.E.E. matches. That was forced upon me the first time I received payment from him. The cricketers went up to him one after the other for their money, and as I was the last in the row I was able to take in all that transpired. Clarke had a heap of gold and silver in front of him, and during the paying-out process you would hear something like this: "Four pounds for you, fifty shillings for you, three pounds for you", the amounts varying according to a player's fame and what he had done in the match. When I approached him he looked up, saying: "Fifty shillings for you"—and then, shovelling the balance into his trousers pockets, and giving a most satisfied smile, added "and thirty-seven pounds for me!" '

By 1849 he had learnt all the ropes and was in full control. From the start of the season to the end of September the Eleven played twenty-one matches; nineteen against odds but, significantly and importantly, Clarke also provided England teams for the Kent-England and Sussex-England eleven-a-side matches. This represented a striking shift of power from local club to entrepreneur. The only threat to his operations lay in a fixture played by 'An England Eleven' of fair strength against Twenty of Norwich and District, arranged by John Lillywhite.

Still Clarke expanded; in 1850 the Eleven had twenty-one matches against odds, spread from 30 April into October; and one eleven-a-side, against Kent at Cranbrook of which Haygarth notes 'This was one of the All-England matches got up by W. Clarke; the other two, at Lord's and Canterbury, were managed (as usual) by the Marylebone Club.' The danger, clearly, had been recognized by M.C.C. and due action taken.

Clarke had the worst of another power-skirmish with Lord's. In 1854 the Eleven was contracted to meet Eighteen of Maidstone at the same time as the Lord's Gentlemen v. Players fixture in which Parr, Caesar and

Caffyn were invited to play. Clarke—because, it was said, he himself had not been asked to play (he was, after all, fifty-five)—refused to release them, and they appeared at Maidstone. Lillywhite, in his *Guide*, noted 'This, it is believed, caused Clarke's name to be scratched from the books of our rulers, signifying that he would not again have the honour of being applied to for his services.' Surely enough, he was never invited to play in that fixture again.

Clarke could not relax. In 1851 there were thirty-four matches, all against odds except that *versus* Kent at Cranbrook. This year the Eleven began its first match on 5 May and finished its last on 16 October. Lillywhite's *Guide* noted that they won 16 matches; lost 8; and 'principally from bad weather, 10 were left unfinished'.

The results, of course, were not really important. These matches were solely of parochial importance. In many cases ordinary club cricketers contributed towards the guarantee or match expenses for a place in the local eighteen sheerly for the privilege of being able to say they had batted against William Lillywhite or bowled to Fuller Pilch. One of *Punch*'s first sallies into cricket was a drawing showing a battered cricketer in bandages and splints saying proudly 'I 'ad a hover of Jackson' (a very fast bowler who played with the Eleven). Nothing could please a provincial crowd more than that their eighteen or twenty-two should beat the 'cracks'—so long as the professionals gave an interesting exhibition of their skills and appeared to be trying.

The members of the Eleven, for their part, must have found it hard to sustain interest through a May-to-October season. They can have had no enthusiasm, for instance, for such pitches as that on which they met Twenty-two of Leamington in 1848, of which Haygarth wrote: 'The ground on which this match was played was now merely a "ridge and furrow" field, but was levelled in the winter of 1848-9. G. Parr and J. Wisden then became joint proprietors.' Pycroft speaks of the professionals being so tired that they welcomed a wet day with no play so that they could rest their weary feet.

Clarke had recognized from the first the problems of entertaining an uninformed public in matches where multiple fields on the one side and superior bowling on the other ensured that scoring would generally be slow. He was at pains to recruit aggressive and enterprising batsmen, yet there are constant references to players making all their runs in singles; another to George Parr taking five hours to make ten runs—though this obviously included extensive stoppages for rain.

The Eleven, and its subsequent competitors, undoubtedly did much good by spreading the gospels of the straight bat, length bowling and keen fielding. They were instrumental, too, in bringing out some good players who might have remained in obscurity but for a convincing demonstration against such opposition. Clarke did not miss, or forget, talent. Certainly these travelling sides went to towns which had never seen a first-class

Sussex v. Kent 1849

team or a three-day fixture before—and, in many cases, have not done so again since the days of the Elevens.

The other side of the coin, however, demands consideration. Haygarth, a sound judge, if something of a traditionalist, notes under the score of Nottinghamshire v. Sussex at Trent Bridge in 1848: 'G. Parr, Guy and W. Clarke did not play for Nottinghamshire, they being engaged in an All-England match—one contest thus spoiling the other, as about this period began to be the case, owing to the quantity of matches played. County and eleven-a-side matches certainly ought to have the preference.' However sound Haygarth's judgment, and at this range it is difficult not to agree with him, the fact remains that play with the All-England was financially rewarding. It was not so profitable for the players as it was for Clarke but, on the whole, he offered regular employment and a wage standard which they could not better elsewhere.

County cricket had been growing steadily in playing standards and public esteem up to the creation of the All-England. After that, however, it laboured under a considerable handicap for almost thirty years.

Clarke's first setback came in 1852. That was an unlucky year for him. He fell in the course of a match and broke his arm which, it was thought,

would end the bowling career of a man of fifty-three; on the contrary, as soon as it mended, he returned to active play. Several of his players had long thought his profit margins excessive and their payments inadequate; and resented his high-handed discipline. In consequence, in 1852, James Dean and John Wisden launched the United All-England Eleven in a tentative programme of four matches. Their main strength lay in defectors from Clarke's cadre, such as Dean and Wisden themselves, Lockyer, Sampson, Tinley, Grundy and Adams. The new team, which protested its goodwill towards county cricket and the availability (not always granted) of its players for county fixtures, prospered sufficiently to extend to fifteen games in the following season. During their second match the breakaway group signed a manifesto that they would never again play in any fixture—apart from county matches—arranged by William Clarke. Clarke was not seriously incommoded. He still had Parr, Guy, Box, Mynn, Hillyer, Felix and himself; in the immediately preceding seasons, too, he had astutely spotted and recruited some outstanding younger men in Caffyn, Caesar, Anderson, Jackson, Diver, Bickley, Stephenson, Tinley and Willsher. Thus he still commanded probably the strongest group of cricketers in the country. Which was the stronger of the two Elevens? That widely canvassed question could not be put to the test while Clarke was in one camp and the 'Manifesto Group' in the other. After Clarke died, in 1856, however, any reason for hostility between the two sides ceased. Clarke's successor, Parr, was popular with players at all levels. So, in 1857, in response to genuine public interest and demand, the two Elevens met in two matches at Lord's; the first in aid of the Cricketers' Benevolent Fund, the second for Dean's benefit (Dean himself stood down from the match in order to take the money at the gate). The batting of Parr in all four innings and the bowling of Willsher and Jackson proved decisive and Clarke's All-England won both matches. For another decade the two annual matches between these two sides were accepted as the outstanding fixtures of the entire domestic season, transcending both Gentlemen *v* Players and North *v* South in importance and public esteem.

This was in many ways a most profound phase of English cricket in terms of development, social, economic and political significance, and, also, perhaps, in character. It was, too, unquestionably the most artistically rewarding period in the history of the game. There are a few outstanding paintings in which cricket is incidental; a gouache landscape with cricket match by Paul Sandby; apart from Hayman's 'Cricket as Played in the Artillery Ground' though, nothing compares for sustained quality with the productions of the eighteen-forties and eighteen-fifties. W. H. Mason's *Sussex v. Kent* is probably the most popular engraving in the history of cricket; it was extensively pirated; used to hang in almost every pavilion in the country; was often thrown out as Victoriana; and now is a rare and expensive picture. The most eminent, however, are the lithographs of strokes by G. F. Watts, and of some sixty of players of the period by 'Felix', John Corbett Anderson, C. J. Basébe and W. Drummond. These were immensely popular in this rich era of lithography: the drawings are sensitive and the reproduction (they were available both plain and coloured) is immaculate. They are now collectors' items, relatively rare, and invariably expensive.

The financial success of the two Elevens soon tempted others into the field and, while the first two were not excelled, five more Elevens reduced profits and diluted the available talent to the damage, in particular, of county cricket.

They were—with their founders and dates—'The New All-England Eleven' (Tom Sherman; 1858–1862); The United South of England Eleven —later the United England Eleven (Edgar Willsher; 1865–1882); United North & South of England Eleven (Secretary G. Baker; 1866–1868); United North of England Eleven (George Freeman and Roger Iddison; 1870–1881); New United South of England Eleven (Tom Sherman and William Caffyn; 1875–1876).

Before the 'cracks' came back from Australia in 1864, three matches against odds were played by 'The English Eleven' managed by Willsher and Stephenson. In the same season, too, 'R. Carpenter, T. Hayward and G. Tarrant's Eleven' played Twenty-two Amateurs of Cambridge and

District on Parker's Piece. Over a couple of decades virtually every professional—and quite a few amateurs—of any genuine ability joined in this remunerative sport-industry. Dean and Wisden's 'United' ceased to exist in 1869; but, although Parr took little pleasure in managing the original All-England, it continued to make a profit after he handed over to Richard Daft, until 1879.

The Elevens, though, had outlived their value before the All-England ceased to exist. Events had already taken place which spelt the end of the single and extremely important phase of cricket history in which the professional players almost took the control of the game out of the hands of the amateur establishment. They had failed through their own short-comings. Despite the protestations of the 'United' they had all gone for the quick profits of an 'Eleven' *versus* Twenty-one of Little Snodbury, and eventually that vein ran out. The provincial public that at first flocked to the one-sided exhibition matches had grown more sophisticated and was calling for the truly competitive game which, even through its relatively unprofitable days, had always remained under the control of the clubs.

Only Clarke of the professionals had been of the calibre to challenge those whom Lillywhite had described as 'our rulers'. Clarke's fault, too, lay in his cupidity; but once he was dead, the professionals in English cricket were, once more, men for hire.

Chapter 5
New dimensions

Three events of the eighteen-sixties presaged new paths in history. In chronological order they were: the first tour to Australia; the legalization of overarm bowling; and the entry of W. G. Grace into first-class cricket. The visit to Australia set in train the whole procession of international cricket; overarm was the last great technical revolution which set the bowler free; and W. G. Grace was to give cricket a fresh dimension.

The official acceptance of overarm was simply recognition of general practice. From the moment roundarm was allowed, some bowlers were delivering from above the shoulder, in some cases much higher. One of the best bowlers of this period was Edgar Willsher, of Kent, left-arm, of lively pace with a sharp breakaway, and described by Haygarth as 'perhaps the most difficult of all'. In 1862 at The Oval, he opened the bowling for England against Surrey and, in his third over, was five times no-balled by the umpire, John Lillywhite (son of William, the main protagonist of roundarm). Willsher threw down the ball and, in hubbub from the large crowd, went off the field followed by all the England players except C. G. Lyttleton and V. E. Walker, the only two amateurs. Eventually play was suspended. No one knows what discussions went on at Lord's that night, but next day Street took over the duties of umpire at Lillywhite's end, and Willsher bowled (indeed, he took six wickets). Lillywhite had deemed it his duty to force the issue, choosing a major bowler and a major occasion to do so. Authority could no longer turn a blind eye to the question and two years later Law X was changed to allow overarm. The way was now clear for bowlers to develop swing, flight, and pace to the fullest and, since bowlers are the true inventors and innovators of cricket, they took that opportunity, and continue still to exploit it. That was the last major legislative change until the change in the lbw law.

Since cricket had grown out from England it was logical that English cricketers would one day go out to play it in its fresh centres. Spread generally by the British navy, army and traders, by 1850 it was played in Australia, America, India, Canada, New Zealand, South Africa, West Indies, Portugal, the Argentine, Denmark, Germany and Italy. We have observed that, but for the outbreak of the French Revolution, the Duke of Dorset's team would have gone to Paris to play in 1789. In the event the Duke—who was then British Ambassador to France—met his team at Dover as he fled from Paris, in time to stop them sailing.

So the first overseas tour undertaken by an English team was that to Canada and the United States in 1859. It was arranged, and its expenses and payments guaranteed, by the Montreal Club. George Parr captained the side, composed of six members of the All-England and six of the United. It was no rest cure; the crossing alone was agony for several members of the party and, once they began to play, the one of the twelve who was not actually taking part in the match was expected to umpire. Each player was guaranteed £50 for the two-month tour; though Caffyn said he eventually cleared £90.

The first Australian tour followed two years later, a speculative venture, sponsored by Messrs Spiers & Pond, the caterers. They had arranged a lecture tour by Charles Dickens and, when he could not undertake it, they fell back on cricket. The side was not so strong as it might have been because the northern players thought the proffered £150 a man in-sufficient. The sponsors refused to increase the offer for—again—a twelve-man party which played twelve matches—all against odds. In the event it made a profit of £12,000 for the promoters. At the end of the tour, Charles Lawrence, of Surrey, remained behind to coach. He returned to England in 1868, bringing a team of Aboriginals who played some semi-serious cricket and gave demonstrations of boomerang-throwing and dancing. The success of the 1861–62 venture encouraged another trip and in 1863–64 the Melbourne Club sponsored one. George Parr captained a side including E. M. Grace—elder brother of W.G.—with ten professionals. Again all their matches were against odds and they returned unbeaten. For this tour the players had a first-class passage and they were guar-anteed £250 each. This time William Caffyn stayed on to coach, first in Melbourne and then in Sydney, with important, beneficial and enduring effect on the game in Australia.

The inscription on the Grace Gates at Lord's says simply

WILLIAM GILBERT GRACE
THE GREAT CRICKETER

He was, without doubt, the greatest player the game ever knew—or ever can know, because he virtually created the modern game. Others may excel at it; but he created it.

There was never any real doubt about his destiny. His father, a Gloucestershire doctor, was a keen and useful club cricketer; his four brothers—he was the fourth—all played, two of them (E.M. and G.F.) for England; his Uncle Pocock, a diligent net bowler and encourager; and his mother was a shrewd enough judge to write to William Clarke that she had a younger son who would be a better bat than E.M.

William Gilbert Grace was just fifteen when he was chosen to play for Twenty-two of Bristol and District against the All-England Eleven. He scored 32 against Tarrant and Jackson—two of the best fast bowlers in the country—and the slow spin of Tinley. His brother, E.M. made 37 and took ten wickets (W.G., one) and, most unusually, a strong All-England side was beaten by an innings.

In the following season, a few days before his sixteenth birthday, W.G. replaced E.M., who was not available, for the South Wales Club against the Gentlemen of Sussex at Brighton; and scored 170 in the first innings, 56 not out in the second. He made another century that season and a number of useful scores; and took wickets steadily. As a result, in the following summer—and before his seventeenth birthday—he had played his first three first-class matches; remarkably, they were for the Gentlemen of the South against Players of the South, and both Gentlemen *v* Players fixtures, at The Oval and Lord's.

Remarkable as the selection of a sixteen-year-old was for these matches, it was equally appropriate; for he, more than anyone else, was to alter the entire balance of power between Gentlemen and Players. At this point his bowling was more impressive than his batting. He made 0 in his single innings for Gentlemen of the South; 23 and 12 at The Oval; 3 and 34 at Lord's in the first match the Gentlemen had won for twelve years. Against Players of the South he bowled unchanged with I. D. Walker through both innings and took thirteen wickets for 84; at The Oval his seven wickets (for 125) included those of Alfred Shaw, Harry Jupp, George Bennett, Tom Hearne and Luke Greenwood. He had two more first-class matches that season; scoring 48 and 34 for Gentlemen of England against Gentlemen of Middlesex; and made 35 of an opening partnership of 80 with E.M. for England v. Surrey. In various club matches, mainly for Clifton, that season he scored 1,972 runs, took 175 wickets and, as well as 17 catches, made six stumpings.

The modern reader can easily overlook the fact that many wickets at this time were extremely rough. That included Lord's, where no groundsman was employed until 1864. Pitches there were usually prepared by turning sheep out to graze them, and when the first mowing machine was introduced, the Hon. Robert Grimston, one of the succession of Lord's autocrats, went out into the St John's Wood Road and tipped some navvies to go in and smash that 'infernal machine' with their pick-axes. 'Steevie' Slatter, whose family was long associated with Lord's, said that, when he was a boy there in the eighteen-fifties, two ponds used to form on the ground during winter; and that he had learned to swim in the one in front of the present Mound Stand. It was there, too, at the 1868 Gentlemen *v* Players that the crowd rose and cheered W.G. for stopping the four shooters from the fast bowler, George Wootton, which comprised the first over of the match. He came into the game when there were still a legion of extremely fast and wild roundarm bowlers operating on wickets which were often terrifyingly rough. In such conditions Grace's scores were as phenomenal as his contemporaries recognized.

In 1866 he identified himself as a great cricketer with two outstanding innings. A fortnight after his eighteenth birthday, he went in third wicket down for England against Surrey and made 224 not out, out of 431 while he was at the wicket. The next day his captain released him from the field to go to the National Olympian Association meeting at the Crystal Palace and run in the 400 yards hurdles—which he won. A few weeks afterwards he made 173 not out (in a total of 297)—and took nine wickets—for Gentlemen of the South against Players of the South.

The next year was one of the few checks in his career. A split finger, a sprained ankle and scarlet fever limited him to four matches in which he did not make a century. He bowled, however, with some distinction, taking eleven wickets for 63 runs when the Players were beaten again at Lord's and took, altogether, 39 at an average of 7.48.

His accession to the position of the best all-round player in England was emphasized in the Gentlemen *v* Players match at Lord's of 1868, when he went in number three on a fiery pitch and, against some outstanding professional bowlers, scored 134 not out in a total of 201. No one else in the match reached 30; and, looking back, he was inclined to think it the best innings of his career. He followed that with six for 50 and four for 31 to win the match once more for the Gentlemen. A few weeks afterwards, for South of Thames against North of Thames, he became only the second batsman—Lambert was the first—to score two centuries in a match. He was now the chief attraction in the game and he was turning out for the United South of England Eleven against odds. He played for payment under a strict contract for each match, with penal clauses if he failed to appear in person. From this period comes the story of the notice on the gate to a country cricket ground—

CRICKET MATCH
ADMISSION 6 PENCE
IF W. G. GRACE PLAYS ADMISSION ONE SHILLING

Six feet tall, wide-shouldered and beginning to thicken with muscle, he was fit and strong; as a batsman he hit extremely hard and had a voracious appetite for runs. In 1869, Lillywhite's *Companion* said he was 'generally admitted to be the most wonderful cricketer that ever held a bat . . . a certain scorer off any bowling and the quickest run-getter in England'.

Apart from 1867, when he was ill, he was constantly top of the batting averages. In 1870 he set a new record aggregate for a season with 1,808 runs at 54.78; only to beat it in the following year with 2,739 at 78.25. Even those figures need setting in perspective of other players. In 1870 the next batsman was Edward Pooley with 1,078 at 22.4; and in 1871, Harry Jupp with 1,068 at 24.12.

In the second of those years, when Grace's 116 against Nottinghamshire was the first century ever scored in a county match at Trent Bridge, factory hands for miles around struck work to go and watch him. Even the wet summer of 1872 could not check him; before he went to America in early August he had already scored 1,485 runs with an average of 57.3 (the next man, Richard Humphrey, had 1,071 at 23.36 for the entire season).

R. A. FitzGerald captained the team of amateurs that made a short, largely social month's tour of Canada and the United States; the cricket was hardly serious. Twelve months later, though, W. G. Grace went on a much less relaxed tour of Australia. He had just married and, in that his wife came with him, the visit was in the nature of a honeymoon. On the other hand, primitive conditions, much travelling and extremely hot weather made it a taxing ordeal. He made all the arrangements, and picked the team, mainly from Gloucestershire and the United South of England Eleven with which the Graces were involved.

Quite apart from the sea voyages between England and Australia, the playing programme began on 1 January, ended on 28 March and included fourteen matches, all against odds, plus the two-way sea voyage for the two Tasmanian fixtures and, often, coach journeys of hundreds of miles between games. The contractual terms must have been stiff because, although the promoters—wealthy members of the Melbourne Club—paid Mrs Grace's expenses, W.G. himself had to take part in every fixture, and single-wicket matches had to be played if the main engagements ended early. He drove a hard bargain with his professionals. He offered them second-class passage—which put off some and rankled deeply with others —£150 for the tour, plus £20 spending money. For such niggardly terms alone he had a few refusals; the side was not as strong as he had wished, and it was beaten twice. Oscroft, at least, though, showed a substantial profit. 'I went out to Australia,' he told A. W. Pullin, 'to make as much money as I could.' He did it by taking out cricket gear 'four times as much as all the rest of the team put together' and selling it to Australians. Fred Grace in his account of the tour published in *Lillywhite* comments: 'The trip on the whole was an enjoyable one for seeing Colonies and meeting good friends; but from a cricketing point of view we were met in a bad spirit as if contending cricketers were enemies.' W. G. Grace was not a man to be put upon; he protested strongly against bad wickets or any attempt to take an advantage, and the atmosphere was often tense. He came back home convinced that such Australian bowlers as Spofforth, Wills, Midwinter, Kendall, Cosstick, Conway and Boyle could be extremely successful against English players and in English conditions. His estimate was soon to be proved sound.

Chapter 6
The international game

The beginning of Test cricket was completely unpremeditated. Some ill feeling sprang up between the players of the two sides during the Grace tour. Standards of play and pitches in Australia had been low, too, and a decade elapsed before James Lillywhite was invited to take a team to Australia and New Zealand in 1876–77.

Conscious of the ill-will aroused by the second-class passages of W. G. Grace's side, he offered first-class travel and a basic £150. There were, too, some extras which, for instance, brought Alfred Shaw—virtually assistant manager—a total of £300. Even that was by no means excessive for a tour which lasted in playing time from 16 November to 4 April.

Australian cricket had grown in strength and resources. The Melbourne Cricket Ground was described by Haygarth as 'the best in the world of its kind'. Fifteen of New South Wales beat the touring team twice; fifteen of Melbourne once and, after the two wins against Grace's side the Australians, at once nostalgic and self-justifyingly aggressive, were anxious to try conclusions with the touring team on equal terms.

It was belatedly arranged that a joint eleven from Victoria and New South Wales would play an extra match, not in the original schedule, at Melbourne when the tourists returned from New Zealand. It was simply a challenge match. Neither side was at full strength for the occasion. No England team without W. G. Grace, E. M. Grace, A. N. Hornby and Ephraim Lockwood could be remotely representative. Moreover the players were so fatigued from their travels, dangers, soaking and hardships in New Zealand as to be far short of match-fit. Indeed Armitage, the Yorkshire slow bowler, was so exhausted that he was hard put to bowl within the batsman's reach. As an additional deprivation, Edward Pooley, the wicket-keeper and accomplished batsman, was in prison in New Zealand. Before the match at Christchurch he played the old trick of the touring elevens and offered a pound to a shilling that he would forecast the individual score of each member of the local eighteen. When a man named Donkin took the bet, Pooley said, simply, 'nought'. Surely enough, there were eleven 'ducks' in the two innings of the eighteen—a profit of £9 15s to Pooley. When he went with two other members of the team to claim the winnings, however, there was an argument and then a scuffle; and Pooley was arrested and remanded for trial for injuring property over £5 and assaulting Donkin. Some time later he was duly acquitted and some embarrassed local residents raised a subscription, gave him a gold watch and fifty guineas. By then, though, he was too late to play in the first Test Match. His deputy, Jupp, was suffering from 'inflammation of the eyes, brought on in various ways' and Selby made an inadequate stopgap.

Australia, for various reasons, were without three outstanding bowlers in Evans, Spofforth and Allan. The match was dominated by Charles Bannerman who took the first ball, and, with defensive support from Thompson and Cooper, scored 165 of the Australian total of 245 before one of a series of fast, short balls from 'Happy Jack' Ulyett, split his finger, and he had to retire. Shaw (three for 51 in 55 overs) was steady as ever; Jupp made 63 in the first innings; Shaw took five for 38 in the second Australian innings, but Kendall (seven for 55) was too much for the English batsmen. Australia had won the historic match described as 'Victoria and New South Wales or Australia *versus* England' by 45 runs.

Again spontaneously, a return was arranged 'for the benefit of the English players'. It, too, was played at Melbourne and this time the batting of the four Yorkshiremen, Ulyett (52 and 63), Greenwood, Emmett and Hill, and the bowling of Lillywhite, Hill and Southerton squared the issue with a four-wicket win.

The dust had barely settled on the tour before Australians were negotiating for a return visit and, in 1878, John Conway managed the first white Australian team to tour England. Consisting of five from Victoria, plus the manager, five from New South Wales and one from Tasmania, it was truly representative of Australia's strength. It had the backing of the home authorities and was financed by contributions from the players, who were to share in the profits, and by the proceeds of matches played on a domestic tour before they left for England.

They were not accorded a representative match, but were given a fixture with an M.C.C. team which, although not the strongest that could have been chosen, included several of the best players in W. G. Grace, A. N. Hornby, George Hearne, Alfred Shaw, Fred Morley and G. F. Vernon. On a lively Lord's wicket Spofforth (six for 4—including the hat-trick—and five for 16) and Boyle (three for 14 and five for 3) put out M.C.C. for 33 and 19 and beat them by nine wickets in a single day. Hornby, with 19, was the highest scorer of the match; Midwinter made 10 for Australia (41 and 12 for 1); W. G. Grace, four and nought. The news amazed all cricketing England.

Lord Harris's side to Australia in 1878–79 was intended to be purely amateur but, when that proved impossible, the bowling was strengthened and the team called 'The Gentlemen of England with Ulyett and Emmett'. As such they played Australia in what is now accepted as the third Test match of the series. The touring side was extremely strong in batting by

First Australian Team in England 1878

English standards but it was routed by Spofforth: with his off-breaks and variations of pace he took six for 48 (including hat-trick) and seven for 62; and Alec Bannerman made 73. England's chief contributions were 33 and 36 by Lord Harris; 52 by C. A. Absolom; seven for 68 by Tom Emmett.

Unhappily, during the tourists' subsequent match at Sydney there was a riot when Murdoch was given out. Lord Harris faced it out and for some time refused to leave the field although he had already been struck and was surrounded by a hostile crowd. He was forthright in his criticism of the authorities and of David Gregory, the Australian captain, and when the Australians came to England under Murdoch in 1880, some of the leading authorities and clubs treated them coolly. Only Surrey offered them a representative match. It was the first Test match played in England (although the term Test Match was not used until 1884—in the *Melbourne Herald*). All three Grace brothers played; W.G. scored 152 and shared an opening partnership of 91 with E.M., G.F.—Fred—caught Bonnor at point reputedly off the third run of what was said to be the highest skier ever seen. ('I ought to have *hit* it,' said Bonnor afterwards.) But G.F. made a 'pair of spectacles' in what proved to be his last cricket match; given a damp bed at Basingstoke, he died a few weeks later. Importantly, if not crucially, Spofforth was injured and could not play for Australia. Grace's century and useful scores from A. P. Lucas, Lord Harris and A. G. Steel took England to 420 and the bowling of Morley and Shaw gave them a first-innings lead of 271. When Australia followed on, Murdoch made 153 not out and carried them from 187 for eight to 327 all out. Though harried by Palmer and Boyle, England won by five wickets.

The concept of international matches was now accepted, although neither their frequency nor their number was fixed. Tours from England were speculative. Alfred Shaw and Arthur Shrewsbury, the two Nottinghamshire cricketers, floated a number of them with varying success. They made £1,400 from the 1880–81 tour; £300 in 1883–84; lost £500 in 1886–87 and as much as £2,400 in 1887–88 when two English sides toured there at the same time (the single Test was played, and won, by an eleven chosen from both parties).

On Shaw's tour of 1881–82, Australia won the only two Tests (of four) to be finished in a series decided by the bowling of Garrett and Palmer. So Murdoch brought his second touring side to England in 1882; but again only one Test—at The Oval—was arranged. In a low-scoring match Australia (63 and 122) beat England (101 and 77) by seven runs. After Peate and Barlow had run through the Australian batting, Spofforth took seven for 46 to limit England's first innings lead to 38. On the second day the wicket was so wet that many thought it unfit for play. Massie, in a bold hitting innings, scored 55 out of 66 and England needed only 85 to win. Despite W. G. Grace's 32, however, before a painfully tense crowd, Boyle kept the other end secure while Spofforth steadily cut down the England batting. So tight was their bowling in the crucial late stages that the last four English wickets mustered only seven runs.

A few days later *The Sporting Times* published its now all too well known mock obituary notice of English cricket with the footnote 'N.B. The body will be cremated and the Ashes taken to Australia'. So, when hot on the heels of the Australians—three series took place within fourteen months— the Hon. Ivo Bligh took out an England team, he was popularly said to be going to recover The Ashes. After Australia had won the first Test, England, for whom W. W. Read batted impressively, Bates took fourteen wickets at Melbourne and Barlow eight at Sydney, took the next two of the scheduled three-match rubber. Accordingly, two ladies—one of whom later married the Hon. Ivo—burnt a bail, put the ashes in a pottery urn and presented it to Bligh. The Australians, however, demanded an extra match, duly won it and claimed to have drawn the series; and so the records show it. The Ashes urn is still in Lord's and remains there whichever country 'holds' it.

By the end of the century the two countries had played 19 Test series (indeed, many Australians argue that only a match between England and Australia is a genuine 'Test Match'): ten in Australia and nine in England, of which England had won eleven and Australia six, with two drawn; of the 56 Tests, England had 26 to Australia's 20.

That period had thrown up a whole hierarchy of great players. After Spofforth, Palmer, Garrett and Boyle (and many English cricketers thought the '82 Australians their strongest side of the century), the Australian bowling passed to C. T. B. Turner ('The Terror'), the durable all-rounder George Giffen (who for South Australia against Victoria once played an innings of 271 and then took sixteen wickets for 166) and Hugh Trumble. All three of them took over a hundred English wickets. J. J. Ferris and Ernest Jones, who bowled through W.G.'s beard. J. McC.

Blackham, 'the Prince of wicket-keepers' and useful batsman, made eight tours to England. The early batsmen, Charles and Alec Bannerman and W. L. Murdoch (captain for seven series against England), were followed by the hitters, G. J. Bonnor and J. J. Lyons; Percy McDonnell, Syd Gregory and Joe Darling.

For England, W. G. Grace lasted throughout the entire period from first encounter to last. A. G. Steel, leg-spinner and all-rounder; W.W. Read of Surrey, batsman; Arthur Shrewsbury—'Give me Arthur' said W.G.—

George Giffen

Richard Barlow, a sound, acceptable all-rounder; Bobby Abel, the young Archie MacLaren, A. E. Stoddart and Ranjitsinhji reinforced the subsequent batting. Among the bowlers, Bobby Peel, second in the succession of great Yorkshire slow left-arm spinners took over a hundred Australian wickets; the mighty and noble Tom Richardson, 88 in 14 Tests; while George Lohmann of Surrey, A. G. Steel, Billy Barnes and Billy Bates qualify as all-rounders. Their records may not endure by comparison with those of later cricketers who played more Tests against more countries. Still, though, for many, relative figures against 'the old enemy' are the true reflection of quality. On those values many of the pre-1900 players compare favourably with their successors.

Through this earlier period, in particular, English professionals tended to resent the more favourable social and financial treatment accorded to the Australians as 'amateurs'. The fact probably influenced some of the labour troubles of the time.

In 1880 seven Nottinghamshire professionals demanded £20 to play against the Australians. The county committee could only give in; but they paid the four who had not threatened strike action £21 apiece. *Lillywhite's Cricketers' Annual*, which was certainly not on the players' side, commented on the subsequent Nottinghamshire county 'strike' of 1881 that 'The readiness with which in many cases rather exorbitant demands of the Australian managers were met by some of our chief clubs probably had some influence in encouraging Shaw and Shrewsbury, who may be considered the leaders of the union movement.'

Seven years later, nine professionals of Surrey and Notts refused to appear for the Players against the Australians at The Oval (from which match the Australians were to take a profit) unless they were paid £20 each. It was argued that the profits made by the so-called 'amateur' Australians justified their action. In the mutually recriminatory correspondence that ensued, it was said for the Players 'we only asked for what we paid the Australians in our benefit match in the Antipodes'.

Then, sixteen years afterwards, also at The Oval, Lohmann, Abel, Hayward and Richardson of Surrey and William Gunn of Notts refused to play in the third Test unless they were paid £20—which seems to have been the magic figure. All except Lohmann and the wealthy William Gunn, however, gave in; and Lohmann subsequently apologized.

Test cricket was a hardy growth: hardy enough generally to be its own justification.

Chapter 7
The county pattern

The last quarter of the nineteenth century saw the rise of the county clubs. It was almost as if they had been in hibernation—as, in a way, they had—and were now emerging into a springtime of activity. At bottom they probably were, and still are, the best units of competition within England; not merely because of their size and population but because they stir deep loyalties. That remains true even after the decisions on boundaries made in 1972 by faceless men in central government.

The counties had been submerged by the 'Elevens' which had a purpose to serve but, by the eighteen-seventies, had discharged it. Meanwhile the counties had limped along a second-class existence. M.C.C. had continued to play matches against them; though whether from lack of alternative opposition, or from any long-term vision or hope for the county clubs, cannot now be ascertained. Certainly no statement of principle seems to have emerged from Lord's. Nevertheless those fixtures in themselves materially assisted the counties to maintain grounds, establishments and professional staffs. Many of those professionals preferred the higher payment for play with the Elevens; but as those returns diminished they were glad to return to the counties.

The demise of Dean and Wisden's 'United' in 1869 marks the turning of the tide. Many of the other elevens continued but the decision of those two hard-headed men recognized the change in public demand. The transition was relatively swift. For many years there had been a popular acceptance of the idea of a Champion County, but no precise figures or rankings had been published. Indeed, for some years after tables began to appear, they were not uniform. There are, however, some clearly acceptable figures. *Scores and Biographies* records 25 inter-county matches in the season of 1872. In the following year M.C.C. published its regulations for county qualifications. In fact they were framed for an abortive knockout cup competition along the lines of the F.A. Cup which had been introduced the year before; but they served for the league-type Championship. From that year positive—though not consistent—Championship tables were published. The nine counties involved were Derbyshire, Gloucestershire,

Gloucestershire 1888

Kent, Lancashire, Middlesex, Nottinghamshire, Surrey, Sussex and Yorkshire; they sustained the Championship through the early years. Methods of assessment varied between 'fewest defeats'—strongly favoured in some quarters—and 'most wins'. A steady growth showed 31 matches in 1873; 32 in 1874; 34 in 1875; 38 in 1876; 42 in 1877; 58 in 1887; and a happily equitable 72—in which each of the nine met every other twice—in 1892. By then, Somerset had replaced Derbyshire, who returned—and Essex, Hampshire, Leicestershire and Warwickshire were admitted—in 1895 (131 matches); Worcestershire in 1899 when 166 matches were played.

From 1873 until the end of the century, the chief powers were first Gloucestershire, followed by Nottinghamshire, and the mounting forces of Lancashire, Surrey and then Yorkshire. The main strength of Gloucestershire's all-amateur team lay in the three Graces. W.G. was captain and the finest batsman in the world and, in 1874, when they were, for the first time, sole champion county, he was top of their bowling averages as well. E.M. was county secretary and a prodigious all-rounder; in 1863 in all matches he scored 3,074 runs and took 339 wickets. G.F., second to W.G. in both batting and bowling averages, was still a rising power when he died at 29. It often seemed that they needed little reinforcement; but J. A. Bush was a capable wicket-keeper, Frank Townsend and F. J. Crooke useful batsmen, and R. F. Miles a lively opening bowler.

Nottinghamshire at this period had a vast potential of talent. The handicraftsmen villages like Burton Joyce, Hucknall, Radcliffe-on-Trent and Sutton-in-Ashfield, where the pieceworkers could adjust their hours to suit their playing patterns, became fertile production grounds for cricketers. Indeed, the Hon. R. H. Lyttelton wrote in the first *Badminton*: 'We have heard that from the county of Nottinghamshire alone several hundred professional bowlers emerge every year and go to fulfil cricket engagements in various parts of the Kingdom.' He was referring to club and school professionals and coaches. This was by no means an unacceptable summer living for the average semi-skilled, or perhaps skilled, workman with a feeling and aptitude for cricket. That amply explains why Nottinghamshire were an outstanding county for almost half a century. They were considered sole Champions four times and joint Champions once in the nine years before the qualifying regulations of 1873; and in the next seventeen seasons they won the title six times and shared it five. It was extremely hard to win a place in their side.

In 1881, five of their leading players, Shaw, Shrewsbury, Barnes, Morley and Selby, refused to sign their contracts unless they were engaged for all matches; the contract included Flowers and Scotton, and Shaw and Shrewsbury were empowered to arrange a Nottinghamshire–Yorkshire match for the players' benefit. The committee reacted powerfully and refused to compromise. The players would sign the contracts offered, or none. Five of them hung on until August before they surrendered in time to play in the last three or four fixtures; but they had already suffered considerable losses. Shaw and Shrewsbury held out; but all seven signed their contracts for the next season, when the reasons for their anxiety were patent. In 1882, ten England players appeared for Nottinghamshire— Billy Barnes, William Gunn, Arthur Shrewsbury, Wilfred Flowers, Alfred Shaw, William Scotton, John Selby, William Attewell, Mordecai Sherwin, and Fred Morley; as well as William Oscroft who played fifteen times and Walter Wright twice, for Players, John Dixon eleven times and Charles Wright seven, for the Gentlemen. In addition, of course, many other Nottinghamshire men had joined other counties. A number of them went to Lancashire which, surprisingly in view of its large population and general enthusiasm for the game, produced very few professionals of any quality in this period. That may have been due to the fact that labour conditions were unduly harsh there. Certainly, though, in an exchange of acid correspondence between supporters of the two counties a note from Nottingham ran:

'Lancashire County Cricket

The only rules necessary for players in the County Eleven are that they shall neither have been born in, nor reside in, Lancashire.

Sutton-in-Ashfield men will have preference.'

Lancashire nevertheless had their successes (two outright Championships and three shared) up to the end of the century; they were at their strongest in the eighteen-eighties. The captain, A. N. Hornby, as Francis Thompson so nostalgically recalled, went in first with Richard Barlow, patient right-hand bat, faithful left-arm medium-pace bowler. In 1895, A. C. MacLaren

A. C. MacLaren

scored 424 for Lancashire against Somerset: still a record for English first-class cricket. They had, too, in Johnny Briggs and A. G. Steel, two great all-rounders; Richard Pilling, one of the best wicket-keepers in the country, and the Rev. Vernon Royle, legendary cover point; while in Crossland—fast—Nash and Watson, slow, they had three effective bowlers who, sadly enough, had suspect actions.

Surrey came late to take the title outright eight times and share it once in the last thirteen years of the century. In that period Bobby Abel and, from the later generation, Tom Hayward, W. W. and J. M. Read (who scored a century in his last innings for the county) were all England batsmen. The bowling was carried by the mighty Tom Richardson, handsome giant of a fast bowler, who in the season of 1895 performed the amazing feat of skill and stamina of taking 290 wickets; with support, according to their mood or fitness, from three more Test bowlers in Bill Lockwood (he and Richardson were said to be the finest pair of bowlers ever to play in the same county side), George Lohmann, a master at medium pace, and the lively Jack Sharpe. Of these Hayward, Lohmann and Lockwood could all be accounted all-rounders.

Yorkshire, with four wins in eight years, were just coming to power under Lord Hawke with the mature Bobby Peel and Ted Wainwright and the younger Stanley Jackson, George Hirst, Schofield Haigh, 'Long John' Tunnicliffe, J. T. Brown and Wilfred Rhodes.

Between 1860 and 1870, the basic match-pay rate for a Surrey player increased from £3 to £5; with a £1 win bonus and £1 travel allowance, £10 for such a fixture as Players *v* Gentlemen; say £80 a season for a run-of-the-mill player, probably £150 for the seniors. That, for a summer cricket season, compared with the average unskilled labourer's £85 for a full year. The professional cricketer was, in addition, free to work in the winter at some other out-of-season job. As a general rule, the more successful did not choose to do so, unless, of course, they had the opportunity of an overseas tour. Traditionally, in the mining areas, cricket meant emancipation. It used to be said that when Nottinghamshire or Derbyshire needed a player one of their officers would go to the nearest pit-shaft and shout down 'send up a fast bowler' (or an opening bat or wicket-keeper) and he would be up in the next cage. Those men, once released from the pit into the cricket world of better pay, fresh air and headlines, liked during the cricket close season to walk down to their local pub at midday, dressed in their best stiff tweeds and shiny boots, and be seen to take a leisurely drink as evidence of their eminence.

For some of them, however, the success proved fragile. A number of professional cricketers, like many others who emerged from the nineteenth-century working classes into semi-prosperity, fell into the traps laid for those with unaccustomed wealth. Alcohol was the usual enemy. Until the end of the century—later in some counties—the professional was not provided with a lunch on match days; that was the privilege of amateurs. All too often, the professionals went down to the bar—where there were many only too happy to buy them more drink than was helpful to a competitive games player.

Bobby Peel, good enough slow left-arm bowler to take 102 wickets in 20 Tests against Australia, had a £2,000 benefit—the highest recorded until then—in 1894, and took a public house. In 1897 he came drunk on to the field, was ordered off by Lord Hawke, and never played for Yorkshire again.

The relationship between many county committees and their players was at best feudal; and the player who could not command a regular team place might well be in financial difficulties. Indeed, as lately as the nineteen-thirties, some of the Somerset professionals could ill-afford the loss of their match pay in August 'when the amateurs came down from the Universities and the teachers from the schools'. In the attempt to balance their precarious budgets, some of the earlier players used to try to economize on gear, or their meagre away-match expense allowance. Sir Home Gordon in his *Background to Cricket* says: 'Some idea of what the old-timers were like may be gathered from what was related to me about them by C. W. Alcock, when secretary at The Oval. He declared that in the seventies the Surrey professionals wore one suit of flannels right through the summer, the shirt often being a coloured one, or dotted with red spots. There was also the instance later of a subsequently prominent Notts player coming up for the first time to Lord's merely bringing his pads and bat strapped together. When it was noticed he had no baggage, he explained that as the weather was fine he intended to sleep each night in some park in his cricket clothes.'

Of course that could not apply to all nineteenth-century professional cricketers. It is known that Wisden, Clarke, the Lillywhites, William Gunn, Barlow, Woof, Frank Sugg, Shaw and Shrewsbury all ended as prosperous men; and many others spent a secure and contented old age. Still, though, Alcock is referring to a metropolitan team: and, until the days of adequate social services, some of the men who wagered the stake of their security on the uncertain game of cricket, forfeited it.

A number of quite eminent players took pubs during or after their playing careers; and several of them died young from the effects of drink. The truth was that many of them, worth enough while they worked in mill or factory, could not stand the spoiling and treating of admirers, or the temptation of drink always at their elbows. Earlier in the nineteenth century, the Yorkshire team, taken over by Lord Hawke in 1883, was described as 'ten drunks and a parson' (Ephraim Lockwood was a lay preacher). When the Yorkshire journalist, A. W. Pullin, who wrote as 'Old Ebor', published his *Talks with Old Yorkshire Cricketers* in *The Yorkshire Evening Post* in 1897, he surprised many of his readers with revelations of formerly famous players existing in poverty. Subscriptions were raised on behalf of some of them. More positively, Lord Hawke, a benevolent despot so far as his players were concerned, decreed that in future the Yorkshire Club would hold back two-thirds of all players' benefit funds and invest the money for them until they retired.

That kind of security, though, was for those outstanding enough to be given benefits. Lesser players were often hard-pressed; especially those who had no skill or business to turn to when they ceased to play. The Cricketers Fund Friendly Society was founded by Parr and a group of the professionals from the 'Elevens' in 1862 and the proceeds of the annual matches between the All-England and the United were paid into it. When that fixture was discontinued, Surrey proffered a North *v* South match for its funds, but it simply was not enough to meet demands. In 1900 Pullin found the old Nottinghamshire and All-England fast bowler, John Jackson, in Liverpool, 'a bent and grisly man of sixty-seven, having no permanent address and always hovering on the threshold of the workhouse.' 'For some years Jackson's main, if not his sole, support has been an allowance of 6s. per week from the Cricketers' Friendly Society and from that sum a subscription of one guinea a year has to be deducted.'

Certainly the average professional could only 'request' a pay increase. The attitude of the Nottinghamshire committee to their seven-man strike indicates the typically nineteenth-century establishment viewpoint. There was, in truth, at that time, an autocratic belief that a professional cricketer was not as other employees.

'A Light Blue Captain', writing in Lillywhite's *Cricketers' Companion* for 1882, commented on the Nottingham strike—'Professional cricketers ought to remember that their relation with county committees is not the ordinary relation of labour and capital, where labourers and capitalists alike seek remuneration and where, in many people's opinion, the labourer is fully entitled, by striking, to get a fair share of the profits. In County Cricket the Professional, who is the labourer, makes a profit: the Committee, which is the capitalist, does not but merely seeks to encourage and support the game. Hence a combination among the labourers for the purpose of getting higher wages is, we think, improper.'

Lord Hawke, who might well have agreed with the writer—after all, he was 'a light blue captain' himself—nevertheless did much to improve not only the lot, but the standing, of the professional cricketer. In Yorkshire he could do it directly; his example, however, produced similar reactions elsewhere. By the end of the century, thanks to the efforts of a few reformers, most professionals were paid wages instead of match-money and averaged some £275, by comparison with less than £100 for the unskilled labourer. The day of the gentleman-player was not far away.

Chapter 8
The price of Grace

When W. G. Grace 'came out' in the eighteen-sixties, the idea of a gentleman player was unthinkable. Grace himself was the son of a doctor, the brother of a doctor, and he proposed to become a doctor. He was potentially, and soon actually, the greatest cricketer the world had—or has—known. He could not face the life of a professional which, in any case—if he aspired to high success—would have involved him leaving Gloucestershire. On the other hand, he could not afford to play as an amateur.

In his time, the generally accepted view of the amateur—partly Victorian hypocrisy but, also, partly the high-mindedness instilled by Dr Arnold and the 'muscular Christianity' school—was of a man above payment. This was not a matter of great concern in most countries; but it was in England where, for instance, a great gap was maintained in football between amateur and professional for a century.

W. G. Grace was paid; and he was paid a great deal; he was paid sums relatively similar to these now paid to the top soccer players. What did his employers get for their money? C. B. Fry probably put it as well as anyone in *The Jubilee Book of Cricket*—which he 'ghosted' for Ranjitsinhji—'There is one great landmark that separates the old batting from the new—the appearance of Dr W. G. Grace in the cricket world. He revolutionized batting. He turned it from an accomplishment into a science. What W.G. did was to unite in his mighty self all the good points of all the players, and to make utility the criterion of style. I hold him to be not only the finest player born or unborn, but the maker of modern batting. He turned the old one-stringed instrument into a many-chorded lyre. Where a great man has led, many can go afterwards, but the honour is his who found and cut the path. The theory of modern batting is in all essentials the result of W.G.'s thinking and working on the game.'

Once, in conversation, Fry, who watched W.G. often and played in his last Test match, referred to the old Gloucestershire joke about him: 'He dab 'em but seldom, but when he dab 'em he do dab 'em for four.' 'That,' said Fry, 'was the truth; he did, positively, block balls for four. A bowler would try to york him; and from his high backlift, he would come down on it, so swiftly—his speed of reaction was bewildering—and so hard that his defensive stroke simply sent it straight, through mid-on or mid-off, for four.'

Huge, black-bearded and of unfailing strength, he was twenty-five when in 1873 he became the first player to perform the 'double' in English cricket, with 2,139 runs—almost twice as many as anyone else and in a wet summer—and 106 wickets. That effectively took Gloucestershire to their first—though shared—Championship title. Then, off on that exhausting tour of Australia. This prodigious feat prompted the comic magazine *Fun* to: 'The Society for the Improvement of Things in General and the Diffusion of Perfect Equality, at a meeting to be held shortly, will submit the following propositions:

'That W. G. Grace shall owe a couple of hundred or so before batting— these to be reckoned against his side should he not wipe them off.'
'That his shoe spikes shall be turned inward.'
'That he shall be declared out whenever the umpire likes.'
'That he shall always be the eleventh player.'
'That he shall not be allowed to play at all.'

He captained England in five Test series, and won four of them. Nevertheless, his batting record in Test matches—all against Australia— is not statistically impressive by modern standards. In 22 Tests and 36 innings he made 1,098 runs, with two centuries and an average of 32.29, which is higher than that of any of his contemporaries except A. E. Stoddart (35.57), Arthur Shrewsbury (35.47) and A. G. Steel (35.29). He took nine wickets at 26.22; and made the impressive number of 39 catches, mainly at point, where his fast reflexes rendered him outstanding. Moreover, for good measure, when, at The Oval, in 1884, Australia scored 551 and England used no fewer than eleven bowlers, and the wicket-keeper, Alfred Lyttelton, took off his pads, bowled lobs, and took four for 19, W.G. kept wicket.

His batting ability was still not in question when he lost his Test place. Days before his fifty-first birthday, he played in the first Test of 1899 at Trent Bridge; he made 28 and one: he batted soundly enough in the first innings; and indeed in the next match, his 50 was highest score but one of either innings for M.C.C. against the Australians. He dropped out simply because his age and his size were such that he could not run in the field: though he did dismiss Clem Hill, top scorer for Australia, with what *Wisden* called 'a brilliant catch by Grace at point, close to the ground, with the right hand.'

Statistics are not always an accurate indication of ability but it is impossible to question the evidence of W. G. Grace's batting average. There have been instances of freak figures based on a few matches. There can, however, be no argument against the eminence of one who, playing

regularly, was top of the domestic batting averages for eleven of the fourteen seasons between 1866 and 1879. In the latter year he qualified as a doctor and was never again able to devote his full time and attention to cricket.

His stature is probably most truly indicated by his performances in Gentlemen *versus* Players, which he changed from a one-sided anachronism to a genuine and important contest and the major fixture of the domestic season. Indeed, he did more; he gave the Gentlemen an advantage they retained despite the changes and development in the professional talent, until his physical powers began to wane. Before his first appearance in these matches in 1865, the Gentlemen had not won for twelve years, and only seven times since 1837.

From his first selection, when he was sixteen, until, in 1900, at fifty-two, he ceased to play regularly in county cricket, he appeared in 79 of these matches; 38 were won by the Gentlemen, 25 by the Players, 15 were drawn, and one tied. He continued occasionally to play in the fixture until 1906; and, over that span of 41 years, in 85 matches he scored 6,008 runs (with 15 centuries) and an average of 42.50; and took 271 wickets at 18.72.

It is difficult now to appreciate what he meant to half a century, not merely of cricket-followers, but of the whole British public. Certainly no sportsman of our era has had such a profound effect on the social life of his time. He was at once a father-figure, a hero, a performer of sporting near-miracles and a well-loved human being. A shrewd, yet uncomplicated countryman, in a day when games were played hard, he could look after himself; and he refused to be put upon. There were some bad umpires and he was not frightened to say so. He was as sharp as the man who tried to fool him; but no one who knew him accepted that he was unfair. One old professional, asked if W.G. ever went outside the rules, paused, thought, and then said, 'Well, no, but it was wonderful what he could do inside them.' He did not suffer fools gladly. Once, captaining an occasional side he asked a young man he did not know, 'What kind of batsman are you?' and received the reply, 'Well, sir, I have never made a duck.' 'Then,' said the Old Man, 'you have played no cricket; go in last.' He made a lot of money—more than any British games player had ever made before—but he was not mean. In fact, it was generally held that he was more generous than any other great player of his time about playing in benefit matches for the professionals.

The public regarded him not only with admiration, but with affection. In his semi-retirement to Crystal Palace he ran and captained the London County Cricket Club, which played a decreasing number of first-class and steadily more minor matches. It had been created precisely for the purpose of presenting him. He had become so firmly established an institution that it was arranged that visitors to London might go—as to the Tower, or any

A. E. Stoddart

other 'sight' of London—to see W. G. Grace batting. For him it was a remunerative, comfortable and—especially when his old friend Billy Murdoch was playing as well—companionable old age.

He had an amazing capacity for rising to an occasion. After his fall to seventh place in the batting averages of 1875, there were some to say—regardless of the fact that he took more wickets (191) than anyone else—that he was 'going off'. The next year, after a slow start, he averaged 57 in July. Then, in August, he played ten innings for 1,249 runs. An unprecedented eight days of batting began on 11 August, against Kent at Canterbury, when he made 17 and Gloucestershire (144) followed on. He batted through the next two days for 344 to draw the match. Back to Bristol, where his 177 against Nottinghamshire won the game by ten wickets. Next, Yorkshire, his old enemies, came to Cheltenham: he went in first, batted for eight hours and carried his bat for 318 in a total of 528. This was the occasion when some of the Yorkshire players refused to bowl. They had suffered at his hands before. As one of them, that ripe character, Tom Emmett, said: 'I reckon he's a nonesuch; he ought to be made to play with a littler bat.' Grace had played three consecutive innings for 839 runs.

Nothing in his entire career was more remarkable than his second flowering when it was generally assumed, even by his admiring public, that he was suffering the decline in power to be expected in a man of his age. It happened in 1895.

He was rising forty-seven, and 1894 had been for him an indifferent season (1,293 runs at 29.38). W.G. practised with some zest in a chilly March; and played himself in with 101 against twenty-four Gloucestershire colts. He did not start his first-class season until 9 May when, for M.C.C. against Sussex, he was caught at slip by Ranji—playing his first match for Sussex—for 13. In the second innings, Ranji dropped him when he had made 14 and he went on to 103. Incidentally, in this match, he bowled Ranji with the first ball he ever sent down to him. Still with M.C.C., at Lord's, he scored only 18 and 25 against Yorkshire. Then, in Gloucestershire's traditional Whitsun fixture with Somerset, at Taunton, 'Flustered for the only time in his career'—'poor Sam Woods could hardly bowl the ball and the Doctor was nearly as bad'—he hit the four that made him the first man to score a hundred hundreds. That statistical milestone celebrated with champagne on the field, he went voraciously on to 288 in 320 minutes without a chance. For an England XI against Cambridge University his only innings was 52. For Gloucestershire against Kent, on 23, 24 and 25 May, he was on the field for every ball of the match: bowled 43 overs to take two for 115, and then, first in, last out for 257: fielded while Kent were bowled out by Roberts and Painter and then made 73 not out for a nine-wicket win. He batted only once for England *versus* Surrey at The Oval when Tom Richardson bowled him for 18. So he went to Lord's with Gloucestershire to play Middlesex with an ag-

The Great Cricketer

gregate of 847 and two days left of May. W.G. won the toss, Gloucestershire batted and, much bothered by the slow leg-spin of E. A. Nepean, he went slowly until lunch, at 58. He grew into the afternoon, reached his century and, with a four to square leg off Nepean, he completed the rare, true, thousand in May: indeed, in the last twenty-one days of May. He went processionally on through the summer: 118 against the Players at Lord's; nine centuries in the season; more runs (2,346) than anyone else in the country; and, of those who played a reasonable number of innings, only MacLaren—by point five—had a better average than his 51.

Still it was not the end. In 1898, Gentlemen *versus* Players at Lord's began on his fiftieth birthday and was declared the 'Match of the Season', drew more than 40,000 spectators and, when Grace led out his team, the whole crowd stood, waving hats and cheering. He was lame and had a bruised hand, but he made 43 in the first innings; in the second, hobbling in at number eight, he held on for 31 not out with Charles Kortright, and they came within five minutes of saving the match before his partner was caught at cover.

The next year was one of exits. Dropped from the Test team, he accepted the decision with quiet dignity. At the end of the season he parted with Gloucestershire. For financial reasons he wished to take over the management of London County while still continuing to captain Gloucestershire. The county did not think it feasible for any man to combine the two posts; he left irritably. As late as 1906 he made his last appearance for Gentlemen *versus* Players. Persuaded to play against his better judgment, he scored only four in the first innings but, in the second, buckling down hard against some capable bowling, he made 74—the highest score of the game for the Gentlemen. It was his fifty-eighth birthday. He was content; he walked into the dressing-room, threw his bat on the table and said 'I shan't play any more'; and he never did in that fixture. His last first-class match was for the Gentlemen of England against Surrey in 1908, when he made 15 and 25. He did not give up the game. He played his last match in 1914, at sixty-six, for Eltham against Grove Park. On a bad pitch he made 69—more than twice as many as anyone else—and was, symbolically, not out. Cricket is essentially human; none more so than that of W. G. Grace; yet figures must eventually argue for all of them. In first-class matches, William Gilbert Grace scored 54,904 runs and took 2,879 wickets; in minor cricket, 44,936 runs, 4,446 wickets. For those who can assimilate them, the complete figures of his 57 years of play are—according to the meticulous records kept by G. Neville Weston: 99,840 runs (221 centuries); 7,325 wickets; 1,512 catches; 54 stumpings. (How easily he might have made those 160 more runs to reach six figures—if he had only known —or really cared.)

This man was a unique asset; in cricket terms, all but priceless to Gloucestershire and the Gentlemen. Under his captaincy, and largely due to his batting, bowling, fielding, and strategy, Gloucestershire won the

Championship outright three times and jointly once; they have never won it since his day. They certainly paid for a *locum* for him; latterly for two during the summer; for he made it quite clear that he could not play cricket and run a practice without assistance for which he was not prepared to pay. He had, too, quite generous expenses from the county. He was a capable and conscientious provincial G.P. and only abandoned medicine in protest against the 1899 changes in the Bristol Parish medical system.

For several years he found United South of England matches a valuable source of income; the single match contracts under which he played were strict, but the returns seem to have been adequate to keep him and pay for his medical studies. His younger brother Fred was, in fact, once excluded from a Gentlemen v. Players match because he had been paid for appearing in a United South match; but to have taken that step a second time—or to have taken it against W.G. at all—would have been promotional suicide. The terms of his first visit to Australia are not known but they must have been substantial to justify his efforts.

On his second visit, in 1891, as captain of Lord Sheffield's team, all his expenses were paid—including a *locum* for his practice—and he received £3,000; equivalent to more than £30,000 in 1977. When he qualified, in 1879, a national testimonial raised £1,500; worth more than £16,000 today. After his great season of 1895—the hundredth hundred, and the thousand in May—no fewer than three testimonial funds were launched for him: they totalled £9,073.8s.3d.; worth some £100,000 now. Finally the London County appointment paid £600 (now £6,000) a year, and comfortable entertainment expenses.

The price was high; but it would not seem too high, *pro rata*, now—for such a performer.

Chapter 9
Edwardian heyday

For over a dozen years before the First World War, England was probably the most idyllic place to live in that any middle class has ever known. It was a country of prosperity, of privilege, of elegance, of literary and artistic enlightenment. At the same time, it had a highly class-conscious society, one of protocol and extravagance. It seemed that all was just a well-bred party—both above and below the salt—before the impending disaster which destroyed that society for ever.

Cricket flourished at every level, nowhere more richly than in the form nostalgically remembered as 'country house cricket'. It existed before and afterwards, but never so typically of a period. On some of the many private country estates of the time, cricket matches—often full 'weeks'— were organized in connection with house-parties. Some of the pavilions— unmistakably Edwardian with their red brick and white woodwork—are still to be seen, with a ground floor clear and roomy enough for dancing. It was the cricket of the wandering clubs, the old boys' striped blazers and caps, strawberries and cream and Sauternes—or champagne. It was a time of manly, curly moustaches, young women with elaborate coiffeurs and long dresses. It was, in fact, the pictorial world in which the cricketing novelist, E. W. Hornung, set his Raffles, the slow left-arm bowler who was 'The Amateur Cracksman'.

First-class cricket, too, flourished. One of its earliest steps was to put its house in order. For twenty years there had been rumblings of complaint about bowlers with illegal actions: Lord Harris had been extremely forthright on the matter. The result of his protests was accelerated in September 1901 when the county captains met at Lord's in a degree of privacy that could hardly be achieved now, and discussed the bowlers whose deliveries they considered unfair.

Over some four or five years C. B. Fry, Mold of Lancashire, Hopkins of Warwickshire, Tyler of Somerset, Paish of Gloucestershire and Capt. E. R. Bradford of Hampshire were all 'called' for throwing and did not bowl in first-class cricket again.

F. S. Jackson

There never was such a period for amateur players, who poured out from the public schools and Oxford and Cambridge in seemingly unending parade. The batsmen were outstanding and individualistic, men like Gilbert Jessop, the most consistent big hitter in the history of the game or the classicist C. B. Fry; the autocratic A. C. MacLaren; the fascinatingly original Ranjitsinhji and the patrician F. S. Jackson. There were R. E.— 'Tip'—Foster, the double international and his Malvern and Worcestershire brothers; the fine athlete J. R. Mason; the stylists Lionel Palairet and Reggie Spooner; and the typically Edwardian, Captain E. G. Wynyard. Among bowlers there were B. J. T. Bosanquet, who invented the googly and won a Test series with it; the hostile Frank Foster of Warwickshire; and Neville Knox—briefly the fastest in the country—along with Walter Brearley and Hesketh-Pritchard. There was, too, an amazing wicket-keeper in Harry Martyn.

What then, of the professionals who, over those fourteen years won sixteen matches to the Gentlemen's eight with seventeen draws? They included Jack Hobbs, successor to W.G. as the finest batsman in England and probably the most complete of modern times; S. F. Barnes, arguably the greatest bowler of all cricket history. A. A. Thomson used to delight to quote 'Who was the greatest all-rounder?' 'Nobody knows, but he batted right-handed, bowled left and he came from Kirkheaton.' That was true of both Wilfred Rhodes, master slow left-arm bowler and Test opening batsman; and George Hirst, fiery swing bowler, sturdy batsman who, in 1906, performed the still unparalleled feat of the double-double— two thousand runs and two hundred wickets in a season. They were contemporaries in the Yorkshire side of the Edwardian period. Frank Woolley and George Gunn scored runs as felicitous as any; Mead was massively and securely prolific; Johnny Tyldesley coolly explosive; Tom Hayward followed W.G. to a hundred hundreds; Len Braund, leg spinner, dominant bat and superb slip fieldsman was another outstanding all-rounder; Dick Lilley, one of the classic wicket-keepers.

Yet against that strength, Australia shared the eight Test rubbers of the period; and—despite having a badly weakened team in 1912—won fifteen Tests to fourteen. This was the period of batsmen like the well-loved Victor Trumper, Joe Darling, Clem Hill and Warren Bardsley; the all-rounders Monty Noble, Charlie Macartney and Warwick Armstrong; and bowlers like 'Tibby' Cotter, Hugh Trumble and H. V. Hordern.

At the end of the nineteenth century a Board of Control was set up to adminster Tests played in England: hitherto teams had been chosen by the ground authority housing the match; and after 1901–2 M.C.C. assumed the responsibility for official overseas tours.

There had been earlier tours to all the main cricketing countries; George Parr's side went on from Australia to New Zealand in 1863–64; Major Warton's team, captained by C. Aubrey Smith to South Africa, 1888–89; G. F. Vernon's to India, 1889–90; and R. S. Lucas's to West Indies,

Wilfrid Rhodes   *George Hirst*

1894–95. The first official M.C.C. teams went to Australia (P. F. Warner) 1903–04; South Africa (P. F. Warner) 1905–06; New Zealand (Capt. E. G. Wynyard) 1906–07; West Indies (A. W. F. Somerset) 1910–11; India (A. E. R. Gilligan) 1926–27. P. F. Warner's to South Africa was not a full strength England team and was well beaten by the remarkable South African group of googly bowlers—Schwarz, Vogler, Faulkner and White. The South Africans under P. W. Sherwell were beaten, however, on their first Test-playing visit to England (1907). None of the early sides to New Zealand or West Indies played Test matches but they indicated imperial interest and benovolence reflected in cricket administration. An Australian Board of Control was established in 1905. After a great deal of suggestion,

Victor Trumper

counter-suggestion and reluctance, the Imperial Cricket Conference was
formed in 1909 with England (represented by M.C.C.), Australia and South
Africa as founder members.

The England–Australia series of 1902 was one of the classic rubbers of
cricket history. In the first Test—also the first to be played at Edgbaston—
England declared at 376 (J. T. Tyldesley 138): on a damaged wicket, the

two Yorkshiremen, Rhodes and Hirst, bowled out Australia for 36 and
made them follow on; but rain prevented the finish. The Lord's match was
washed out and, in the only Test ever played at Sheffield, Trumper and
Clem Hill gave Noble (11 for 103) Trumble and Saunders elbow room to
bowl out England for a win by 143 runs.

Old Trafford saw one of the finest cricket matches of all history. On a
wet wicket Victor Trumper scored a century before lunch on the first day;
then Australia collapsed before the bowling of Rhodes and Lockwood
(Hirst had been dropped from the side in a shabby piece of cricket politics).
England, too, collapsed, but Jackson and Braund mounted a rescue operation before Lockwood and Rhodes again bowled out Australia. They were
saved from complete rout by Darling (dropped by Tate) but England
needed only 124 to win and reached 92 before the fourth wicket fell.
Saunders and Trumble broke through; rain came and at the end, in the
often told tale, Tate was bowled and Australia took the match and
retained The Ashes by three runs. This was Fred Tate's first and last Test
match. Tate's son, Maurice, was in the team that recovered The Ashes in
1926.

Also in that 1902 series, England won the fifth Test when, after needing
263 to win, they were 48 for five; then Jessop struck 104 in 75 minutes and

Trumper in action

the two historic Yorkshiremen, Hirst and Rhodes, made 15 for the last wicket to see England home. Both those epic matches were completed in three days, despite stoppages for rain.

The 1911–12 series in Australia was arguably England's finest in that country. They had lost the two previous rubbers, home and away and, unable to master the leg spin and googlies of Dr Hordern, they were conclusively beaten in the first Test. In the second, at Melbourne, Barnes, on the first morning, had figures of 9 overs; 6 maidens; 3 runs; 4 wickets—those of Kelleway, Bardsley, Hill and Armstrong. Barnes (8 for 140) and Foster (7 for 143) swept on to win the match by eight wickets; and, in conjunction with the batting of Jack Hobbs and Wilfrid Rhodes (who set the then record 323 for a Test opening partnership), the next three as well. In the entire series, Barnes took 34 wickets and Foster 32; and Hobbs made 662 runs at an average of 82.

The England team came home to the first, and so far the only, Triangular Tournament ever played in England. Conceived and enthusiastically supported by Sir Abe Bailey, it was a tournament between England and touring teams from Australia and South Africa, each of whom met the other two in three matches. The idea was not a bad one; but two pieces of ill-luck made it a failure. In the first place it was a dismally wet summer. Secondly, a dispute in the constantly troubled Australian Board of Control resulted in Trumper, Hill, Armstrong, Cotter and Ransford—half the main strength of any Australian team at that time—not making the trip. England, captained by C. B. Fry, thus had a rather hollow win in their last pre-war series with Australia.

If Australia 1911–12 was the peak of Barnes's long and successful career, South Africa 1913–14 gave him his most impressive Test figures. A tall, strong, determined man, he played his first first-class match in 1895, his last in 1930; yet he had only two full seasons of County Championship cricket. Indeed, his total of 44 Championship matches contrasts with his 27 Test matches, in which he took 189 wickets at 16.43. He would have been more than welcome in any team as a bowler; but in his determination to have his rights he fell foul of the cricketing establishment. In consequence he spent most of his career in minor counties cricket—for Staffordshire (1,441 wickets at 8.15) and the leagues, where every club he ever played for won its competition and, within a space of 45 years, he took 4,069 wickets at 6.08.

He believed that a cricketer was a cricketer, a view that he lived to see officially accepted. In his playing time, however, he lived abrasively with authority. In a hotel dining-room during the 1911–12 tour he asked for asparagus, was refused and insisted on it. 'Plum' Warner leant across to the waiter and said simply 'He must have asparagus; he's got to bowl for me tomorrow.' The asparagus was served. In the first Test of that series, Douglas, acting captain in place of Warner who was ill, took the new ball with Foster and used Barnes as first change. Asked about the decision years afterwards Barnes called it 'a misjudgement'; but, at the time, he saw it as a slight—that Douglas thought himself the better bowler—and that threw him into a fury. In fact, it was then that he passed the remark which was repeated by Parkin in similar circumstances years later—'Go on, then, you bowl them in and then expect me to bowl them out.'

In South Africa in 1913–14, Barnes simply cut down the South African batsmen with the exception of Taylor—arguably the best batsman ever produced by that country—who averaged 50 but was five times out to Barnes. He did almost everything with the ball. Once 'Tiger' Smith, who kept wicket to him in Australia in 1911–12, said 'I believe you bowled everything except the googly, Syd'. 'I never needed the googly' said Barnes without a smile. The matting wickets in South Africa gave him high pace and steep rise from the pitch, and in the first four Test matches he took 49 wickets (still the record for any Test series) at 10.93. He refused to play in the final Test because the South African authorities would not provide the accommodation he wanted for his wife and son. He never played for England again, though he was asked to go to Australia in 1924–25 but refused because M.C.C. would not pay for his family to go with him.

He was quite remarkably durable. In 1929, at the age of fifty-six, he bowled for Minor Counties against the South African touring side and in an unbroken spell of 32 overs, took eight for 41. The South African batsmen were unanimous that they faced no better or more accurate bowling on the tour.

In the fifteen seasons to the outbreak of War, Yorkshire won the Championship six times, Kent four; Middlesex, Lancashire, Nottinghamshire (through the bowling of Hallam and Wass in the wet summer of 1907), Warwickshire (the first winner from outside the original nine to do so) and Surrey once each. Northamptonshire were admitted in 1905. Yorkshire were outstandingly equipped in the bowling of Rhodes (whose 4,184 wickets aggregate has never been approached), Hirst, Haigh, and F. S. Jackson, all of whom could be accounted all-rounders. Add the batting of Denton, Tunnicliffe, Ernest Smith and Oldroyd; the bowling of Myers, Ringrose and Kilner; the wicket-keeping of first Hunter and then Dolphin, and you have a strong eleven indeed.

Kent had considerable amateur strength especially in batting with J. R. Mason, K. L. Hutchings, C. J. Burnup, A. P. and S. H. Day, E. W. Dillon and C. H. D. Marsham. Among the professionals, Seymour, Hardinge and Woolley—the last a genuine all-rounder—made runs. Their bowling was varied; both Colin Blythe—unlucky to be a contemporary of Rhodes —and Woolley bowled slow left-arm; Bradley and Fielder were fast, Fairservice steady medium-pace. 'Daddy' Carr was the leg-spinner who came into county cricket at the age of thirty-seven and played in a Test against Australia after only seven first-class matches. In 1910 Kent won the Championship by 12 August—the earliest it has ever been achieved.

Apart from Kent and Yorkshire, Surrey were the most consistent county over those years. Their batting, with Hobbs, Hayward, Hayes and, from time to time, J. N. and V. F. S. Crawford, the Australian Marshal, and Raphael, was massive. Before he retired in 1904, too, Bobby Abel set up new records for the number of centuries in a season (12 in 1900) and for aggregate (3,309 in 1901). As Richardson and Lockwood dropped out, the bowling was not quite strong enough: the pace of Knox, Lee and Hitch, the spin of 'Razor' Smith and J. N. Crawford were never all available together.

Wisden for 1916 and 1917 tells what happened to so many of that generation of country house cricketers and their potential successors. Slim volumes, they would be slimmer still but for the 82 and 75 pages which record the deaths of some three thousand cricketers—Lieutenants and Second Lieutenants most of them, the school players of only two or three years earlier, now nineteen to twenty-two—who hurried into khaki in time to be at Ypres, Loos, Verdun, the Somme.

It is not true that *Wisden* 1916 is a rare book; it only seemed so briefly while bereaved parents sought it urgently as a last memorial.

Chapter 10
Between the Wars

The problems of the greater world outside were mirrored in the cricket of the inter-war years. Economic and political problems, the slump, the merging of Empire into Commonwealth, the extension of the suffrage, the Hollywood-bred star system, all those had their parallels in cricket. There was the disappearance of the true amateur from the first-class game, the admission of West Indies (1928), New Zealand (1929–30), India (1932) to Test status; of professionals to the conference of power; there were 'ghosted' reminiscences, commercial recommendations and intensive press coverage for outstanding players. There was, too, the same failure to settle major problems in the inability of bowlers to achieve a balance of power as on over-perfect pitches three great batsmen and some of lesser calibre hammered capable bowlers with something near impunity.

Certainly, bowlers made every attempt to deal with the conquering batsmen; indeed, that is the recurrent theme of the period. They attempted varying degrees of intimidation by pace, from Gregory and McDonald in 1921 to Larwood and Voce in 1932–33. There was inswing to a leg trap, practised by Arthur Jaques (killed in the War) and the slightly slower Bill Greswell of Repton and Somerset before 1914; but only perfected by Fred Root with his sharp, late controlled swing and the 'one that went the other way' in the mid-nineteen-twenties. Warwick Armstrong tried a different leg theory with leg-breaks bowled from round the wicket in a partly successful attempt to check stroke-making. Despite all this, Jack Hobbs, Don Bradman and Walter Hammond set up their batting records.

In the inter-war period the influence of the press on the game increased far beyond anything dreamt of in the Edwardian era. W. G. Grace had towered over the Victorian scene as the outstanding performer. Now, though, the newspapers, through what was to be known as the 'star system' inflated reputations, sometimes distorted critical standards and in some cases violated privacy, but also brought financial benefits to outstanding players. The period saw the beginning of radio commentary, first in Australia and then in England; originally largely as an information service but soon as an established form of listening.

E. A. McDonald

In the post-war confusion of personal enthusiasm and administrative unpreparedness, it was hastily decided to play long hours and two-day matches in the Championship. The idea was a failure; ironically enough, immediately before the next World War broke out, a 'timeless' Test played in South Africa had to be left drawn after ten days.

Between 1920 and 1938, England and Australia played 10 Test series of which Australia won six, England three and one was tied for Australia to retain The Ashes; in the 49 matches (one was abandoned without a ball bowled) Australia won 22 to 15.

The Australians called for an early resumption of Test cricket. They sent an 'Australian Expeditionary Force' of demobilized soldiers to tour England in 1919, and asked for an English team to visit them in 1919–20. M.C.C. knew they were not ready and deferred the tour until 1920–21 when, as in 1946–47, they sent out a team of relatively elderly players. In their first post-war Test match, England used only four players new to international cricket while Australia had seven. Australia won all five matches by substantial margins. Macartney had a batting average of 86, Armstrong 77, Gregory 73, Collins 61 and Pellew 53. For England, only Hobbs (505 runs at 50.5) offered any effective batting resistance to Mailey (36 wickets at 26), Gregory (23 at 24) and Kelleway (15 at 21). The two most successful English bowlers were Fender (12 at 34.16) and Parkin (16 at 41.87). In the rubber of the following, heat-wave summer the English selectors, unlucky to be deprived of Hobbs who was first injured and then ill, vacillated, using thirty players. Despite some bold batting resistance by Mead, Russell, Tennyson, Brown and Woolley, the two fast bowlers McDonald (27 wickets at 24) and Gregory (19 at 29) effectively

J. M. Gregory

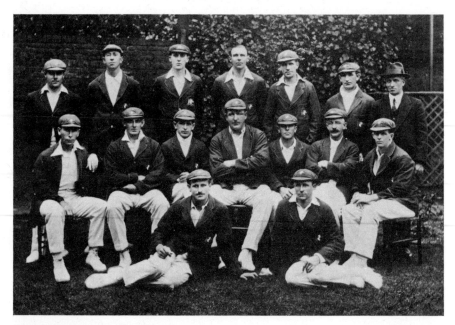

Australians in England, 1921

won the series by three matches to none. Bardsley, Macartney and Andrews batted soundly and Armstrong was a hostile and effective captain.

English cricket, duly chastened, set out to rebuild. There existed one firm foundation in Jack Hobbs, the best batsman on either side. There was, too, valuable talent in Cecil Parkin, Frank Woolley and Patsy Hendren. Unfortunately Parkin, a versatile bowler but a man of moods, resented not being given the new ball at Edgbaston in 1924; his reaction as expressed in a newspaper cost him any more England caps. He wrote some humorous books, went early and well-paid from the first-class game to league cricket in Lancashire, leaving behind a reputation as a compulsive joker and a fine bowler.

Jack Hobbs had been an outstanding and brilliant stroke-making batsman from his entry into county cricket, with Surrey in 1905; and had scored 65 centuries when War broke out. When cricket recommenced in 1919, however, he was thirty-six years old. He could hardly have dared even to hope that he would score another 132 centuries, but he did. He adapted his methods to increasing age but remained essentially a stroke-maker and, despite the interruption of war, two years lost to injury or illness and two or three tours turned down for family reasons, he scored 61,237 runs—over 6,000 more than W.G.—in first-class cricket, and more than anyone else seems likely to approach.

A quiet, courteous man, he came from a poor family, and always declared himself grateful for the prosperity and fame cricket had brought him. Beneath his gentle manner and extremely moral behaviour, there

Sir John Berry Hobbs

was an immense streak of determination which served him well under pressure and when his team was in trouble. He seems only to have been put off his game once; when he came within one of W. G. Grace's record of 126 centuries, reporters and newsfilm cameramen began to follow him to every match. He had rattled up twelve centuries in the previous eleven weeks but now he could not score another for almost a month; and, in his gentleness, he feared he was failing his entourage. Then he managed 101 against Somerset at Taunton and equalled Grace's figure. The newsmen and cameras departed and, in the second innings—with the tension lifted—he made another 101—and passed Grace.

In 1919 he decided to invest the proceeds of his benefit in a sports goods shop in Fleet Street. By dint of extremely hard work and sound trading he built a substantial business; as he said 'To make sure my children are never as poor as I was.' In time he became relatively well-off. Indeed, the scale of his business was such that he did not need to play cricket for a living. Yet he never contemplated becoming an amateur; and, to his dying day, he always referred to every amateur he ever played with as 'Mr'. He it was, too, who courteously and without effort, broke the social barrier between amateur and professional. No professional's wife had ever been allowed to accompany her husband on an M.C.C. tour; and the privilege was accorded only rarely to an amateur. Jack Hobbs, however, was a most devoted husband and, in 1924, he refused the official invitation to go to Australia with M.C.C. but agreed to go on 'Solly' Joel's private tour of South Africa with his wife. The news, of course, reached Lord's and Lord Harris, the autocrat of the day, enquired if it was correct. Jack Hobbs' reply, as he spelt it out, was 'Yes, the privilege of going with my wife having been granted, I find it possible to go to South Africa, and that is why I cannot accept the invitation to Australia.' By cricket standards, he could not be spared. Lord Harris conceded that he might take his wife—provided, of course, that Jack and not M.C.C. paid her expenses. Hobbs agreed, but stipulated that no one should lose his place in the party to accommodate him. He would not even accept a change to the South African party for anyone else. Firmly but quietly he insisted 'That doesn't seem to me fair; an Australian tour and an African tour are very different. There is nothing like an Australian tour—nothing in all cricket.' He went as the 'extra' player in the M.C.C. team to Australia; and took his wife with him. One wonders whether if he had been a lesser batsman, the two concessions would have been granted: and the conclusion must be that they would not. Yet he was no greater asset than S. F. Barnes: only he asked less—and more politely—than 'Barney'.

The season of 1926 was one of the high points of Jack Hobbs' career. He had deeply wanted to be again in a winning side against Australia. It was, too, of considerable importance that he should have been co-opted—with Wilfred Rhodes—on to the selection committee. Moreover, when Arthur Carr, the English captain, became ill at Old Trafford, although there was

A Famous Partnership: Hobbs and Sutcliffe

an amateur (Greville Stevens) in the side, Hobbs was asked to take over the captaincy.

He had succeeded where all previous professionals had failed; he had turned the flank: without belligerence, without even insistence, indeed with infinite dignity. He was the eldest of the twelve children of a Cambridge net bowler; he scored more runs and more centuries—and more runs and centuries for England against Australia—than anyone else. In 1953 he became the first professional games player to be knighted; he was made an honorary member of Surrey and of M.C.C., and he lived to see the

Hobbs Gates erected in his honour at The Oval. He had been the finest batsman in the World; and he played against his successor.

In 1924–25 in Australia, Hobbs and Sutcliffe established themselves as the greatest of all opening pairs and Maurice Tate, son of Fred, an eager fast-medium bowler, set a new record of 38 wickets in an England-Australia series. England at last won a Test—though they lost the rubber by 4–1. In the following home series—of 1926—their elderly team under a young captain, Chapman, won the only Test that was finished and took The Ashes. They held them in 1928–29 by 4–1, through the batting of Hammond (905 runs at 113) supported by Hobbs, Sutcliffe and Hendren; and the tenacious bowling of White, Tate, Larwood and Geary. In that series Australia selected, dropped and then recalled, Don Bradman who finished the series with a century in the match they won. He averaged 66.85; the other young batsman, Archie Jackson, who was soon to die tragically, averaged 69; but apart from the spinners Grimmett and Blackie, their bowlers found their task too great.

What followed has been justly and accurately described as The Bradman era. In England in 1930 he not only set up astronomic new records but proved the effective—winning—difference between Australia and England.

At Trent Bridge, where England won the first Test, he made 8 and 131; at Lord's he trumped Duleepsinhji's 173 with 254 (1 in the second innings) and Australia won by seven wickets; at Leeds, 334, but a thunderstorm gave England a draw; in the rain ruined Old Trafford match, 14; at The Oval, 232 and Australia won by an innings. His aggregate was 974, his average 139.14; both far beyond anything anyone had achieved before.

Before the England tour of 1932–33, Bradman had scored 447 at 74 against West Indies; 806 at 201.50 against South Africa. Accordingly, Douglas Jardine, who took the 1932–33 team to Australia, and Arthur Carr, captain of Nottinghamshire, evolved a tactic to counter him. It was 'fast leg-stump attack'; called by the Australians 'Body-line', bowled by Harold Larwood right-arm and Bill Voce left-arm, the opening bowlers of Nottinghamshire. At need, Bill Bowes of Yorkshire was in support; with G. O. Allen as an orthodox fast bowler, and Hedley Verity of Yorkshire, slow left-arm. Bradman played in only four of the five Tests, and the tactic reduced his average to 56. Larwood took 33 wickets (Bradman's four times) at 19.51; Allen 21 at 28; Voce 15 at 27; Verity 11 at 24. For England, Paynter averaged 61, Sutcliffe and Hammond 55. O'Reilly, the Australian leg-spinner, took 27 wickets at 26, but England won the series, 4–1. The ill-will engendered was vented at cabinet level and the entire concept of 'fast leg theory' was ruled out of court. Larwood never played for England again, and Jardine never again appeared against Australia.

In England, in 1934, Bradman scored 758 at 94.75 (Ponsford 569 at 94.83), and Australia won by 2–1; in Australia in 1936–37 he made 810 at 90, and Australia won by 3–2; in England, 1938, 434 at 108; but Hutton

Sir Donald Bradman

for England scored 473 at 118 and the series was tied, one all. In this period England had such players as Kenneth Farnes, the physically magnificent Essex fast bowler; Hedley Verity, fourth in Yorkshire's sequence of great slow left-arm bowlers (he won the Lord's Test of 1934 on a turner with 15 for 104); Douglas Wright, lively leg-spinner; Voce, Bowes and Allen. Hammond was outstandingly the finest of the domestic batsmen after Hobbs; and, but for Bradman, might have dominated the international scene.

West Indies won one and drew one of the two series played there, but lost the three in England through the weakness of their batsmen—except

George Headley—against the swinging ball: and their shortage of finger spin bowlers. South Africa won one home and one away series by the only match finished and drew one. Otherwise England contrived to win their rubbers, though standards everywhere were rising, and the Indian pace bowlers in 1932 and 1936 looked capable.

Yorkshire were easily the outstanding county; in the twenty-one seasons from 1919 to 1939 they won the Championship twelve times; Lancashire five times, Middlesex twice; Nottinghamshire and Derbyshire once each. Worcestershire—under severe financial stress—did not take part in the two-day-match Championship of 1919. Glamorgan were admitted to the competition in 1921; since then the same seventeen counties have taken part. The poor relations of the inter-war period were Northamptonshire, bottom eight times (they did not win a match between the beginning of 1935 and May 1939); Worcestershire five times; Glamorgan three times.

The Yorkshire side in the early twenties was based on Herbert Sutcliffe and his highly capable partner, Percy Holmes, supported by the tough left-hander, Maurice Leyland, and Edgar Oldroyd, a fine player on bad wickets. Rhodes and the left-handed Roy Kilner were all-rounders; Abe Waddington was the fast bowler; George Macaulay bowled fast-medium or off-cutters, and Emmott Robinson, medium pace. Arthur Dolphin was wicket-keeper. In the late thirties, Sutcliffe and Leyland were still there, but Len Hutton, Wilfred Barber and Arthur Mitchell were newcomers as batsmen. Verity, slow left-arm, remained; Bill Bowes was still fast. Cyril Turner was the left-arm stock bowler, Ellis Robinson, the off-spinner and Arthur Wood, wicket-keeper. Both these sides were—the first under a sequence of captains, the second with Brian Sellers—highly professional teams, most of the players capped by England, all extremely well organized.

Lancashire, typified by the tenacious, extremely technically and defensively correct batsman, Harry Makepeace, were a hard side to beat. Among their best batsmen were the cultured Ernest Tyldesley, the left-handed Charles Hallows and Eddie Paynter. There were two all rounders, who both bowled slow left-arm, Jack Iddon and Leslie Hopwood; there was Ted McDonald, the Australian fast bowler, with the young Dick Pollard and Eddie Phillipson both capable of lively pace. After Parkin's departure, the corpulent Dick Tyldesley came in to bowl leg-breaks; while George Duckworth, for a dozen years, was the best wicket-keeper in England.

Middlesex won twice, in 1920 and 1921, the last year of Plum Warner's captaincy and the first of Frank Mann's. Each time they won by beating Surrey at the end of the season; the second time when Surrey would have taken the title if they had won. It was an historic recovery. The Middlesex bowling was thin; Durston and Haig with the new ball; 'Young Jack' Hearne with his leg spin had little support for years, until Ian Peebles and

Walter Robins, also leg-spinners, came along. A series of talented amateurs were only irregularly available. Hendren, though, was a wonderfully consistent batsman, and Frank Mann a powerful hitter capable of turning a match.

Nottinghamshire under Arthur Carr relied much on the pace of Harold Larwood and Bill Voce; but they were supported by Fred Barratt, also of brisk pace, and Sam Staples, off-breaks. The best of their batsmen were the near-genius George Gunn, 'Dodge' Whysall, the immaculate Walter Keeton, stylish Joe Hardstaff junior, and Carr himself.

Derbyshire won largely by bowling; the pace of Copson and the wrist spin of Tommy Mitchell was supported by the off-breaks of Townsend, the seam bowling of the Pope brothers, Alf and George, and the general purpose of Bert Rhodes; all four all-rounders. The main batsmen were Stanley Worthington, Denis Smith and Albert Alderman.

One of the most consistent sides of the inter-war period were Kent: seventeen times in one of the first five places, without taking the title. 'Tich' Freeman—only 5 feet 2 inches tall, and with remarkably small hands—took more wickets—3,776—than anyone else except Rhodes. He bowled high-tossed leg-breaks, googlies and top-spinners to an accurate length and line; and in 1928 he took 304 wickets, in 1933, 298. He rarely got out the top batsmen but he was deadly among those of lesser quality who simply destroyed themselves with catches to his deep fieldsmen or stumpings to Leslie Ames. In August he had the support of a rather faster leg-spinner in C. S.—'Father'—Marriott and they proved an immensely effective pair. Otherwise the Kent bowling was not strong enough to take them to the title. In the nineteen-seventies Freeman would not take a remotely similar number of wickets, simply because present-day batsmen do not hit slow spinners in the air to fieldsmen. He was, though, symptomatic of the twenties, when so many county batsmen would always attempt to hit a tossed up ball for six. Leslie Ames, the pre-eminent wicket-keeper batsman, was the first to perform the double of a hundred wicket-keeper wickets and a thousand runs in a season. Their batting, with Percy Chapman, the captain, a great fieldsman and spectacular left-handed hitter, Woolley, the most graceful of left-handers, Wally Hardinge, Aidan Crawley, Brian Valentine and Arthur Fagg, was constantly long and strong. Sussex, under Duleepsinhji, Scott and Melville; and with Tate, the Langridge brothers and Bowley, pressed both Yorkshire and Lancashire hard in the middle thirties.

Apart from the success of Freeman, another significant aspect of cricket between the two wars was batsmen's deliberate and, indeed, increasingly skilful, use of the pads in defence. The off-spinner or the fast inswinger could beat the stroke and still see the batsman push his back pad safely into a ball which had pitched even fractionally outside the off stump. Frustration from this tactic produced an attitude of mind which drove bowlers to inslant, bouncers and body line.

This was a fruitful period for the cricket professional. The separate gates for pros and amateurs were abandoned; the difference between the two were often apparent only in selection for Gentlemen *versus* Players. Socially and financially, too, his position was better than that of his generally comparable competitor, the professional footballer. Several leading cricket players of the period had a choice: Walter Hammond, for instance, preferred to concentrate solely on cricket.

Hammond was one of the great athletes of British history: a quite regal cover driver from front foot and back, and a batsman of poise and sporting intellect; a distant man but a superb performer; a great batsman, a gloriously relaxed and certain slip fieldsman who could have been a great bowler or, for that matter, probably a great golfer, footballer or tennis player.

By the acceptable criteria of the time, the established cricket professional in the thirties could afford to run a motor car: the average professional footballer could not. Cricket in 1939, however, was in an uncertain financial state; its aristocratic patrons were growing fewer and, simply enough, less wealthy.

Learie Constantine, son of the foreman of a Trinidad sugar plantation—'Old Cons' who also came to England with a West Indian team—made the tours of 1923 and 1928. In 1928, his spectacular fast bowling and hitting reversed and won a match for the West Indian touring team against Middlesex at Lord's. It made him, in a day, a national figure. He went to play—extremely successfully—as professional for Nelson, where he became very popular in the life of the town. He used his earnings to study law, and became a barrister. He played for West Indies in eighteen Tests: bowling first extremely fast, then at much varied pace; from time to time batting brilliantly and fielding quite remarkably. Indeed, he probably was the finest fieldsman the game has ever known. More importantly, he became a spokesman for his people and did more in their interest in Britain than anyone else. High Commissioner for Trinidad and Tobago in Britain, he was knighted in 1962 and created a baron—Lord Constantine of Trinidad and Tobago—in 1969.

To chronicle and explain the changes in the laws of cricket and in the regulations governing county cricket would alone demand a book. Larger wickets, a smaller ball; the countless concertina-like lengthening, shortening and stretching again of the number of overs before another new ball could be taken—were made to reinforce the bowler in face of the growing strength and prosperity of the batsman. Those changes to County Championship regulations, qualifications, point-scoring, bonus points; the follow-on introduced, adjusted, abolished, re-introduced; first innings lead and limitation of first innings were aimed first at the poaching of players, then towards a just outcome, and the entertainment of spectators.

No change, however, was more important than that to the 1935 lbw law by which the batsman could be lbw to a ball pitching outside the line of the off stump, provided the point at which his pad or body was struck was in the line of wicket-to-wicket. It was the product of an argument which had been constantly and strongly posed since the eighteen-eighties. Simply enough, the original eighteenth-century lbw law had specified 'that the batsman puts his leg before the wicket with a design to stop the ball': but later legislation ignored that factor of intent. The experimental law of 1972, under which the batsman may be out although the point of interception is outside the line of the wickets, if he has made no attempt to play it, is simply a logical extension of that thinking.

The supporters of the 1935 law argued enthusiastically that it would give the bowler a just reward for his labours and, by forcing batsmen to play outside the off stump recapture the earlier glory of off-side stroke play and would encourage spin bowling. At the time only R. E. S. Wyatt clearly foretold the outcome. The bowlers did gain some just advantage. On the other hand, with their instinctive hunger for opportunity against their natural enemy, the batsman, they soon found out how to exploit it, to use inswing, inslant, and tight off-spin restrictively. Thereupon batsmen began to play more to the leg side; and to take unorthodox, but often effective, risks, to hit slow bowlers there. As a result, true slow bowlers have all but disappeared from English cricket in favour of slow-medium spinners to whom flight is an unknown art.

In the nineteen-thirties, however, bowlers still attacked. When Bradman had made two hundred, Maurice Tate still set an attacking field and tried to get him out. As soon as the new law was adopted, fewer batsmen scored 2,000 runs and fewer 1,000; more bowlers took 200 wickets and more 100. Nevertheless, Herbert Sutcliffe, who had been suspicious of it, gave the new law a season's study and announced that he found it fair and effective (he was second in the averages with 2,494 runs at 48.90): and the editor of *Wisden* 1936 devoted four pages to 'Success of the lbw Experiment'.

It was all to be put in perspective once more by war. In August 1939, the West Indian touring team took ship for home as soon as they had finished—and lost—the three-Test rubber; and the Second World War broke out on 3 September. Only one county match was in progress at the time. It was Sussex *versus* Yorkshire at Hove, played for Jim Parks senior's benefit. After rain Hedley Verity took seven for nine, bowled out Sussex for 33 and gave Yorkshire the Championship. That was Hedley Verity's last first-class match. He was killed in Italy. For the second time cricket took cover; this time for a six-year 'duration'.

Chapter 11
Post War euphoria and reality

Cricket began after the Second World War in a general euphoria generated by relief and nostalgia. There had been more play during that War than the earlier one, if only because of the different nature of warfare and different treatment of members of the Forces. Somewhat surprisingly, though, Services cricket threw up few discoveries; Jim Laker—a strong rumour from North Africa—and Maurice Tremlett—reported from the Rhine—were almost the only fresh names to emerge.

The prevailing sense of bloodless revolution did not sweep through cricket so completely as through many other spheres. The cricket establishment tends to be politically conservative in politics and traditionalist in method; and, while some reforming zeal creeps in, it is invariably in a marked minority, and change has never been easily achieved. Once more, though not easily, it proved faithful to its society. This was the age of the media and, if cricket had to be tugged into it at first, it eventually was captivated by its money. The outstanding pre-war English commentator, Howard Marshall, was not allowed to broadcast from within Lord's. When Verity bowled out Australia in 1934 Marshall had to run from the match and broadcast an account from a microphone installed in a house in Grove End Road. Even in the early post-war years, Lord's held aloof from radio and even more from television. By the nineteen-seventies, however, M.C.C. members were to be seen in the pavilion watching the Lord's Test on the set provided by the BBC rather than the actual event which was taking place a few steps away. Above all, television and the sponsorship it brought were to stabilize the finances of the game.

Australia was again anxious for a rapid resumption of Test play but, while cricket had progressed there, it had been static in England. Thus, for their first post-war Test (against India) England produced players new to international cricket—Ikin, Smailes and Alec Bedser. In the following winter, Australia had eight in Morris, Miller, McCool, Johnson, Tallon, Lindwall, Tribe and Toshack, but again England had only four who had not been capped before the War.

Ray Lindwall   *Keith Miller*

England had an easy passage against India in 1946 and won the only Test to be finished, but they learned little from the three-day Tests in which nineteen players took part. They suffered a salutary series of defeats in Australia. It was not certain that Don Bradman intended to continue in post-war cricket; and, although he played in the first Test, it was regarded as a personal try-out to decide whether or not he should retire. In the early and highly tentative stages of his first innings, he edged Voce to slip, where Ikin made what he thought to be a clean catch. On appeal the umpire gave Bradman not out and he went on to make 187, and play through that series and the next against England. If he had been given out, at least Australia would probably have batted on the subsequent rain-damaged wicket. In the event, Miller and Toshack bowled on it and put out England for 141 and 172 for Australia to win by an innings and 332 runs.

Australia now had one of the strongest of all their teams. The pre-war batting strength of Barnes, Bradman, Hassett and, at need, Brown, was reinforced by the all-rounder, Miller, and a 'tail' in which all but one was a capable batsman. In echo of Gregory and McDonald in 1921, they had a superb pair of fast bowlers in Lindwall and Miller, who were similarly to stalk England wreaking destruction. Moreover, their variety of spin was so great that their selectors' problem was really that of who should be left out. They won three matches of the series and, given a little more time, would probably have won the two left drawn.

For England, Hammond's failure after his brilliant domestic season of 1946—a batting average of 84—16 more than the next man—was a bitter —almost historic—disappointment. Neither his mind nor his heart were in his cricket and he retired on his return to England. Only the batting of Hutton, Compton and Edrich; the bowling of Wright and the still immature Bedser, and the wicket-keeping of Evans, gave reason for hope.

The English cricket season of 1947 was a kind of cloud cuckoo land for the cricket enthusiast returning to a normal post-war life. In retrospect, at least, the sun shone all and every day and there are figures to prove that there were some quite prodigious batting performances and exciting cricket. The South Africans made a happy and friendly tour, and Middlesex under Walter Robins won the County Championship. In the course of the tour and title both Denis Compton and Bill Edrich broke Tom Hayward's forty-one-year-old record aggregate of 3,518. Compton scored 3,816 and Edrich 3,539; and, quite strikingly, those two made over 2,000—Compton 1,187 and Edrich 869—against the South African touring team alone. England won the three Tests that were finished. The Championship was a triumph for Robins' enterprise. Although his side was short of bowling, his batsmen—primarily Robertson, Brown, Edrich and Compton—scored so quickly that matches were won by weight of runs, and Lord's became a place of happy resort.

In the following winter, English cricket received another sharp setback when West Indies won two Tests and had the better of two draws. It was a poor England party, captained by G. O. Allen who, at the age of 45, was not even remotely match fit; in Tests he scored 94 runs at 18.80 and took five wickets at 41. Robertson, Hutton, Hardstaff, Place and, to his surprise, Griffith with his first century, as batsmen; Laker and Howorth as bowlers, maintained resistance against a far stronger side.

Thus there was little hope for anything but defeat from the 1948 Australians who, under Bradman, proved as strong as any to have visited England. The already weighty batting was made quite massive by the addition of the young Neil Harvey; Barnes, Morris, Bradman, Hassett, Miller, Harvey, Loxton (who made 93 at Leeds) and Lindwall (77 at Leeds) was a disheartening sequence for English bowlers. (Seven of their batsmen had Test averages between 44 and 87.) In their attack, Miller and Lindwall were now supported by the tall Bill Johnston, who bowled left-arm swing, cut or spin over a range of paces; the stock bowling of Toshack, the fast medium Loxton, or leg-spinner, Ring. Three bowlers took 67 wickets at between 19.62 and 23.33. Tallon was a great wicket-keeper and the fielding of Miller, Harvey, Lindwall, Barnes and Hassett was superb.

Australia won four Tests, two by an innings, the others by seven and eight wickets; rain ended the only match England had an opportunity of winning. Compton, who made a brave 145 not out after being injured at Old Trafford, Washbrook, Hutton (who at one period suffered a complete loss of confidence) and Edrich all batted well on occasions, but not often enough; and Alec Bedser, as so often in those years, laboured prodigiously (18 wickets at 38.22). Despite England's overwhelming defeat, this tour aroused immense public interest. Such Australian performances as their 721 runs in a few minutes short of a full day against Essex, and the fast bowling of Lindwall and the divertingly athletic Miller drew huge crowds, and they took home an amazing profit of £75,000.

Before the tour began Don Bradman announced that he would retire at the end of it; and in the Australian season of 1948–49 appeared only in three Testimonial matches. He played from 1927 to 1949, and all his first-class cricket was in Australia and England. In 234 matches he had 338 innings and made 28,067 runs (highest score 452 not out) at an average of 95.14; his 117 centuries represent an incidence of better than one every third innings. In Test Matches he had 80 innings for an average of 99.94; like W.G., no doubt he would have liked to have made the figure a round one. As Sir Donald Bradman he continued as administrator and thinker, to serve cricket valuably.

The winter tour of South Africa was more restful; England won the two Tests finished but, in the first, all four results were feasible at the start of the final over—bowled by Tuckett—and it was won by a leg-bye off Gladwin's thigh from the last possible ball of the match.

In 1948 Glamorgan, the last county to enter the County Championship, won it, largely through fine fielding to the spin bowling of Len Muncer, Stanley Trick and John Clay. Wilfred Wooller was a hard-going, hard-driving captain; John Clay, who played in their first season, of 1921, was in the team that ensured the title at Bournemouth.

The magnificent batting of the left-handed Martin Donnelly helped New Zealand to draw all four of their three-day Tests in 1949; and that spelt the end of three-day Tests.

Another event of 1949 was Denis Compton's benefit which brought him some £12,000 but had even more important repercussions. Compton's aversion to 'paper work' led to Bagenal Harvey, an accountant from Cork, being asked to set the correspondence and accounts of the benefit fund in order. At the same time he found himself dealing with Compton's other business affairs. He soon became aware that payments to sportsmen by publicity firms were negligible. A few enquiries showed him that an agency wanting to use a photograph of a film actor for advertising purposes was prepared to pay £100; but they would offer a cricketer only £5. All Harvey did was to insist that his principal was treated as well as actors. He was successful, and the happy coincidence of an improvement in English sporting fortunes, found him the first English agent for sportsmen. He has handled the affairs of many successful cricketers, footballers and golfers in respect of newspaper columns, books, radio, television and public appearances to their—and no doubt his own—healthy profit.

The 1950 West Indies were beaten in the first Test on a terrifyingly dusty wicket at Old Trafford where Evans scored a century of mixed luck and genius. They won the next three. They had—somewhat unusually for them—a sound sheet-anchor batsman in Alan Rae; and, more usually, some glorious stroke makers in the three Barbadians, Everton Weekes, Frank Worrell and Clyde Walcott. The matches were won for them by two spin bowlers, Alf Valentine, remorselessly accurate slow left-arm, who spun until his spinning finger bled, and still spun; and 'Sonny' Ramadhin, basically an off-spinner with an occasional leg-break which no English batsman was able to 'pick'. In the four-Test rubber they took 59 of the 77 English wickets that fell to bowlers; Valentine 33 at 20.42; Ramadhin 26 at 23.33; and inspired a calypso which still echoes.

England, beaten four-one in Australia in 1950–51, and held to a one-all draw in India, were now at the lowest level they had so far known in their Test history, and needed to rebuild. At this juncture, amid an atmosphere of more than debate, it was decided—at a much higher level than that of the selection committee—to appoint a professional as captain. The position had been half prepared by the election of twenty-six professionals to honorary life membership of M.C.C. in 1949, the appointment of Leslie Ames, former professional and manager of Kent as a selector in 1950, and of Compton as vice-captain in Australia in 1950–51. Now Len Hutton was named as captain immediately for the home series of 1952 with India, but looking ahead to Australia in 1953, West Indies in 1953–54 and Australia again in 1954; punctuated in 1954 by a visit from Pakistan, newly admitted to the then Imperial Cricket Conference.

Although James Lillywhite, Alfred Shaw and Arthur Shrewsbury had captained some of the 'mercenary' sides of the nineteenth century in Australia, no professional had ever held the post of captain of England in England, or anywhere since M.C.C. and the Board of Control took over. The establishment had come to terms with the times, but many of their supporters had not.

Much unofficial—and some quasi-official—opposition to the appointment was surprising and all but shocking. In some quarters reaction towered far above that form of team-support which is sometimes called patriotism. Len Hutton never did anything braver, sounder or more balanced than keeping his eye firmly on his objective and ignoring this malevolent snobbery. He had always been a believer in pace as a weapon, and now he had it to his hand in a somewhat technically and temperamentally erratic, but unquestionably fast, twenty-one-year-old Yorkshireman, Fred Trueman. There was rain at Leeds during the first Test with India. Trueman (three for 89 in the first innings) bowled on a difficult wicket in the second and Hazare came in to prevent a hat-trick with the score board reading nought for four—and not, as a newspaper sub-editor

Point of Delivery: F. S. Trueman

Point of Delivery: Brian Statham

rang his correspondent to confirm, four for nought. Trueman's figures for the innings were four for 27. At Lord's, where Mankad counter-attacked, he took four for 72 and four for 110. At Manchester there was rain again and India were bowled out twice on Saturday for 58 and 82: with Trueman eight for 31 and one for nine (Bedser five for 27, Lock four for 36). Rain once more at The Oval where India—no doubt to their relief—were only able to bat once when they were put out for 98 (Trueman five for 48).

Despite this success Trueman was not in Hutton's basic eleven against Australia in 1953; in fact, only two fast bowlers were used; Statham in the second Test and Trueman in the last. Hutton's designed side was himself, Edrich, Graveney, Compton, Watson, Bailey, Evans, Laker, Bedser, with either Lock or Wardle and one of the fast bowlers, or an extra batsman. Bailey, the new, genuine and highly combative all-rounder, balanced the team effectively. England won the rubber by the solitary finished Test—the last. Already, though, it had been heroically saved. At Lord's on the last morning, England, 73 for four, needed another 269 to avoid an innings defeat and there were five hours left to play when Watson (109) and Bailey (71) began their epic stand of 163 which lasted more than four hours and saved the match. At Old Trafford, on the last afternoon, in earnest of 1956, Wardle and Laker took between them six for 18 on a wet turning wicket. Leeds was a draw, and so to The Oval with an extra day available for a finish. The bowling of Bedser and Trueman and the batting of Hutton and Bailey gave England a first innings lead of 31. Then the two spinners, Laker and Lock, on their home pitch, took nine wickets for 120; England needed only 132 to win and made them for two wickets. Happily enough Edrich and Compton were together when the winning hit was made and England held The Ashes for the first time for twenty years.

The series in West Indies during the following winter was even more savagely contested. West Indies, with Walcott, Weekes and Holt in fine batting form, and Ramadhin puzzling as ever, won the first two Tests; England the third; and the fourth was drawn. Hutton, in a final mighty effort, made 205 (he averaged 96.71 for the series) which, with the superb bowling of Bailey (seven for 74 on the first day) won the fifth and drew the rubber.

The medium-paced cutters of Fazal Mahmood on a difficult pitch at The Oval enabled Pakistan to draw their low scoring inaugural Test series in England. Hutton's mind, however, was already on Australia where, in the first Test, at Brisbane, he took the risk of a green wicket on the first morning and, when he won the toss, put Australia in to bat. England went into the match without a slow bowler; Morris, dropped, made 153; Compton broke a finger; and Australia won by an innings and 154.

Hutton decided to pin his faith to pace. He left out Alec Bedser, who had shingles, and settled for a team of himself, Edrich or Graveney, May, Cowdrey, Compton, Bailey, Evans, Wardle, Tyson, Statham, Appleyard; and they won him the rubber by three to one. After Brisbane, Tyson—

in the most splendid performance of his life—and Statham took between them 43 wickets for 799 runs. The Australian batsmen with little pace in their domestic game found such a pace-bowling confrontation irresistible. May, Bailey, Cowdrey and Hutton made enough runs. Hutton had achieved his ambition, beaten Australia home and away; held out against West Indies. The strain had been heavy; he handed on the captaincy to May, and took his appropriate knighthood.

After a narrow—three-two-win over Cheetham's well-drilled South African side in 1955, England faced Australia again in 1956. In a wet summer Australia won on the only good pitch of the series, at Lord's, when Benaud's forcing batting and the fast bowling of Miller and Archer were decisive. Laker, who also took all ten Australian wickets in an innings in their county match against Surrey, took six for 87 in the draw at Trent Bridge; three for 64 at Lord's; eleven for 113 in England's innings win at Headingley. Then, at Old Trafford, incredibly and without parallel in the records of first-class cricket, but backed by superb catching, nine (for 37) in the first innings and then all ten for 53, when England again won by an innings. He ended with seven for 88 in the rain induced draw at The Oval.

Before the second throwing purge of the century Australia won the series of 1958–59 with Rorke and Meckiff; while between them, Australian captains Benaud, Simpson and Lawry kept The Ashes for another fifteen years and eight series, until 1970–71. England beat a strangely disheartened West Indies in England in 1957 but, far more impressively, did so for the first time in West Indies in 1959–60. In 1961 South Africa left the British Commonwealth and relinquished membership of the International Cricket Conference.

Over the seventeen years from the end of the Second World War among the counties Surrey were consistently strong. They shared the title with Lancashire in 1950 and then won it outright for seven consecutive seasons from 1952 to 1958. Their main strength lay in bowling: Loader and Bedser at some pace; the spin of Jim Laker and Tony Lock with assistance, when needed, from Stuart Surridge at fast medium, or the off-breaks of Eric Bedser. Essentially an attacking side under the splendidly impatient Stuart Surridge, they finished their match with Warwickshire at The Oval in a single day; and on a number of occasions won within two days. As with the England side, May, in 1957, inherited a winning team, and won the title for two more seasons; Surrey did not win again until 1971.

Yorkshire won in 1946 with the remnants of the pre-war team but they did not do as much again for thirteen years—many of them traumatic, with constant changes of team and, after Norman Yardley's retirement, of captains also. In 1959, the stopgap disciplinarian captain, Ronnie Burnett, saw them take the title once more in a stirring finish—215 runs in 100 minutes against Sussex—and then handed over to Vic Wilson, their first professional captain since before Lord Hawke. He repeated the feat in the next season. Hampshire, with the ebullient, popular—and shrewd—Colin Ingleb-Mackenzie won their first title in 1961; Warwickshire, with the wise and capable Tom Dollery, their second in 1951.

Surrey, though, were the major power of the period. It was, therefore, disquieting that, while they were still at their strongest, playing purposeful cricket and achieving positive results, attendances at The Oval were decreasing.

The nostalgia for the game that was so widespread in 1947 had disappeared. Yet, in that very year, when some sports were suspended altogether in midweek because they affected the production drive, the Home Secretary decided that the number of people watching cricket (it was 3,000,000 man-days in 1947) could not have any perceptible effect. In 1953, moreover, the Chancellor removed the entertainment tax on cricket. Widespread car ownership had freed the vast captive audiences of the nineteenth-century cities. Cricket was no longer the sole spectator sport in major population centres; and television could provide action and spectacle in the home. Hard times lay ahead for all sections of the entertainment industry and it was in the entertainment industry that cricket's future lay. The day when the Lord Lieutenant of the County was also President of the county club and would settle an annual deficit of a hundred or so pounds out of his own pocket was gone. It became obvious that if first-class cricket could not sell itself, it would perish.

Chapter 12
Economics, politics and sponsorship, 1963-1977

If a wall separating—and protecting—cricket from the outside ever existed, it had never seemed lower than in the early nineteen-sixties. In the next four years the game was to know the same problems as those of the rest of society—racism; violence; wage demands; over-exposure to the media; commercial rivalries; 'plugging'; unrestricted movement of labour; and even the 'streaker'. In a time when female equality was conceded, it was completely appropriate that the English women cricketers should be given a match at Lord's against those of Australia.

The three-day game, the mainstay, always the training ground, and essentially, the heart-form of cricket, was no longer a viable entertainment. Yet it was the traditional—and apparently the only—method of sustaining international cricket without which the entire economy of the sport in England would be ruined.

In 1963 the distinction between amateur and professional in English cricket was abolished. It had long been meaningless; many 'amateurs' of the nineteenth century were paid to enable them to play first-class cricket. So were a number who could not afford to play without payment, and were paid to be captains or secretaries of their clubs. All were now free to negotiate their own terms with their employers.

This was in turn a reflection of the fact that a former major source of amateur players, 'Oxbridge', was drying up. It was no longer simple for a young athlete to gain admission to Oxford or Cambridge on the strength of his cricket record at his public school; and, once there, he was expected to study or go. For a few years after the war there was a steady stream of outstanding performers—Donnelly, Whitcombe, Pawson, Kardar, Carr, Smith, Dewes, Doggart, Sheppard, Insole, Bailey, May, Subba Row, McCarthy and Warr—but soon post-war society and official educational policy imposed their shape on the University game, and there was no remotely comparable crop of talent until 1976. A few won blues and became professionals in the county game, where several of them rapidly became disenchanted. By comparison with its great days, however, University cricket has become a backwater.

In the same season, over-limit cricket, which had long been known at club level as 'knock out', was admitted among first-class clubs. The Gillette Cup met with instant success—and publicity for its sponsors at a far cheaper rate than cricketing authority was prepared to concede later. While there was rapid public reaction in favour of such a competition—it had always been popular locally—many, including a number of county players, took a strongly traditionalist attitude. Their arguments were mainly based on its probably destructive effect on techniques. There had already been something of a technical revolution since the War. It was often attributed to M. J. K. Smith but he was less its creator than the observant pragmatist who used unorthodox methods—quite simply, to hit the ball where there were no fieldsman. He would, for instance, swing the left-arm breakaway out on the leg side—which is not easy, but demands infinite judgment, skill and timing.

This batting tactic led in its turn to 'slow' bowlers adopting a 'flat' trajectory so that the batsmen could not 'get at' them. As a further consequence, flight was more rarely practised and, soon, spin bowlers were regarded as a luxury in some county class teams. Since it follows that boy and junior players tend to copy their 'seniors' of the first-class game, spin bowling is often rejected in favour of medium pace: and therefore tends to die out.

It was argued, too, and with some justification, that soon the competition would be less about which side could make the most big hits than of which could keep the other batsmen in the tightest check. (Incidentally, it is interesting that the 'perfect' knock-out bowling analysis—eight overs for no runs—was achieved by a slow bowler, Brian Langford of Somerset.)

It was thought, too, that young players would 'learn bad habits' which would prove dangerous when they played under pressure in the 'full' game. Certainly it is true that there is much restrictive bowling in over-limit cricket. After all, its aim—as distinct from that of the 'full' game—is to restrict the opponents' scoring; that is to say, a bowling side does better to hold the other side to 49 for no wicket than to bowl them all out for 50.

Nevertheless, it was soon apparent that this 'one-day' entertainment demanded special aptitudes and skills. The first specialists were Sussex, who won the Gillette in the first two years. Their main assets were the forcing batting of Jim Parks and Ted Dexter, linked to the foraging sheet-anchor of Ken Suttle; and accurate bowling to defensive field-placings. Kent with their considerable reservoir of talent, were likely to succeed in this, as in any other form, of the game. Soon, however, the ultimate experts were Lancashire who, under the astute and intensive captaincy of Jackie Bond, demonstrated the value of meticulous and fast fielding. They had, too, a sequence of all-rounders, more than the minimum number of bowlers, and some fine forcing batsmen. They continue to excel in over-limit rather than three-day play.

During 1966, Fred Rumsey the Somerset, Worcestershire and occasional England, fast left-arm bowler, began to canvass the idea of a 'union' for cricketers. It was not unanimously accepted, but in 1968 *The Daily Express* paid the expenses of a meeting at which The Cricketers Association was formed, with Rumsey as secretary and Jack Bannister of Warwickshire as treasurer. For brief periods Jim Parks and Roger Prideaux held office; but the Association first found its feet with Bannister, and then Mike Edwards, of Surrey, as chairman; and in 1971 Bannister became perm-anent secretary as an exception to the rule that only active players could be members. Its first testing was in 1975 when, in demanding some share of the game's now considerable income from television and radio for the players, there was a threat of industrial action of mounting intensity. As a result, it was agreed that a proportion of the proceeds of media pay-ments would be granted to the players. The Association has consistently pressed the players' right to a point of view, and is now represented on the disciplinary committee, the qualifications sub-committee and the crick-eters' pensions committee; as well as being invited regularly twice a year to the Chairman's Advisory Sub-committee in a consultative capacity.

The T.C.C.B., or Test and County Cricket Board, is that section of the Cricket Council responsible for the first-class game. The Council was formed in 1968 to take over from M.C.C., the Board of Control and the Advisory County Cricket Committee in the administration of the game in this country. So far as names are concerned, it looks as if no change has taken place but, in fact, there has been a transfer of power.

The year 1968 was to prove historic in several ways. In the first case, in the perpetual search for means of increasing the income of county clubs, it was decided to waive the normal two-year qualification period for one overseas player per county. The move was successful; players like Clive Lloyd (Lancashire), Mike Procter (Gloucestershire), Barry Richards (Hampshire), Rohan Kanhai (Warwickshire) gave play in England an immense fillip. Once a first player had been also qualified by residence, another could be added. In consequence Lancashire added Farook Engineer; Warwickshire, Lance Gibbs, Alvin Kallicharran and Bill Bourne, as well as Kanhai. That tendency, in conjunction with the argument that the number of overseas players was restricting the develop-ment of young English players, caused the ruling to be amended so that, however many overseas players may be on a county's staff, ten of their eleven for every match must be qualified to play for England; which, under the new regulations, demands ten years' residence. There can be no doubt, however, that the presence of the imported star players has done—

and is still doing—much to make English cricket more entertaining and of a higher standard than it would be without them.

Australia had previously allowed the introduction of overseas cricketers into the Sheffield Shield competition. Such legislation introduced in the jet age meant that outstanding performers could play all the year round. There was no finer player of the time than Garfield (later Sir Garfield) Sobers of Barbados. Indeed he was, beyond reasonable argument, the finest all-rounder the game has ever known. He bowled left arm fast-medium, orthodox finger-spin and wrist spin; was a splendid batsman (he scored more runs—7,932—in Tests than anyone else); an outstanding close fieldsman; and captain of his country. In addition to Barbados and West Indies, the speed of jet travel enabled him to play in League cricket in

Barry Richards

England, for South Australia and Nottinghamshire, Rothmans Cavaliers and on various sponsored overseas tours. Even his splendidly athletic and wiry strength, though, could not sustain that strain; and he was physically and nervously burnt out before he retired from first-class cricket in 1974.

The other far-reaching event of 1968, of which the repercussions are not yet over, was what has been known as 'The D'Oliveira Case'. Basil D'Oliveira is a Cape Coloured, born in Cape Town and, in his own country, South Africa, not allowed to play cricket with or against white people. In non-white cricket, however, he had some quite outstanding batting and bowling performances to his credit. In 1960 he first came to England, hoping to learn about cricket and to become a coach and help the cause of 'non-white' cricket in South Africa. His passage money was raised by a local testimonial. He was only able to live in England on his wages as professional for Middleton in the Central Lancashire League. After a poor start there, his improving form led to the renewal of his contract and the interest of some shrewd judges in his unsophisticated but genuine talent. He toured Rhodesia in 1961–62 and 1962–63; and Pakistan in 1963–64, with Commonwealth XIs; and in 1964, joined Worcestershire. His entire life had been changed; he was free to live among white people and to play cricket with people of any race—except white South Africans in South Africa. Although he continually returned on visits, he was not prepared to submit his wife and children permanently to the intolerable regime of apartheid, and he became a British citizen. He qualified for Worcestershire in 1965 and was capped in the same season. In the next, he played for England against West Indies, when he faced the immense fast bowling of Wesley Hall and the frequently illegal pace of Griffith with such skill and courage that he averaged 42.66 for the series. In the two-tour summer of 1967 his figure was 83.00 against India, 50.00 against Pakistan. He had, though, a poor tour in West Indies with Cowdrey's determinedly successful team in the following winter with a batting average of 22.83 and, for bowling, 97.66. Nevertheless, once he had been chosen for the first Test of 1968 against Australia, and made 87 not out— the only score over fifty in either England innings—in a round defeat; there seemed no justification for leaving him out of the side subsequently. He was, however, brought in as a replacement for the unfit Prideaux for the last Test, at The Oval, with Australia leading by one-nil in the rubber. After Edrich had given the innings a sound start, D'Oliveira, missed at 31, went on to make an enterprising 158 which, by the speed of its making, gave England a chance to win. That opportunity seemed lost when a cloudburst on the last day flooded the ground with Australia 85 for five. When the rain stopped, a crowd of volunteers mopped the ground and made an hour-and-a-quarter's play possible. When it started, Cowdrey used Brown, Snow, Illingworth and Underwood before he turned to D'Oliveira who, in his second over, and with only 35 minutes left, hit Jarman's off-stump with a leg-cutter. Cowdrey brought back Underwood who took the remaining four wickets to give England a win by 226 runs with only six minutes left.

D'Oliveira had effectively won the match. Yet, at a selection committee meeting held that night, he was not included in the M.C.C. team to go to South Africa in that winter. There was immediately strong protest and suggestion that he had been omitted to accommodate South African political opinion. Almost at once *The News of the World* announced that it had engaged D'Oliveira to report the tour. Then Cartwright, one of the originally selected team, had to cry off as unfit; and the selectors nominated D'Oliveira—whom they had originally stated had been evaluated and rejected for the tour solely as a batsman—as replacement for a stock bowler. Mr Vorster, the South African Prime Minister, at once announced that South Africa was not prepared to accept a team imposed upon her 'by people with certain political aims'. M.C.C. had no alternative but to cancel the tour.

At a special general meeting of M.C.C. the Rev. David Sheppard, and J. M. Brearley proposed motions critical of M.C.C.'s handling of the matter and asking that no further tours of South Africa be undertaken until there was evidence of progress towards non-racial cricket. The motions were carried easily within the hall but lost on the postal ballot.

So, for the moment, the matter rested.

It was revived a year later in a movement to stop the projected South African cricket tour of England in 1970. A body of opposition led by the new Bishop of Woolwich, the Right Rev. David Sheppard, Sir Edward Boyle, Lord Constantine, Jeremy Thorpe, Reg Prentice, and Father Trevor Huddleston was insistent that it should not take place. On the other side, the Cricket Council launched an appeal for £200,000 to protect the tour; appeals were launched, too, for vigilantes to protect grounds. Eventually it was decided to go ahead with a limited tour of matches to be played on 'defensible' grounds protected by barbed wire, guard dogs and police. Already, however, the matches of the touring South African rugby team had shown how easy it was for demonstrators to interrupt play of less than two hours on a ground which might be less immaculate. What chance had a cricket ground to be kept inviolate for five days? It cost £8,985 to protect a single rugby match at Manchester in November 1969.

Mr Denis Howell, Minister for Sport, said four important questions to be considered were the effect of the proposed tour on race relations; the threat to law and order; the implications for the Commonwealth Games in view of the reactions of other member-countries; and the long-term interests of sport.

There were extremists on both sides but the T.C.C.B. was obviously determined to go on with the tour regardless of expense, risks or damages to any external relations since this 'had the support of the majority', and despite an appeal by a body which asked them to cancel the tour 'to demonstrate their sense of responsibility as citizens and at the same time their concern for the future of international cricket'. Simultaneously the International Olympic Committee formally expelled South Africa. Lord's 'noted' the decision. The Royal Commonwealth Society stated its concern 'at the harm that would be done by the tour to multi-racial sport and good relations within the Commonwealth'. The matter was debated in the Commons and, at the last, the Home Secretary summoned represent-atives of the Cricket Council and formally requested them to cancel the tour. They did so, qualifying it with a statement that they 'sustain the invitation to the South African cricketers issued four years ago'. They later said that they would not renew relations with South African cricket until they had satisfactory evidence that multi-racial cricket was permitted there. So the situation stands.

The revenue lost by the cancellation of the tour could hardly have been less than the expense of protecting it. A series of 'Rest of the World' matches against England were played, but they produced no comparable revenue and, by now, the resources of the county clubs were so low that several of them stood within sight of bankruptcy.

In the nineteen-sixties, Bagenal Harvey promoted for Rothmans, the cigarette makers, a series of cricket matches played by a team of inter-national cricketers called Rothman's Cavaliers. They played over-limit matches against sides of first-class county strength for substantial money prizes to ensure genuine competition with all the play and a result fitted into a four-and-a-half-hour television 'slot'. It proved such popular entertainment that, after a few years, the cricket establishment cast eyes upon it; and killed it as a Harvey promotion by forbidding any registered county cricketer to take part in the matches. That decree might have been circumvented but it would have been a difficult and complicated operation. Surely enough, it was officially taken over in the name of the Cricket Council; the sponsorship sold to John Player, the John Player League founded, shaped and launched on television with genuine success and profit.

The John Player League prompted the demand for another one-day competition which materialized in the form of the Benson and Hedges Cup on a league and knock-out system. In both, too, there is a valuable financial off-shoot in the exposure of advertisements to television, which provokes an almost laughably cynical jockeying for position on the lines most likely to be taken by the cameras.

The newest idea was formulated for the Prudential Insurance Company, which had already sponsored one-day internationals between England and each touring side. In 1975, however, they promoted the Prudential Cup, for one-day competition between England, Australia, West Indies, India, Pakistan, New Zealand, Ceylon and East Africa. It was eventually won by West Indies in a splendid final against Australia and, blessed by almost incredibly good weather and followed and attended enthusiastically, it was an immense success in every possible way.

Jeff Thomson

Over this same period, England had mixed fortunes in Test cricket. Illingworth, like Hutton, a Yorkshireman, and a professional, plastered over the cracks in the English façade, beat West Indies in England in 1969; won The Ashes series of 1970–71 in Australia and, after being beaten two-one by the Indian spinners, held Australia with a draw in England in 1972. Eventually the edifice crumpled in abject defeat by West Indies in England in 1973. Tony Lewis took the side that was beaten two-one in India in 1972–73.

Michael Denness of Kent had mixed fortunes as Lewis' successor as captain; and lost the post to Tony Greig not only through an error of judgment over the toss at Edgbaston in 1975 which cost the series with Australia but, ultimately, because of his own and England's vulnerability to the pace bowling of Lillee and Thomson. West Indies, in 1976, won conclusively in a blaze of strokes by Richards, Greenidge and Fredericks and, above all, by the terrific fast bowling of Holding, Roberts, Daniel and Holder. Great side as West Indies were, after that series, England stood lower in the comparative table of world cricket than ever before: but Greig, still unbowed, retained credibility.

All through the nineteen-forties, fifties and sixties the comparative differences in strength among the counties had been growing steadily smaller. So, in the fourteen seasons of this survey, nine different counties have won the Championship. The title has never gone round so widely in any previous comparable period. Yorkshire, at their best in spirit, and probably in technique, under Brian Close, took it four times. Worcestershire, one of the poor relations of previous years, three times. For the rest, Leicestershire, a rising power under first Lock and then Illingworth, have won it once (and, lately the Benson & Hedges twice, and the John Player League) so have Glamorgan, Hampshire, Surrey, Warwickshire and, most lately, Middlesex, under the thoughtful captaincy of Mike Brearley. Kent, surprisingly for a team of so many, rich and varied talents, have taken it once only. Yet this is the true prize for the best teams, which may explain why Michael Denness left the captaincy after the 1976 season in which they won the Benson & Hedges Cup and the John Player League. Northamptonshire, another of the lesser powers between the wars, have challenged strongly in recent years and, in 1976, found some consolation in their first honour, when, against the odds, they beat Lancashire in the final of the Gillette Cup.

English cricket has many problems; not least a lack of such outstanding talent as is available to Australia, West Indies, Pakistan and, in spin bowling, India. For the moment, however, it is in such a state of financial prosperity as its most informed and truest friends hardly dared to hope for a decade ago. It has had its hard times; yet it has endured over two hundred years in public esteem; all that time it has been faithful to the people among whom it existed. Illogical as it may seem, that fidelity may yet preserve it.

Chapter 13
The future

Cricket, like many other present day British activities, lies at the mercy of an unpredictable economy. Like a number of other sports, it is not viable in itself. It is dependent on sponsorship, publicity, and payments from the media, none of which are necessarily permanent. It is not capable, though, of continuing to exist on its 'natural' revenue from subscriptions and gate money. A by no means impossible cutback in the national economy could see the loss of sponsorship and publicity. A change in public taste or a cheaper form of entertainment could—though improbably—remove or reduce the payments from television, in which, unfortunately for cricket's negotiators, there is no competition. Commercial television companies have shown clearly that they are not interested in cricket; if they were, and cricket could play off one against the other as the football authorities do, they would be in a far stronger negotiating position.

A possible solution lies in greater use of cricket grounds and their buildings for other purposes such as golf driving ranges; social clubs; squash or other indoor sports; bars; cinemas; or, as at Trent Bridge and Old Trafford, restaurants.

An equally grave and relatively new problem, however, is that of the standard of playing ability. It is beyond question that there is no such inflow of talent now as had existed for well over a century until the abolition of the maximum wage for professional soccer players in 1961. There will always be a few gifted cricketers who, through parental direction, or singleness of mind or talent, will play cricket. Most British boy ball-games players, however, tend to be versatile, to play at least cricket in the cricket season, football in the football season; increasingly probably, in present times, golf or tennis as well.

It must be difficult for the parent of a gifted boy to advise him to adopt cricket as a profession in preference to one of the other three. A really gifted tennis player can make an income astronomically far above anything a cricketer could hope to earn. The same is true of a successful tournament golfer; but even the golf professional who does not reach that level can make a steadier, longer and generally larger income as a club pro than a county cricketer. Footballers, too, can earn vastly greater sums. The average Football League professional earns three times the income of a capped county cricketer; and there are two thousand professional League footballers in England alone by comparison with, at most, 180 capped county cricketers.

The final question is economic. If cricket cannot afford to pay its players a wage comparable with those available in the competing sport-industries, it will always come off worse than they do. When it is asked, where is the former cricket talent, the answer is all too obvious. It lies in the young men who are playing soccer for far more money than is paid to cricketers.

In the early twenties, the then Southampton football club manager begged Wally Hammond—who lived on the Isle of Wight—to sign forms for his club. Hammond haughtily told him that he preferred the wage he had been offered to qualify on the ground staff for Gloucestershire. It is difficult to believe that if a comparable situation arose now, a player of Hammond's gifts could afford to play cricket. The same would apply to Willy Watson, Arthur Milton, Patsy Hendren, Denis Compton, probably Fred Trueman and Brian Close, if they were now at seventeen with sufficient ability at football to be offered five to ten times as much as a county cricket club can pay its ground staff boys.

Cricket will always be played. First-class cricket will continue to flourish in countries like India and Pakistan and, probably, West Indies, where there are still large, unmotorized captive audiences. The same is not necessarily true in England; to make its future certain, the game must become truly viable of itself: and, despite all the shifts and expedients which still sustain it, it has not yet found out how to pay its own way in the nineteen-seventies.

Cricket:
an anthology

Gilbert Phelps

An opening invocation

Hail Cricket! glorious, manly, British game!
First of all Sports! be first alike in fame!
To my fir'd Soul thy busy transports bring,
That I may feel thy Raptures, while I sing;
O thou, sublime Inspirer of my Song!
What matchless Trophies to thy Worth belong!
Look round the Globe, inclin'd to mirth, and see
What daring Sport can claim the Prize from *thee!*

Not puny Billiards, where with sluggish Pace
The dull Ball trails before the feeble Mace,
Where no triumphant shouts, no clamours dare
Pierce thro' the vaulted Roof and wound the Air;
But stiff Spectators quite inactive stand
Speechless, attending to the Striker's Hand:
Where nothing can your languid Spirits move,
Save when the Marker bellows out Six love!
Or when the Ball, close cushion'd slides askew,
And to the opening Pocket runs, a Coup.
Nor yet that happier Game, where the smooth Bowl,
In circling Mazes, wanders to the Goal;
Not Tennis self, thy sister Sport, can charm,
Or with thy fierce Delights our Bosoms warm.
Tho' full of Life, at Ease alone dismay'd,
She calls each swelling sinew to her Aid;
Her echoing Courts confess the sprightly Sound
While from the Racket the brisk Balls rebound.
Yet, to small Space confin'd, ev'n she must yield
To nobler Cricket the disputed Field.

O parent Britain! Minion of Renown!
Whose far-extended Fame all Nations own;
Nurs'd on thy Plains, first Cricket learn'd to please,
And taught thy Sons to slight inglorious Ease;
And see where busy Counties strive for Fame,
Each greatly potent at this mighty Game.
Fierce Kent, ambitious of the first Applause,
Against the World combin'd, asserts her Cause;
Gay Sussex sometimes triumphs o'er the Field,
And fruitful Surrey cannot brook to yield.
While London, Queen of Cities! proudly vies
And often grasps the well-disputed Prize.

James Love, 1744

These lines are extracted from Cricket: An Heroic Poem, *one of the earliest verse tributes to the game. The complete poem runs to over 300 lines (in three books). Its author's real name was James Dance. He changed it when (after leaving St John's College, Oxford) he took to writing and acting for the theatre—as a compliment to his wife, whose maiden name was Lamour. The poem was inspired by the match between Kent and All-England, played on the Artillery Ground, Finsbury Square (venue of many of the important matches of the period) on 18 June 1744. It is the first big match of which we have the detailed score. Kent won by one wicket. Special tickets for admission were issued, one of which still survives, in the possession of the M.C.C.*

Ticket of Admission 1744

Origins of Cricket

A game played with a crooked stick, later called a bat. According to
Mr Samuel Looker, one of the game's many enthusiasts, anthologists and
historians, it was first mentioned in the poetic writings of Joseph of
Exeter, AD 1180:

> The youths at cricks did play
> Throughout the merry day.

In Joseph's time the knights batted and bowled at two sticks or wickets,
with a third across the top: the wicket-keeper was a serf and presumably
other fielders were also less than gentlemen. During the Middle Ages
cricket was popular but frowned upon by those engaged in raising military
forces: it interfered with the practice of archery.

Ivor Brown: From *A Book of England*, ed. Ivor Brown, 1958

*We have to remember, though, that English as a literary language did not
exist in 1190, so the lines attributed to Joseph of Exeter must be a translation
made at a much later date—and the mention of 'cricks' may well be an
anachronism of the translator's. At the same time there is no doubt that
cricket is of very early origins. There is pictorial evidence that in its elementary form of club-ball it was being played as early as the middle of the
thirteenth century. It gradually evolved into the more mature form that prevailed throughout the eighteenth century and the early decades of the nineteenth.
There are records, for example, that show that about 1550 the game was being
played by the boys of the free school of Guildford.*

An historian looks at eighteenth-century Cricket

In Stuart times cricket had grown up obscurely and locally, in Hampshire
and Kent, as a game of the common people. The original method of
scoring, by 'notches' on a stick, argues illiteracy. But in the early eighteenth century cricket enlarged both its geographic and its social boundaries. In 1743 it was observed that 'noblemen, gentlemen and clergy' were
'making butchers, cobblers or tinkers their companions' in the game.
Three years later,* when Kent scored 111 notches against All England's
110, Lord John Sackville was a member of the winning team of which the
gardener at Knole [ie, *Knole Park*] was captain. Village cricket spread fast
through the land. In those days, before it became scientific, cricket was the
best game in the world to watch, with its rapid sequence of amusing
incidents, each ball a potential crisis! Squire, farmer, blacksmith and
labourer, with their women and children come to see the fun, were at ease
together and happy all the summer afternoon. If the French *noblesse* had

[* *The Kent versus All-England match was in fact in 1744.*]

been capable of playing cricket with their peasants, their chateaux would never have been burnt.

Until the later years of the century the two wickets each consisted of two stumps, only one foot high, about twenty-four inches apart, with a third stump or bail laid across them. The space between the stumps was known as the 'popping hole', into which the batsman thrust the end of his bat, before the wicket-keeper could 'pop' the ball into it at the risk of a nasty knock for his fingers. The bowler trundled the ball fast along the ground against the low wicket; when, as often happened, the ball passed between the stumps without hitting them, the batsman was not out. The bat was curved at the end like a hockey-stick. Towards the end of the century the game was radically altered by abolishing the 'popping hole', adding a third stump, and raising the height of the wicket to 22 inches. The straight bat was soon adopted as the result of these changes.

G. M. Trevelyan: From *English Social History*, 1944

Game of Cricket 1740 by Boitard

Verses in praise of cricket

Assist all ye muses, and join to rehearse
An old English sport, never prais'd yet in verse;
'Tis Cricket I sing of, illustrious in fame,—
No nation e'er boasted so noble a game.

Great Pindar has bragg'd of his heroes of old—
Some were swift in the race, some in battle were bold;
The brows of the victors with olive were crown'd;
Hark! they shout, and Olympia returns the glad sound!

With boasting of Castor and Pollux, his brother!
The one fam'd for riding—for bruising the other!
Compar'd with our heroes they'll shine not at all;
What were Castor and Pollux to Nyren and Small?

Reynell Cotton

The verses are from a song attributed to the Rev. Reynell Cotton, when in 1790 the Hambledon Cricket Club had 100 copies specially printed and framed; but there are several versions, apparently of a somewhat earlier date.

Men of Hambledon

Hambledon, the Hampshire village some seven miles south-west of Petersfield, has often been referred to as 'the cradle of cricket'. In fact the title more properly belongs to the hamlets of the Eastern Weald. During the first half of the eighteenth century it was Kent which enjoyed the ascendancy in cricket, though Sussex had a great cricket nursery at Slindon, and a notable champion of the game in Richard Newland—who was captain of the 'All-England' team in 1744. Newland was also cricket tutor to Richard Nyren, the moving-spirit behind the Hambledon Cricket Club, which played its first recorded game in 1756. The club certainly deserves all the glory that has attended its memory. Broad Half-Penny Down—and later Windmill Down, nearer the village—were the scenes of many historic matches, and the arenas of cricketers of genius. In June 1777, for example, the men of Hambledon defeated an England XI by an innings and 168 runs—though it was not until 1786 that they met and beat Kent. They played their last recorded match in 1793—at Thomas Lord's cricket-ground in Dorset Square, where the Marylebone Cricket Club had been established in 1787. The exploits of the Hambledon Cricket Club have been immortalized in the prose of Richard Nyren's son John, whose *Cricketers of My Time*, together with *The Young Cricketer's*

Tutor, was edited by Charles Cowden Clarke (friend of the poet John Keats, who was himself an enthusiast for the game) and published in 1833. The book contains vivid pen-portraits of the heroes of the Hambledon Cricket Club. Here is a selection of them:

Richard Nyren

Richard Nyren was left-handed. He had a high delivery, always to the length, and his balls were provokingly deceitful. He was the chosen General of all the matches, ordering and directing the whole. In such esteem did the brotherhood hold his experience and judgment, that he was uniformly consulted on all questions of law or precedent; and I never knew an exception to be taken against his opinion, or his decision to be reversed. I never saw a finer specimen of the thoroughbred old English yeoman than Richard Nyren. He was a good face-to-face, unflinching, uncompromising, independent man. He placed a full and just value upon the station he held in society, and he maintained it without insolence or assumption. He could differ with a superior, without trenching upon his dignity, or losing his own . . .

Hambledon Cricketers by Shepheard

William Beldham

We used to call him 'Silver Billy'. He was a close-set, active man, standing about five feet eight inches and a half. No one within my recollection could stop a ball better, or make more brilliant runs all over the ground; besides this, he was so remarkably safe. I hardly ever saw a man with a finer command of the bat, and he rapidly attained to the extraordinary accomplishment of being the finest player that has appeared within the latitude of more than half a century. One of the most beautiful sights that can be imagined, and which would have delighted an artist, was to see him make himself up to hit a ball. It was the *beau ideal* of grace, animation, and concentrated energy.

'Silver Billy' Beldham

David Harris

He was a muscular, bony man, standing about five feet nine and a half inches. It would be difficult, perhaps impossible, to convey in writing an accurate idea of the grand effect of Harris's bowling; they only who have played against him can fully appreciate it. First of all, he stood erect, like a soldier at drill; then, with a graceful curve of the arm, he raised the ball to his forehead, and drawing back his right foot, started off with his left. His mode of delivering the ball was very singular. He would bring it from under the arm by a twist, and nearly as high as his arm-pit, and with his action *push* it, as it were, from him. He never stopped in the least in his delivery, but kept himself upright all the time. His balls were very little beholden to the ground when pitched: it was but a touch and up again; and woe to the man who did not get in to block him, for they had such a peculiar curl that they would grind his fingers against the bat.

Tom Walker

Tom Walker was the driest and most rigid-limbed chap I ever knew. His skin was like the rind of an old oak, and as sapless. I have seen his knuckles knocked handsomely about, from Harris's bowling, but never saw any blood upon his hands. You might just as well attempt to phlebotomize a mummy. He had a wilted, apple-john face; long, spider legs, as thick at the ankles as at the hips, and perfectly straight all the way down.

George Lear

George Lear, of Hambledon, who always answered to the title among us of 'Little George', was our best long-stop. So firm and steady was he, that I have known him stand through a whole match against Brett's bowling, and not lose more than two runs. The ball seemed to go into him, and he was as sure of it as if he had been a sand-bank. His activity was so great and, besides, he had so good a judgment in running to cover the ball, that he would stop many that were hit in the slip, and this, be it remembered, from the swiftest bowling ever known. The portion of ground that man would cover was quite extraordinary. He was a good batsman, and a tolerably sure guard of his wicket; he averaged from fifteen to twenty runs, but I never remember his having a long innings. What he did not bring to the stock by his bat, however, he amply made up with his perfect fielding. Lear was a short man, of a fair complexion, well-looking, and of a pleasing aspect. He had a sweet counter-tenor voice. Many a treat have I had in hearing him and Sueter join in a glee at the Bat and Ball on Broad Halfpenny:

> I have been there, and still would go;
> ''Twas like a little Heaven below!'

John Small

Upon coming to the old batters of our club, the name of John Small, the elder, shines among them in all the lustre of a star in the first magnitude . . . He was the best short runner of his day, and indeed I believe him to have been the first who turned the short hits to account. His decision was as prompt as his eye was accurate in calculating a short run. Add to the value of his accomplishment as a batter, he was an admirable fieldsman, always playing middle wicket; and so correct was his judgment of the game, that old Nyren would appeal to him when a point of law was being debated. Small was a remarkably well-made and well-knit man, of honest expression, and as active as a hare.

He was a good fiddler, and taught himself the double bass. The Duke of Dorset having been informed of his musical talent, sent him as a present a handsome violin, and paid the carriage. Small, like a true and simple-hearted Englishman, returned the compliment, by sending his Grace two bats and balls, also *paying the carriage* . . .

An epitaph

John Small (1737–1826)

Here lies, bowled out by Death's unerring ball,
A cricketer renowned, by name John Small.
But though his name was Small, yet great his fame,
For nobly did he play the noble game;
His life was like his innings, long and good,
Full ninety summers he had death withstood.
At length the ninetieth winter came, when (fate
Not leaving him one solitary mate)
The last of Hambledonians, old John Small,
Gave up his bat and ball, his leather, wax and all.

Pierce Egan (1772–1849)

Pierce Egan is chiefly remembered for his Life in London; or the Day and Night Scenes of Jerry Hawthorn and his elegant friend Corinthian Tom, *a treasure-house of information about the period. In 1824 he began the issue of a weekly paper* Pierce Egan's Life in London and Sporting Guide, *which later developed into the well-known sporting journal* Bell's Life in London. *Egan was devoted to most sports, and wrote a book on boxing.*

Above *An Exact Representation of a Game of Cricket 1758 Artist Unknown*
Below *Cricket at Moulsey Hurst c. 1790 Artist Unknown*

Top left *Rural Sports, or a Cricket Match Extraordinary, by Thomas Rowlandson 1811*

Bottom left *The Grand Jubilee Match, Lord's 1837*

Above *Cricket at Eton 1840 Artist Unknown*

Above *The Eleven of England 1847 by Nicholas Felix*
Opposite page *Surrey Players (Sherman, Caesar, Caffyn, Lockyer) by
J. C. Anderson 1852*
Below *Lord's 1874*

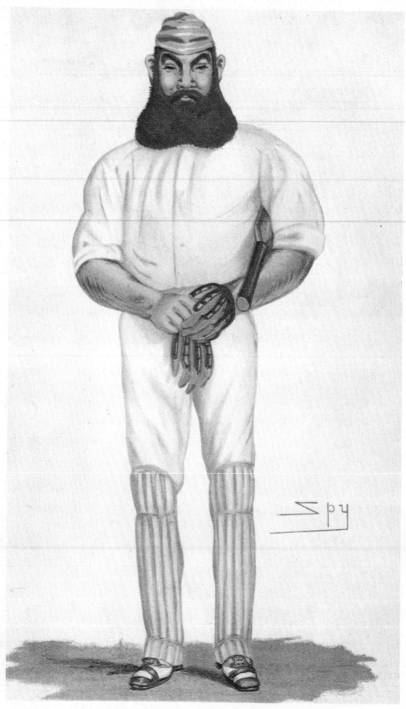

William Gilbert Grace by Spy 1877

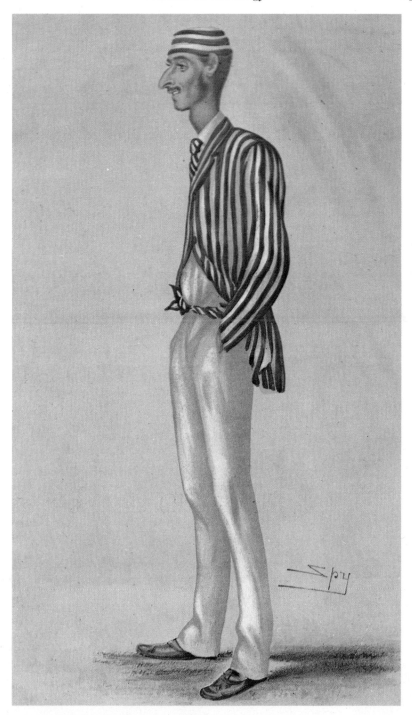

The Demon Bowler (F. R. Spofforth) by Spy 1878

Left *Sir Donald Bradman by Arthur Mailey 1948*

Right *Andy Roberts by Patrick Eagar 1976*

Hambledon—Cricket, Lovely Cricket!

There was high feasting held on Broad-Halfpenny during the solemnity of one of our grand matches. Oh! it was a heart-stirring sight to witness the multitude forming a complete and dense circle round that noble green. Half the county would be present, and all their hearts with us—Little Hambledon, pitted against All England was a proud thought for the Hampshire men. Defeat was glory in such a struggle—Victory, indeed, made us only 'a little lower than angels'. How those fine brawn-faced fellows of farmers would drink to our success! And then, what stuff they had to drink! Punch—not your new *Ponche à la Romaine*, or *Ponche à la Groseille*, or your modern cat-lap milk-punch—punch be-devilled; but good, unsophisticated, John Bull stuff—stark!—that would stand on end —punch that would make a cat speak! Sixpence a bottle!

The ale too!—not the modern horror under that name, that drives as many men melancholy-mad as the hypocrites do—not the beastliness of these days, that will make a fellow's inside like a shaking bog, and as rotten; but barley-corn, such as would put the souls of three butchers into one weaver. Ale that would flare like turpentine—genuine Boniface!— This immortal viand (for it was more than liquor) was vended at twopence per pint. The immeasurable villainy of our vintners would, with their march of intellect (if ever they could get such a brewing), drive a pint of it out into a gallon. Then the quantity the fellows would eat! Two or three of them would strike dismay into a round of beef. They could no more have pecked in that style than they could have flown, had the infernal black stream (that type of Acheron!) which soddens the carcass of a Londoner, been the fertilizer of their clay. There would this company, consisting most likely of some thousands, remain patiently and anxiously watching every turn of fate in the game, as if the event had been the meeting of two armies to decide their liberty. And whenever a Hambledon man made a good hit, worth four or five runs, you would hear the deep mouths of the whole multitude baying away in pure Hampshire—'Go hard!—go hard!—*Tich* and turn!—*tich* and turn!' To the honour of my countrymen, let me bear testimony upon this occasion also, as I have already done upon others. Although their provinciality in general, and personal partialities individually, were naturally interested in behalf of the Hambledon men, I cannot call to recollection an instance of their wilfully stopping a ball that had been hit out among them by one of our opponents. Like true Englishmen, they would give an enemy fair play. How strongly are all those scenes of fifty years by-gone, painted in my memory!—and the smell of that ale comes upon me as freshly as the new May flowers.

John Nyren: From *The Young Cricketer's Tutor* and *Cricketers of My Time*.

Sonnet

Dear fellow Traveller! here we are once more.
The cock that crows, the smoke that curls, that sound
Of Bells, those boys that in yon meadow ground
In white-sleev'd shirts are playing by the score,
And even this little River's gentle roar,
All, all are English. Oft I have looked round
With joy in Kent's green vales; but never found
Myself so satisfied in heart before.
Europe is yet in bounds; but let that pass,
Thought for another moment. Thou art free,
My Country! and 'tis joy enough and pride
For one hour's perfect bliss, to tread the grass
Of England once again, and hear and see,
With such a dear Companion at my side.

William Wordsworth

*This sonnet was composed on 30 August 1802, when William Wordsworth
and his sister Dorothy (the 'Dear fellow Traveller' and 'dear Companion' of
the poem) landed at Dover after a visit to the Continent. That the game played
by the boys in their 'white-sleev'd shirts' is cricket we know from this note in
Dorothy Wordsworth's* Journal *for 1820: 'When within a mile of Dover, saw
crowds of people at a cricket-match, the numerous combatants dressed in
"white-sleev'd shirts", and it was the very same field where when we "trod the
grass of England" once again twenty years ago, we had seen an assemblage of
Youths engaged in the same sport'. The words 'playing by the score' are
perhaps a little puzzling: it may be that more than eleven players were
engaged on one, or both, sides: old score cards often refer to a 'XXII'. In 1802
the short-lived Peace of Amiens was in force between England and France,
but on 3 August of the same year Napoleon Bonaparte had been appointed
First Consul for life (becoming Emperor two years later) and Wordsworth by
now saw Napoleon's rule as a tyranny compared to the 'freedom' of England.
It was not the last time an English cricketing scene was to be seen as a symbol
of freedom and peace.*

Cricket at Harrow

High, through those elms, with hoary branches crown'd,
Fair Ida's bower adorns the landscape round;
There Science, from her favour'd seat, surveys
The vale where rural Nature claims her praise;
To her awhile resigns her youthful train,
Who move in joy, and dance along the plain;
In scatter'd groups each favour'd haunt pursue:
Repeat old pastimes and discover new;
Flush'd with his rays, beneath the noontide sun,
In rival bands, between the wickets run,
Drive o'er the sward the ball with active force,
Or chase with nimble feet its rapid course.

Alonzo! best and dearest of my friends . . .

. . . when confinement's lingering hour was done,
Our sport, our studies, and our souls were one:
Together we impell'd the flying ball;
Together waited in our tutor's hall;
Together join'd in cricket's manly toil.

George Gordon, Lord Byron

These lines come from 'Childish Recollections', one of the longer poems in Hours of Idelness, *Byron's first volume of poems, published, while he was still an undergraduate at Trinity College, Cambridge, in 1807 (when he was nineteen years old). Two years before, on 2 August 1805, Byron had played cricket for Harrow against Eton at Lord's. He wrote in a letter shortly after: 'We have played Eton, and were most confoundedly beat: however, it was of some comfort to me that I got eleven notches in the first innings and seven in the second, which was more than any of our side, except Brockman and Ipswich, could contrive to hit.'*

In fact, Byron, like many another schoolboy in similar circumstances, exaggerated his scores—which were really seven and two (though in these days of club-like bats and under-arm bowling low scores were the rule rather than the exception). John Arthur Lloyd, the captain of Harrow, declared that Byron was in the Eleven against his wishes, and that he played 'very badly'. But we have to remember that Byron was lame, and needed a runner.

Cricket—and Mr Jingle—at Dingley Dell

Mr Pickwick and his friends are the guests of Mr Wardle at Dingley Dell. While they are there Mr Wardle takes them to see the annual cricket match between Dingley Dell and Muggleton. When they arrive at the ground they run into the mysterious—and loquacious—stranger whom they had met on the coach when they first set out on their adventures.

'Well; and how came you here?' said Mr Pickwick, with a smile in which benevolence struggled with surprise.

'Come,' replied the stranger—'stopping at Crown—Crown at Muggleton —met a party—flannel jackets—white trowsers—anchovy sandwiches— devilled kidneys—splendid fellows—glorious.'

Mr Pickwick was sufficiently versed in the stranger's system of stenography to infer from this rapid and disjoined communication that he had, somehow or other, contracted an acquaintance with the All-Muggletons, which he had converted, by a process peculiar to himself, into that extent of good fellowship on which a general invitation may be easily founded. His curiosity was therefore satisfied, and putting on his spectacles he prepared himself to watch the play which was just commencing.

All-Muggleton had the first innings; and the interest became intense when Mr Dumkins and Mr Podder, two of the most renowned members of that most distinguished club, walked, bat in hand, to their respective wickets. Mr Luffey, the highest ornament of Dingley Dell was pitched to bowl against the redoubtable Dumkins, and Mr Struggles was selected to do the same kind office for the hitherto unconquered Podder. Several players were stationed, to 'look out', in different parts of the field, and each fixed himself into the proper attitude by placing one hand on each knee, and stooping very much as if he were 'making a back' for some beginner at leap-frog. All the regular players do this sort of thing;—indeed it's generally supposed that it is quite impossible to look out properly in any other position.

The umpires were stationed behind the wickets; the scorers were prepared to notch the runs; a breathless silence ensued. Mr Luffey retired a few paces behind the wicket of the passive Podder, and applied the ball to his right eye for several seconds. Dumkins confidently awaited its coming, with his eyes fixed on the motions of Luffey.

'Play,' suddenly cried the bowler. The ball flew from his hand straight and swift towards the centre stump of the wicket. The wary Dumkins was on the alert; it fell upon the tip of the bat, and bounded far away over the heads of the scouts, who had just stooped low enough to let it fly over them.

'Run—run—another.—Now, then, throw her up—up with her—stop there—another—no—yes—no—throw her up, throw her up!'—Such were the shouts which followed the stroke; and, at the conclusion of which All-

Muggleton had scored two. Nor was Podder behindhand in earning laurels wherewith to garnish himself and Muggleton. He blocked the doubtful balls, missed the bad ones, took the good ones, and sent them flying to all parts of the field. The scouts were hot and tired; and bowlers were changed and bowled till their arms ached; but Dumkins and Podder remained unconquered. Did an elderly gentleman essay to stop the progress of the ball, it rolled between his legs, or slipped between his fingers. Did a slim gentleman try to catch it, it struck him on the nose, and bounded pleasantly off with redoubled violence, while the slim gentleman's eyes filled with water, and his form writhed with anguish. Was it thrown straight up to the wicket, Dumkins had reached it before the ball. In short, when Dumkins was caught out, and Podder stumped out, All-Muggleton had notched some fifty-four, while the score of the Dingley Dellers was as blank as their faces. The advantage was too great to be recovered. In vain did the eager Luffey, and the enthusiastic Struggles, do all that skill and experience could suggest, to regain the ground Dingley Dell had lost in the contest;—it was of no avail; and in an early period of the winning game Dingley Dell gave in, and allowed the superior prowess of All-Muggleton.

The stranger, meanwhile, had been eating, drinking, and talking, without cessation. At every good stroke he expressed his satisfaction and approval of the player in a most condescending and patronizing manner, which could not fail to have been highly gratifying to the party concerned; while at every bad attempt at a catch, and every failure to stop the ball, he launched his personal displeasure at the head of the devoted individual in such denunciations as 'Ah, ah!—stupid'—'Now butter-fingers'—'Muff' —'Humbug'—and so forth—ejaculations which seemed to establish him in the opinion of all around, as a most excellent and undeniable judge of the whole art and mystery of the noble game of cricket.

'Capital game—well played—some strokes admirable,' said the stranger as both sides crowded into the tent, at the conclusion of the game.

'You have played it, sir?' inquired Mr Wardle, who had been much amused by his loquacity.

'Played it! Think I have—thousands of times—not here—West Indies —exciting thing—hot work—very.'

'It must be rather a warm pursuit in such a climate,' observed Mr Pickwick.

'Warm!—red hot—scorching—glowing. Played a match once—single wicket—friend of the Colonel—Sir Thomas Blazo—who should get the greatest number of runs.—Won the toss—first innings—seven o'clock, AM —six natives to look out—went in; kept in—heat intense—natives all fainted—taken away—fresh half-dozen ordered—fainted also—Blazo bowling—supported by two natives—couldn't bowl me out—fainted too —cleared away the Colonel—wouldn't give in—faithful attendant— Quanko Samba—last man left—sun so hot, bat in blisters, ball scorched

Cricket Match at Muggleton by Buss

brown—five hundred and seventy runs—rather exhausted—Quanko mustered up last remaining strength—bowled me out—had a bath, and I went out to dinner.'

'And what became of what's-his-name, sir?' inquired an old gentleman.

'Blazo?'

'No—the other gentleman.'

'Quanko Samba?'

'Yes sir.'

'Poor Quanko—never recovered it—bowled on, on my account—bowled off, on his own—died sir.' Here the stranger buried his countenance in a brown jug, but whether to hide his emotion or imbibe its contents, we cannot distinctly affirm.

Charles Dickens: From *The Posthumous Papers of the Pickwick Club*, 1847.

Felix on the bat

Nicholas Felix (1804–1876) was the great-nephew of Nicolas Wanostrocht, a Belgian teacher and educationalist, who came to England as a tutor in a noble family in 1770, and later founded a school at Camberwell—which his great-nephew eventually inherited when he was nineteen and ran for the next thirty years. Young Nicholas was a scholar, a writer, a draughtsman and painter, a gifted amateur musician and actor—and a great cricketer, who was one of the stars of the 'All-England Eleven', the travelling cricket 'circus' of distinguished performers, founded by William Clarke (North-country businessman and one of the finest slow bowlers of his day) in 1846. For his cricketing persona Wanostrocht adopted the name of Felix, partly because of the difficulty of pronouncing his Flemish name, and partly perhaps because he thought that the parents of his pupils might disapprove of a Headmaster so directly associated with a game still not considered as entirely respectable—and in fact his cricketing activities were largely responsible for the ultimate failure of his school. Felix was the inventor of various items of cricketing equipment, including the catapulta, *based on the Roman siege-engine, which propelled a ball, to a selected length, direction and speed, for batting practice. His book* Felix on the Bat—*to use its main title—was first published in 1845, but was twice revised, in 1850 and 1855. Though not the first book of cricket instruction, it was the first really practical and well-illustrated manual—as well as being one of the most attractive and entertaining books on the subject.*

It requires nerve of no ordinary character to possess yourself of sufficient self-command to walk from amidst the assembled thousands of Cricketing *cognoscenti*, and advance singly to the post made vacant by the destructive influence of the enemy fire. It is, however, for you now to summon up all presence of mind; and as you walk before the wondering speculations of the congregated critics, bear in mind this useful hint, 'to be composed'; satisfied to defend. You will find the realization of this little suggestion of immense value. Defend until the excitement of your important position in the game shall subside. After playing one or two overs with 'comparative' firmness, your sight will become curiously and quickly accustomed to perform the astounding duties which it has to encounter.

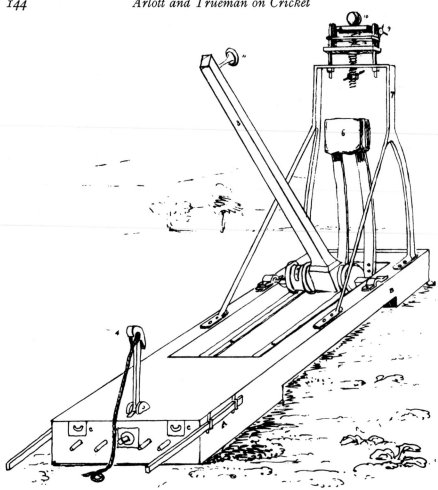

The First Bowling Machine? The Catapulta from 'Felix on the Bat' *1850*

Astounding is a term not half powerful enough to describe the electrical rapidity with which the eye communicates to the nerves, and the nerves to the muscles the word of command. The marvellously rapid judgment of the eye, and the extraordinary quick response whereon to calculate to a nicety where and when the convexity of the cricket-ball shall be met by the convex surface of the bat, to be laid dead at the feet, or to be driven forth, swimming through the 'field', baffling all attempts to arrest its winged flight, is what may be termed quick decision. And before we shall touch upon the delicious consequences of this quick decision, we must prove the efficacy of that position, or attitude, which shall to the greatest degree facilitate the operation of this 'quick decision'.

I feel some delicacy in insisting upon this part of my preamble; for, in so doing, I shall be obliged to argue against many attitudes which have been adopted by some of the best batsmen of the old and of the modern times.

All persons, Cricketers or not, will agree with me, I think, that a man standing (as a soldier does with his musket) bolt upright, cannot jump off the ground without bending the knees; and the more they are bent, the higher will be the jump. Observe the first position in Fencing, *'En garde!'* How beautifully every limb of the body is prepared for action! The knees are bent, and the body, well balanced, is prepared either to be thrown forward in the instant of straightening the hinder knee, or thrown backward upon straightening the knee of the leg in advance. I strongly recommend that you practise this lounge with the bat, just as the fencing-master orders you *'En garde!'*, 'Lounge!' And often, when on the full extent of this action, hold the bat firmly, so that it does not move from its perpendicularity, and walk in front of it to see if your lounge is perfectly carried out. Another good way of practising this lounge is to do it before a looking-glass.

It is only a curious fact, but you will observe, by the figures in the following Plate, that the attitude of *'En garde'* of the left-handed swordsman, is the attitude of 'Play' for the right-handed batsman; and, *vice versa*, the attitude of 'Play' of the left-handed batsman is the *'En garde'* of the right-handed swordsman. I have found it a good plan, the moment the bowler begins to advance, to raise the blade of the bat about half a foot from the ground, keeping it well before the wicket, so as to screen it as much as possible from the eye of the bowler. From analogy to the first position in fencing, and from experience, which is one of the greatest tests of truth, I venture to assert, that no attitude will be found so convenient, or so well suited for action, as that which we recommend by the bending of both knees . . .

All England Men

And yet, although old Messieurs DEATH and TIME
Are sure to come off winners in the end!
There's something in this 'game of LIFE' that's pleasant;
For though 'to die!' in verse may sound sublime
(*Blank* verse I mean, of course—not doggrel rhyme),
Such is the love I bear for LIFE and CRICKET,
Either at single or at double wicket,
I'd rather play a good long game—and spend
My time agreeably with some kind friend,
Than throw my bat and bail up—JUST AT PRESENT!

Pierce Egan

Curious Match of Cricket between *Twenty-two Greenwich Pensioners*—eleven men with one leg, against the same number with one arm

From the novelty of the advertisement announcing a cricket-match to be played by *eleven Greenwich Pensioners with one leg against eleven with one arm*, for one thousand guineas, at the new cricket ground, Montpelier Gardens, Walworth in 1796, an immense concourse of people assembled. About nine o'clock the men arrived in three Greenwich stages, about ten the wickets were pitched, and the match commenced. Those with but one leg had the 1st innings, and got ninety-three runs. About three o'clock, while those with but one arm were having their innings, a scene of riot and confusion took place, owing to the pressure of the populace to gain admittance to the ground: the gates were forced open, and several parts of the fencing were broke down, and a great number of persons having got upon the roof of a stable, the roof broke in, and several persons falling among the horses were taken out much bruised. About six o'clock the game was renewed, and those with one arm got but forty-two runs during their innings. The one legs commenced their second innings, and six were bowled out after they got sixty runs, so they left off one hundred and eleven runs more than those with one arm.

A match was played on the Wednesday following, and the men with *one leg* beat the *one arms* by one hundred and three runnings. After the match was finished, the *eleven one legged men* ran one hundred yards for twenty guineas. The three first divided the money.

Original report, 1796

Extraordinary female cricket match

In a field belonging to Mr Story, at the back of Newington Green, near Ball's Pond, Middlesex, on Wednesday 2 October 1811, this singular performance, between the Hampshire and Surrey Heroines (twenty-two females) commenced at eleven o'clock in the morning. It was made by two noblemen, for 500 guineas aside. The performers in this contest were of all ages and sizes, from *fourteen* to *sixty*, the young had shawls, and the old long cloaks. The Hampshire were distinguished by the colour of *true blue*, which was pinned in their bonnets, in the shape of the Prince's plume. The Surrey were equally as smart—their colours were *blue*, surmounted with *orange*. The latter *eleven* consisted of Ann Baker (sixty years of age, the best runner and bowler on that side), Ann Taylor, Maria Barfatt, Hannah Higgs, Elizabeth Gale, Hannah Collas, Hannah Bartlett, Maria Cooke, Charlotte Cooke, Elizabeth Stocke, and Mary Fry.

The Hampshire eleven were Sarah Luff, Charlotte Pulain, Hannah Parker, Elizabeth Smith, Martha Smith, Mary Woodrow, Nancy Porter, Ann Poulters, Mary Novell, Mary Hislock, and Mary Jougan.

Very excellent play took place on Wednesday; one of the Hampshire lasses made forty-one innings, before she was thrown out; and at the conclusion of the day's sport, the Hampshire eleven were 81 a-head. The unfavourableness of the weather prevented any more sport that day, though the ground was filled with spectators. On the following day the Surrey lasses kept the field with great success; and on Monday, the 7th, being the last day to decide the contest, an unusual assemblage of elegant persons were on the ground. At three o'clock the match was won by the Hampshire lasses, who not being willing to leave the field at so early an hour, and having only won by two innings, they played a single game, in which they were successful. Afterwards they marched in triumph to the Angel, at Islington, where a handsome entertainment had been provided for them by the Nobleman that made the match.

Original report, 1811

Ice stopped play ?

We have all come across cricket in strange places, but I have never been more surprised than to find it as portrayed in this print, a steel engraving, from a drawing by Captain Lyon, engraved by Findon, the frontispiece to Parry's *Journal of the Second Voyage for the Discovery of a North-West Passage*, published in 1824. The game was played during the second, and last, winter spent by Captain Parry's two ships, *Fury* and *Hecla*, inside the Arctic Circle. They were frozen in at Igloolik throughout that long winter, hard put to it to maintain health and avoid boredom in a desert of snow and ice.

Cricket in the Arctic 1822

By the start of November the temperature was 30 degrees below zero and the sun barely appeared above the horizon. In fact, for a fortnight in January they did not see the sun at all: but still the light from the snow enabled them—of all the English things you can imagine—to play cricket on the ice in their full winter clothing. It is strange that, of all that historic journey, it should have been this incident that so stood out as to be chosen, of all Lyon's drawings, as the frontispiece of the book.

John Arlott

Full of half-and-half

On Tuesday, in July 1828, on Clapham Common, a match took place between eleven blacksmiths, of Clapham, and a similar number of Wandsworth Vulcans, for a supper. The parties wore white leather aprons, brand new for the occasion; and after a well-contested match the Clapham men won with three wickets to go down. Dr Beech, one of the Clapham heroes, happened to get quite full of half-and-half, and, being upwards of twenty stone in weight, he was placed for a long stop, but, in pursuing the ball, he frequently tumbled, and rolled about like a sick elephant. The supper was placed on the table at Mr O.N.'s, the Windmill, Clapham Common, and was well served up . . .

Original report, 1828

Right hand, left hand . . .

The grand match between eleven right-handed, and eleven left-handed players, commenced on Monday, in July 1828, at Lord's Ground, St John's Wood; and, from the interest it excited, the ground, throughout the contest, was thronged by the amateurs and admirers of the noble game, from Norwich, Brighton, Kent, and other parts of the country, among whom were an unusual assemblage of distinguished spectators. The match did not terminate till Wednesday evening.

    The following is a correct statement of the game:

Right-handed	First Innings	Second Innings
Mr J. Broadridge	0	71
Matthews	22	7
W. Broadbridge	35	0
Beagley	20	9
Ward	57	20
Hooker	11	4
Brown	18	24
Pilch, not out	47	5
Kingscote	21	19
Lillywhite	9	0
Howard	3	7
Wide balls	4	14
Byes	1	3
Total	248	183

Left-handed

Mr Maynard	3		0
Boyer	0		5
Mellersh	5		0
Wenman	7		1
Searle	33		10
Marsden	10		6
Saunders	27		18
Woolhouse	13		3
Pierpoint	6		0
Slater	13		10
W. Slater	12		23
Wide balls	3		3
Byes	0		0
Total	**132**		**73**

From the above, it will be perceived the right-handed players scored in their two innings the enormous number of 431 runs; and their opponents only gaining 205, they were consequently left in a minority of 226 runs and byes. The excellent batting, however, of the losing party, was apparent to every one, throughout the match; but they, unquestionably, had not any bowlers of so superior a description as their antagonists, who had six of the best in the kingdom; and, from the left-handed players having to contend against so great a disadvantage, may be attributed their coming off in so disproportionate a manner.

Oldest known scorebook: Oxford v. Cambridge 1829

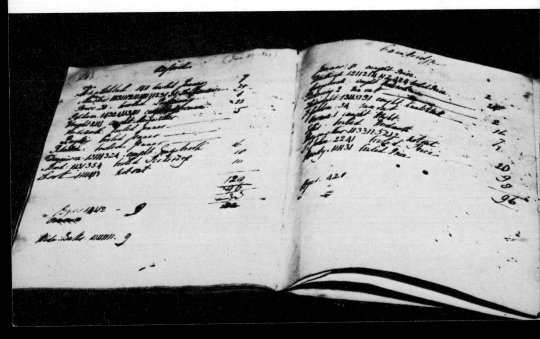

Remarks.—The right-hand hitters against the left naturally brought to the wicket most of the very best players in the world. From the *striking* qualities of Marsden, Searle, Woolhouse, Saunders, Mellersh, &c, the latter had hosts of friends: but when we look on the opponent side, we may well parody the dramatist, and say

> 'The bowler's quality is a tower of strength,
> Which they upon the adverse faction want.'

This was literally the case, for here were Lillywhite, who quite retrieved his character, by beautifully effective deliveries, Howard, Matthews, Broadbridge, and Pilch, against Marsden, and, at most, Searle and Pierpoint. The consequences were inevitable—viz., an innings of great power (248) on the part of the Right-handers, and in which the average was more than a score to each bat. Marsden certainly bowled well; and, in comparison with those at the other wicket, much fewer runs were booked from his balls; but the state of the score will show how utterly useless it is to look for success without effective strength in the bowling department. Pilch, a fine young player from Bury St Edmund's, showed great capabilities, both in the field and with the bat; though early down in the second innings, Mr Ward recalled the remembrance of his best days, playing, not only effectively, but with caution and precision. Marsden, upon whom those who had 'their right hands put on the wrong side' (as the famous *left-handed* north country coachman once told the writer upon mounting his box) much depended, was very unfortunate, being caught (as . . . were the majority of the best bats, not being able to *hit down* Matthews, nor *hit out* Lillywhite's bowling) when commencing well. When it is considered he scored 114 from his own bat, at Leicester, we may consider him a player. Woolhouse wanted confidence to *lash* as he should have done; and Mellersh was new to the ground and players. The Slaters and Saunders were, however, as steady and active as ever, and the latter in particular worthy of his hire. Indeed, Mr Aislabie, who backed this party, was not dissatisfied with his men throughout, but cheered them to the last; in fact, he was aware their capabilities, or the want of them, and not their will, consented to the defeat. The weather, to use a cant word of the day, was very 'untoward', and much delayed the completion of the match. As it turned out, it is much to be regretted that the left-handed hitters did not have the first *ingo*, and quite as much that the dinner-folks in the Pavilion should not have given up, on Monday, a little more time than they did, and have *fed* when the storm had no respect for cricket, rather than when Sol shone encouragement to bats, stumps, and balls, or, at least, not have wasted so much *longer a period than usual* at the festive board.

Original report, Circa 1828

The making of a cricketer

I cannot remember when I began to play cricket. Respect for the truth
prevents me from saying I played the first year of my existence, but I have
little hesitation in declaring that I handled bat and ball before the end of
my second. My family was known as a cricketing family a quarter of a
century before I was born. My brothers Henry, Alfred, and E.M. were
respectively 15, 8 and 7 years of age when I appeared, and though my
mother did not lay claim to being considered a player, I am inclined to
believe, judging by the light of later years, she knew how to play as well
as any of them; she was certainly most enthusiastic, and ever ready with
sound counsel and cheering words. And I know in her heart she hoped
that I should be a credit to the family.

I have been told that I was an easy subject to teach; always willing to
listen to words of wisdom, but rather casual in carrying them out, and
looking as if I had a theory of my own about playing the game. Perhaps
even at that age I realized the duty resting on every cricketer who desires
to add a page or two to cricket history . . .

My father and mother were married in the year 1831, and settled down
in Downend, Gloucestershire, where they lived the rest of their lives . . .
My father had to make his way in life, and was at the beck and call of
every sick person within a radius of twelve miles. He had not an hour he
could call his own. The early morning saw him riding six miles eastward;
at midnight he was often six miles to the west.

There was not much time for cricket. The village had not a club of its
own; so my father had to be satisfied with running into Bristol now and
again to look at the matches of the Clifton and Bristol clubs—about the
only two at that time within available reach.

My brother Henry, the eldest of the family, was born on 31 January
1833. At eight years of age he was sent to school, and every time he came
home he would talk of nothing but cricket. My father realized that he
would be compelled sooner or later to create time to help him, if he desired
to keep in touch with him physically as well as mentally. He was strong
in the belief that if you want to educate and influence a boy thoroughly
it is as important to play with him as to work with him; so he took time
by the forelock, and had a cricket-pitch laid in front of the house. It was
not much of a pitch, nor was it full size; but it was sufficient to teach the
rudiments of the game.

The villagers and surrounding neighbours began to take an interest in
cricket, and nothing would satisfy them but that my father must take the
initiative in forming a club. Why should not Downend have a club of its
own? It was not strong enough to form one; so the neighbouring villages
were invited to help, and a club was established and named 'The Mangotsfield'. Rodway Hill was the most convenient spot for the majority of the
players, and, indeed, about the only place where ground could be had. It

was common ground; but the members set to work with a will, and levelled and railed in about forty yards square at considerable expense. The West Gloucestershire club was formed about a year later . . .

Downend House, where my father and mother had been living since Henry's birth, had now become rather straitened in accommodation, and a move was made to 'The Chestnuts' across the road some time in 1850, where my father and mother lived for the rest of their lives.

The change was an improvement in many ways. For one thing there was an orchard attached to it, which meant for my brothers and myself a more convenient pitch on which to practise. My father, Henry, and uncle set to work early in 1851, and had a good wicket ready by the beginning of the cricket season. The orchard was about eighty yards in length, and thickly studded with apple trees, a few of which had to be sacrificed. On the left of it was a high wall; on the right, Mr Cave's wood and a deep quarry full of water.

The first year or two the pitch was small; but E.M. enlarged and improved it as he grew up, and I cannot remember when it was not in a condition worthy of a first-rate club. There was no restriction on our hitting, but undoubtedly the situation was its greatest attraction: we only had to step out of the house and begin play, and that to a medical family whose duties took them so far from home was a priceless boon. Many a time my father and brother Henry returned from their work too pressed for time to be able to go to Rodway Hill, and so had to give up the desire of half-an-hour's practice. That was obviated now. They could partake of a hasty lunch, and join in the practice that was carried on most days during the season. I should say during most months of the year, for we commenced as early as March and did not leave off until October. To my father and mother there was a great charm in the new arrangement, for it kept the entire family together. Rarely did we practise without my mother being present as an onlooker. My sisters did not play the game . . . but my mother and they fielded the ball if it travelled their way, and bowled a ball or two occasionally to Fred and myself when we were boys . . .

My uncle made a point of coming to Downend frequently to coach us, and an excellent coach he made. His bowling was not fast enough to frighten us, but straight and accurate enough to enable us to learn the first principles of batting; viz., a good defence. Very fortunately, at that period of my life I was given a bat to suit my strength. I say fortunately, for my uncle and Henry tell me a mistake had been made with regard to E.M. in that respect. Who was to blame, I know not but E.M., long before he reached manhood's years, was in the habit of using a full-sized bat, and to that they attribute in some measure his cross-hitting . . . Good players can be reckoned by the score, who will tell you that a mistake of that kind was made with them in their early days, and that they never got thoroughly over it . . .

I should like to be able to say that I had no difficulty in learning, and that proficiency came to me much easier than it comes to other boys. The reverse is the truth. I had to work as hard at learning cricket as I ever worked at my profession, or anything else. Very quickly I learned that there was no royal road there, and that if I wanted to be a good cricketer I must persevere. I was fortunate in having a good tutor, and a strong gift of perseverance; that is as much as I can say to students of the game.

For the next two or three years I had to be satisfied with short innings in family practice games. The rule was, fifteen minutes each to the senior members, five minutes to the juniors or more if time allowed; however I had plenty of fielding, and worked hard at it. E.M. kept us busy in that way; and as Mr Cave's wood and the quarry were in the direction of long-on, it suited his pull from the off beautifully, and he took a special delight in hitting the ball there.

From first to last we had three dogs, whose services were invaluable: Don, Ponto, and Noble. Noble was a most intelligent retriever, and would go into the water for the ball without hesitation. Ponto took his position at the side of the bowler, and watched the flight of the ball with as much care as the batsman; and when it was hit over the trees, would listen carefully until he heard it crash among the branches and then make straight to the spot where it fell. His instinct was remarkable, and with a little training we got him to do wonders. A ball bowled to the off he expected to be hit on that side, and he did not take kindly to E.M.'s pulling. They had plenty of pluck, too; for they would present their chest to the ball, no matter how hard it was hit, and time after time I have seen them catch it on the bound with their mouth . . .

The appearance of the All-England Eleven at Bristol against twenty-two of West Gloucestershire, in June 1854, was my first experience of first-class play. I was nearly six years old, and had paid more than one visit to the field at the back of the 'Full Moon' Hotel, Bristol, while it was being relaid for this special match, and the names of Clarke, Parr, Caffyn, Julius Caesar, Anderson, and Willsher, were discussed constantly at home. My father, uncle Pocock, and brother Henry were playing, and with boyish eagerness and delight I sat in the pony-carriage by the side of my mother and watched the play . . .

By the time I was nine years old I had got over the elementary stage of stopping the ball, and was slowly acquiring power in meeting it firmly and playing it away. Playing with a straight bat had become easy to me; and my uncle told me I was on the right track, and patiently I continued in it. In my tenth year I could play a ball from my wicket with a fair amount of confidence. 'Do not allow the bowler to stick you up, or it is all over with you,' he said. I could now play forward as well as back; but, of course, had to be content with less firmness in that stroke, quite satisfied if I could meet the ball with a straight bat.

The next year saw me still improving, and I was considered good enough to play for the club . . .

The year 1860 saw E.M. in great batting form for the West Gloucester-shire Club, and I too helped to swell the total of the scoring-sheet. Against Clifton the Club did a good performance, scoring an aggregate of 381, and winning easily. E.M. and my uncle went in first, and made 126 before they were parted. Altogether E.M. scored 150 without the semblance of a chance, and his hitting was clean and hard. I was down on the sheet as eighth man, and at the end of the first day scored 35 not out—very patiently and correctly, they say; and the next day added 15 more. I was not quite twelve years of age . . .

The West Gloucestershire Club, while it owed much of its early success to my cousins, W. Rees and George Gilbert, was at its best between 1860 and 1867. In those years, E.M. was a host in himself; Henry, Alfred, and my uncle as good as they had ever been; and Fred and I improving every year. We all played in the eleven in 1863, and I could show at the end of the season an average of 26.12 for nineteen innings . . .

. . . I made great progress in batting, scoring freely against our crack local clubs—Clifton, Landsdown, and Knole Park—and was looked upon as one of the principal bowlers of the West Gloucestershire Club . . . On 31 August, 1 and 2 September, of the same year, I played my first match against first-class bowling. The All-England Eleven played Twenty-two of Bristol, at Durdham Down, on those days, and I was anxious to measure my strength against players who ranked so high . . . Before I began batting in this match I practised for a little during the luncheon hour, and Tarrant was kind enough to bowl to me for five or ten minutes, a kindness which turned out very useful. When I began my innings Jackson and he were the bowlers; and being nearly of the same pace, in an over or two I felt quite at home, played confidently, and hit out. Tarrant was shunted, and Tinley took his place and bowled lobs. A change from fast round-arm to lob-bowling has never affected my rate of scoring. E.M. bowled lobs at home as long as I can remember, and I used to hail the change with delight.

Tinley's first over I played carefully; in the second I decided to hit, and hit him into the scoring tent. The hit was loudly cheered; I was pleased, felt elated, got over-confident, and paid the penalty. In my haste to repeat the stroke, I ran out too far in the third over, missed the ball altogether, and was clean bowled. I had scored 32, at 15 years of age, against the All-England Eleven, the heroes of the cricket world, and there is no need to say I was delighted . . .

To be asked to play for the All-England Eleven may be considered a distinct step forward. That was my position in the early part of 1864, when I was in my sixteenth year . . . I received an invitation to bat against Eighteen of Landsdown on 30 June . . . I batted sixth man, which I considered rather a high compliment in so strong a team, and was in for over half an hour while I made 15. Just when I got set an unfortunate mistake of Lillywhite's caused me to be run out. But I did not mind that: I had played for the All-England Eleven, and had helped defeat a strong local Eighteen by an innings and 22 runs.

Ten days later I made my first appearance in London, playing at the Oval for the South Wales Club. Henry and E.M. had played repeatedly for the same club; but E.M. was still on his homeward journey from Australia, and they had to do without him this match. My uncle and brothers were well known in Wales, having played at Newport, Cardiff, and elsewhere against the All-England Eleven, and that led to their connection with the South Wales team, with whom they made an annual trip to town for years. Henry suggested I should take E.M.'s place . . .

. . . The Brighton match was played on the old Hove ground, on the 14, 15, and 16 July . . . South Wales won the toss, and I batted first wicket down. Before the second wicket fell, Mr Lloyd, the South Wales captain, and myself raised the score to close upon 200 runs; and at the end of the day the total was 356 for nine wickets, of which I had scored 170 . . . The Gentlemen of Sussex scored 148 first innings, and had to follow on. They gave us a fine bit of leather-hunting in their second innings, scoring 341, and leaving us 134 to win. Time did not permit us to finish; but at the end of the third day we had scored 118 for five wickets, of which I had made 56 not out.

They gave me a bat, which I have today and am very proud of. The handle and the blade are of one piece of wood: it was the only one to be had on the ground at the end of the innings; however, I value it for the reason it marks the date of the beginning of my long scores. I was not quite sixteen years of age, and had gained my first experience in playing steadily and consistently through a long innings . . .

I began to play an active part in first-class cricket in 1865. I was only sixteen years of age, but I was over 6 feet in height and 11 stone in weight . . . On 22 June I played in my first representative match. The Gentlemen of the South met the Players of the South at the Oval on that day, and it was my good fortune to be on the winning side . . . I need not say that I was anxious to do well and was chagrined at being stumped without scoring . . . but I was on better terms with myself at the end of the match, having bowled with success unchanged through both innings. In the first innings I took five wickets for 44 runs, in the second eight wickets for 40 . . .

I have often been asked if I had much faith in myself before I commenced my big innings of 224 not out for England v. Surrey, at the Oval, on 30 July (1866). My memory is a blank in that respect. I was a little over eighteen years of age at the time . . . I know I travelled up to town the same morning, and felt slightly nervous the first over or two; everything afterwards I have forgotten, except the shouting which followed at the end of the innings, late in the afternoon of the second day. And I remember Mr V. E. Walker, the captain of the England team, was kind enough to let me off the last day to compete in the 440 yards' hurdle-race of the National Olympian Association Meeting at the Crystal Palace, which I won in 1 minute 10 seconds over 20 hurdles . . .

The West Gloucestershire Club . . . had almost become a family club for some years before it stopped playing . . . It ceased to exist owing to the many first-class engagements which we had offered to us, and which my father and mother thought we ought to accept in the interests of the game. It had fulfilled what my father had in view when he formed the Mangotsfield Club—to spread a knowledge of the game in the district, and to teach his boys to play. That its success as a club gave him pleasure I do not require to say. My uncle and he little thought their efforts would bear such fruit, or that the orchard at Downend would be cherished so dearly. They had watched their boys grow into men, able to hold their own on the cricket-field, and accepting defeat and victory in the right spirit. It was a stern school to learn in, but it was thorough. We pursued it earnestly, never grumbling at the work to be undertaken . . . When we took to first-class cricket, play and practice suffered to some extent in the orchard at Downend; but we kept the wicket in good condition until the home was broken up, and always used it a month or two before the season began.

We kept in constant touch with the home-circle right through the season; either wiring the result of every first-class match, or posting the scoring-card at the end of every day's play. That much they expected, and I think we rarely disappointed them.

My father died in the year 1871. He had lived to see his sons grow up to manhood's years, taking part in the duties of life, and occupying a high position in the game he loved so dearly. His last effort was to establish the Gloucestershire County Club on a sound basis, which he was successful in doing in the year 1870. My mother remained among us thirteen years longer, and was present at every county match at Clifton College. She took great interest in cricket all round the neighbourhood, and treasured every telegram and report of our doings. Local papers did not give much space to cricket twenty years ago, and rarely reported matches played outside the county; and as London papers did not reach Downend till late in the day, we made a point of telegraphing or writing to her the result of every match played from home. E.M. and I were playing for Gloucestershire v, Lancashire, at Manchester, on 25 July 1884, when we received the telegram announcing her death. It came with painful surprise to us, and for the moment we knew not what to do; but my friend and comrade of many years, A. N. Hornby, the captain of Lancashire Eleven, grasped the situation, and, with a promptness and consideration which E.M. and I never forgot, immediately stopped the match, and we hurried home to have the last look at her who had loved us so wisely and well.

From *Cricket:* by W. G. Grace, 1891

'W.G.'

Dr. W. G. Grace
Had hair all over his face.
Lord! how all the people cheered
When a ball got lost in his beard!

E. C. Bentley

One Grand Old Man about Another

Sometimes he (W.G.) would play, at the height of his fame, in a country cricket match in some village in the West of England. And from far and wide the folk would come, on foot, in carriages, and homely gigs. On one of these occasions Grace had made a score of twenty or so when he played out at a ball and missed it. The local wicket-keeper snapped up the ball in his gloves triumphantly, and swept off the bails and—seeing visions of immortality—he screamed at the umpire: 'H'zat!'

The umpire said: 'Not out; and look 'ee 'ere, young fellow, the crowd has come to see Doctor Grace and not any of your monkey-tricks.'

I have always been amused that W. G. Grace became famous while the Victorians were endowing cricket with moral unction, changing the lusty game that Squire Osbaldeston knew into the most priggish of the lot, and stealing rigour, temper, and character from it. Cricket was approved at the private schools for the sons of gentlemen; the detestable phrase, 'It isn't cricket', was heard in the land. The game acquired a cant of its own, and you might well have asked why two umpires were necessary at all, and why the bowler ever appealed for leg-before-wicket. W.G. could not have contained his large humanity in any genteel pursuit; he was of more than ordinary human bulk, and therefore he had more than ordinary frailty. He exercised his wits, went about the job of winning matches with gusto.

'Did the old man ever cheat?' I once asked an honest Gloucestershire cricketer, who worshipped Grace.

'Bless you, sir, never on your life,' was the quite indignant answer. 'Cheat? No, sir, don't you ever believe it—he were too clever for that.'

If a man is going to give his whole life to a game, let him play it like a *full* man, with no half-measures and no repressions. Cricket was a battle of wits with Grace, first and last. His enormous technique was saved from mechanical chilliness because he never practised it without some artful end in view; he larded the green earth wherever he played; he dropped juicy flavours of sport; he loved an advantage, and hated to be beaten . . .

At the present time, nearly all the performances of W. G. Grace have been surpassed by cricketers here and there . . . Yet the fact of Grace's posterity remains to this moment: he is still the most widely known of all cricketers amongst folk who have seldom, if ever, seen a match. After all, he really did transcend the game; . . . I cannot, and nobody possible could, contain the stature of the man within the scope of bat and ball. Nobody thinks of Grace in terms of the statistics recorded of his skill; like Dr Johnson, he endures not by reason of his works but by reason of his circumferential humanity. I always think of him as the great enjoyer of life who, after he had batted and bowled and fielded throughout the whole three days of a match between Gloucestershire and Yorkshire, was at the end of the third afternoon seen running uphill from the ground, carrying his bag, in haste for the train to London—running with a crowd of cheering little boys after him, and his whiskers blowing out sideways in the breeze.

Neville Cardus: From 'William Gilbert Grace' in *The Great Victorians*, 1932

On a great batsman

As the gull conceals in easeful glide
The inborn gift to curb and ride
The gale—merging the sea-wind's force
With lovely movement on a chosen course—
So, in timed swoop, he moves to charm
The ball down-swirling from the bowler's arm
Along some glissade of his own creation,
Beyond the figures' black and white rotation.

Recorded centuries leave no trace
On memory of that timeless grace.

John Arlott

'Play up, play up, and play the game'—the solemn view

'Out! Bailey has given him out—do you see, Tom?' cries Arthur. 'How foolish of them to run so hard.'

'Well, it can't be helped; he has played very well. Whose turn is it to go in?'

'I don't know; they've got your list in the tent.'

'Let's go and see,' said Tom, rising; but at this moment Jack Raggles and two or three more came running to the island moat.

'Oh, Brown, mayn't I go in next?' shouts the Swiper.

'Whose name is next on the list?' says the Captain.

'Winter's, and then Arthur's,' answers the boy who carries it; 'but there are only twenty-six runs to get, and no time to lose. I heard Mr Aislabie say that the stumps must be drawn at a quarter past eight exactly.'

'Oh, do let the Swiper go in,' chorus the boys; so Tom yields against his better judgment.

'I dare say now I've lost the match by this nonsense,' he says, as he sits down again; 'they'll be sure to get Jack's wicket in three or four minutes; however, you'll have the chance, sir, of seeing a hard hit or two,' adds he, smiling, and turning to the master.

'Come, none of your irony, Brown,' answers the master. 'I'm beginning to understand the game scientifically. What a noble game it is too!'

'Isn't it? But it's more than a game. It's an institution.' said Tom.

'Yes,' said Arthur, 'the birthright of British boys, old and young, as *habeas corpus* and trial by jury are of British men.'

'The discipline and reliance on one another which it teaches is so valuable, I think,' went on the master; 'it ought to be such an unselfish game. It merges the individual in the eleven; he doesn't play that he may win, but that his side may.'

'That's very true,' said Tom; 'and that's why football and cricket, now one comes to think of it, are such much better games than fives or hare-and-hounds, or any others, where the object is to come in first or to win for oneself, and not that one's side may win.'

'And then the Captain of the eleven!' said the master; 'what a post is his in our School-world! almost as hard as the Doctor's; requiring skill and gentleness and firmness, and I know not what other rare qualities.'

Thomas Hughes: From *Tom Brown's Schooldays*, 1857

Gentleman cracksman and cricketer

. . . Raffles may or may not have been an exceptional criminal, but as a cricketer I dare swear he was unique. Himself a dangerous bat, a brilliant field, and perhaps the very finest slow bowler of his decade, he took incredibly little interest in the game at large. He never went up to Lord's without his cricket-bag, or showed the slightest interest in the result of a match in which he was not himself engaged. Nor was this mere hateful egotism on his part. He professed to have lost all enthusiasm for the game and to keep it up only from the very lowest motives.

'Cricket,' said Raffles, 'like everything else, is a good enough sport until you discover a better. As a source of excitement it isn't in it with other things you wot of Bunny, and the involuntary comparison becomes a bore. What's the satisfaction of taking a man's wicket when you want his spoons? Still, if you can bowl a bit your low cunning won't get rusty, and always looking for the weak spot's just the kind of mental exercise one wants. Yes, perhaps there's some affinity between the two things after all. But I'd chuck up cricket tomorrow, Bunny, if it wasn't for the glorious protection it affords a person of my proclivities.'

'How so?' said I. 'It brings you before the public, I should have thought, far more than is either safe or wise.'

'My dear Bunny, that's exactly where you make a mistake. To follow crime with reasonable impunity you simply must have a parallel ostensible career—the more public the better. The principle is obvious . . . And it's the one and only reason why I don't burn my bats for firewood.'

Nevertheless, when he did play there was no keener performer on the field, nor one more anxious to do well for his side. I remember how he went to the nets, before the first match of the season, with his pocket full of sovereigns which he put on the stumps instead of bails. It was a sight

to see the professionals bowling like demons for the hard cash, for whenever
a stump was hit a pound was tossed to the bowler and another balanced
in its stead, while the man took £3 with a ball that spread-eagled the
wicket. Raffles's practice cost him either eight or nine sovereigns; but he
had absolutely first-class bowling all the time, and he made fifty-seven
runs next day.

Ernest William Hornung (1866-1921): From 'Gentlemen and Players':
Raffles, The Amateur Cracksman, 1899

King Willow

After bats had ceased to be of a shape not far removed from that of an
Indian club they were curved at the bottom end, so that they resembled
a combination of the golf clubs and hockey sticks of the present time.
The length depended upon the whim of the batsman, and most of them
were far bigger than those of today. A big proportion of the weight was in
the curve, planned to block or scoop away the primitive bowling in vogue,
which was of the fast under-hand variety, the type known in later years
as 'sneaks', 'grubs', 'grounders' and 'daisy cutters'.

Even after the curved end was abandoned, probably because artifice
had entered into bowling and the 'sneak' no longer predominated, the bat
continued to be made with a slope from handle to blade in the manner of
a champagne bottle. It was not until 1773 that John Small, whom John
Nyren, oracle of the Hambledon Men, described as 'a remarkably well-
made and well-knit man, of honest expression and as active as a hare',
introduced the blade with shoulders almost square; yet even at that
period the size of the bat was not subjected to any fixed rule. In the
following year, however, an incident occurred which led to the standard-
izing of width and length. A player called 'Shock' White went to the
crease armed with a monstrosity wider than the wicket, and the obvious
absurdity of the proceedings which followed stirred Authority into
action. As a result the width of the bat was limited to $4\frac{1}{4}$ inches, a measure-
ment which has not since been altered. It is astonishing that the necessity
of a fixed size had not been realized earlier, but we may assume that the
matter was governed by some unwritten law accepted by the makers and
that 'Shock' White brought about a crisis by ignoring a custom.

The length of the bat has been fixed at 38 inches for over 150 years,
and it is a point of interest that within this limit the blade may be as long
as any player pleases. There is nothing to prevent him wielding a bat
entirely composed of blade if he fancies that such a weapon would suit
his style.

Although measurements of breadth and length have not been changed
since the eighteenth century, the bat has been altered in other ways.
Cane handles were introduced in 1853, sections of indiarubber and whale-

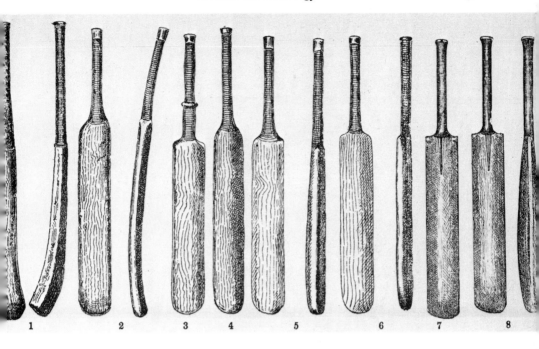

1   2   3   4   5   6   7   8

Bats—Old Style and the New: The drawings of Bats 1 to 6 are taken, by permission, from 'Echoes from Old Cricket Fields', *by Mr. F. Gale. The approximate dates are as follow:—No. 1, 1743; No. 2, weighing 5 lbs., 1771; No. 3, 1790—this is a double-handed bat, and belonged to Robinson, a man with a crippled hand, who wore an iron strapped on to his wrist; No. 4, marked on the back 1792, and named 'Little Joey', belonged to Ring of Dartford, an old Hambledon man, to whose style of play is attributed the origin of the law l-b-w; No. 5, weighing about $2\frac{3}{4}$ lbs., 1800; No. 6, marked on back with brass brads 1827—belonged to John Bower, and weighed about $2\frac{3}{4}$ lbs.; Nos. 7 and 8 are in my possession, and are of present date; they weigh 2 lbs. $5\frac{1}{2}$ ozs., and illustrate the plan of splicing, No. 7 in addition showing the whale-bone. Figures 1, 2, 5, 6, and 8, show the front and edge of bat, and figures 3, 4, and 7, front only.*

bone have since been added to increase the spring, and the covering of indiarubber over the string binding has come as saving of hands. Far more important is the alteration in the character of the blade. Until the later years of the last century bats were practically the same thickness from splice to base, but gradually they were given a bulge in the part where the ball is met by a correctly executed stroke. The extra weight is counteracted by a better balance. Whether the ball can be hit to greater distances by the present type of bat than those used by the later Victorians is doubtful. Certainly the great players of the eighties made drives which carried as far as those of present-day cricketers, but men who have had practical experience of both the 'thin' blade and the 'fat' say that the latter puts more force into a purely defensive stroke.

Willow even in the remote days of the Hambledon Club was the wood chosen for bat making. There is no known substitute; but the quality of the trees varies considerably, while much depends upon the way the wood is seasoned. In these times white willow is preferred by most players to the red from which the old cricketers, down to the later stages of Dr W. G. Grace's career, obtained their scores. Prince Ranjitsinhji wrote in 1897: 'It will generally be found that the white willow is softer than red, but it is not so durable'. Durability, apparently, is no longer considered of importance, and whereas cricketers of old could proudly point to a scarred red blade with which they had obtained 2,000 runs or over, batsmen of the present often use—and cheerfully break—half a dozen or more white blades in a season.

H. J. Henley: From 'Implements of Cricket', in *The M.C.C. 1787–1937*: Reprinted from *The Times M.C.C. Number, May 25, 1937*

To Charles Wordsworth in reply to the present of a bat

That bat that you were kind enough to send,
Seems (for as yet I have not tried it) good:
And if there's anything on earth can mend
My wretched play, it is that piece of wood.

Henry Edward, Cardinal Manning (1808–1892)

Henry Edward Manning, who became Archbishop of Westminster in 1865, and a Cardinal in 1875, was captain of the Harrow Eleven in 1826. Charles Wordsworth, nephew of William, was at Harrow with Manning, and gave his friend a bat as a leaving present. Manning's reply of twelve stanzas includes this verse. Charles Wordsworth while at Oxford organized the first official Inter-Varsity match, which was played at Lord's on 4 June 1827. It was only by pleading the need of a visit to his dentist that Wordsworth was able to obtain the Dean's permission to go to London.

Willow the King

Soft, soft the sunset falls upon the pitch,
The game is over and the stumps are drawn,
The willow sleeps in its appointed niche,
The heavy roller waits another dawn—
Bowled is the final ball again,
Hushed is the umpire's call again,
The fielders and the batsmen cease to run—
But memory will play again
Many and many a day again
The game that's done, the game that's never done.

In happy dreams we'll see each ball re-bowled,
And mend the fault that robbed us of some prize,
In dreams we'll hold the catch we failed to hold,
And see our duck-eggs swell to centuries—
In dreams we'll take the field again,
In dreams the willow wield again,
And see the red ball spinning in the sun—
Ah, memory will play again
Many and many a day again
The game that's done, the game that's never done.

Herbert Farjeon

Father to H. G. Wells

In registering his son's birth in the parish church, just behind Atlas House, on 17 October [1866], Joe described himself as 'Master China Dealer', but his heart and skills were not in the trade. Behind the three panes of the front window, and under the centre display stand, the crockery was pushed aside to make room for the cricket goods which Joe found a more congenial line. When a new delivery came in from Duke's, his cousins at Penshurst who made cricket gear, bats and balls were even stacked in the parlour behind the shop . . .

He was a country boy, who could swim and fish and use a fowling-piece; he learned to write, to do sums, and above all to read. He had a great liking for books, but his passion was cricket . . . When Joe had his first job, at nearby Redleaf, he would run a mile into Penshurst after the day's work was done to get half an hour of cricket before the twilight failed. He was a small man, only five feet eight, but he was a fast left-handed bowler—a round-arm 'slinger' in the days when under-arm bowling was on its way out, and the cricket world was convulsed with debate about the legality of over-arm delivery . . .

The sale of cricket goods was just about enough to keep the shop in business. For a number of years, moreover, Joe Wells earned a modest extra income as a professional bowler and coach. At Box's Brunswick Cricket Ground in Hove on 26 June 1862, playing for Kent against Sussex, he was the first player ever to take four wickets with four consecutive balls. But within a year he went back to club cricket, earning about ten pounds a season for bowling at nets for members of the Bickley Park and then the Chislehurst Clubs, and for several summers going off for a term to Norwich Grammar School as a resident professional. He was probably happiest when he hung up the sign in the shop window which read 'Gone to Cricket. Back at 7', and wandered across the field behind the White Hart which had served as the Bromley pitch since 1751. There, by the Booze Tent, run by old Brazier, the barman from the Bell, this short, stocky man, with a ruddy complexion and a short crisp beard, could sit with his cronies—for a few hours a local worthy of modest but recognized status . . .

Wells said his father 'was never really interested in the crockery trade and sold little, I think, but jam-pots and preserving jars to the gentlemen's houses round about, and occasional bedroom sets and tea-sets, table glass and replacements'. Joe's sense of priorities in his business emerges clearly from his advertisement in the *Bromley Record* around the time Wells was born.

CRICKET! CRICKET! CRICKET!

Joseph Wells has an excellent selection of all goods requisite for the noble game, are of first-class quality and moderate prices. His cane-handled Bats specially selected by himself are acknowledged to be unsurpassed in the trade. Youths' bats of all sizes, &c&c, at his

OLD ESTABLISHED CHINA AND
GLASS WAREHOUSE
High Street, Bromley, Kent

Norman and Jeanne Mackenzie: From *The Time Traveller: The Life of H. G. Wells*, 1973

A famous stanza

It is little I repair to the matches of the Southron folk,
Though my own red roses there may blow;
It is little I repair to the matches of the Southron folk,
Though the red roses crest the caps, I know.
For the field is full of shades as I near the shadowy coast,
And a ghostly batsman plays to the bowling of a ghost,
And I look through my tears on a soundless-clapping host
As the run-stealers flicker to and fro,
To and fro:—
O my Hornby and my Barlow long ago!

Francis Thompson: From 'At Lord's', 1907

These lines, some of the most famous in the poetry of cricket, form the first and last stanzas of the poem. The title, 'At Lord's', calls for an explanation. Francis Thompson, who was born at Preston in 1859, was in his boyhood an ardent Lancashire supporter. The match of July, 1878, between Lancashire and Gloucestershire at Old Trafford made a particularly profound impression on him, and as late as 1900 he could still, despite the intervening years of destitution, illness and drug addiction, recite the names of twenty of the cricketers who had played in it. Not long before his death in 1907, while he was living in London, he was invited to Lord's to see his beloved Lancashire play. He could not bring himself to go, but his remembrance of the match of 1878 revived and so he wrote a poem about it, and entitled it 'At Lord's' as a token of gratitude to those who had invited him.

Francis Thompson wrote other poems about cricket, but they were of a lighter kind. He also wrote an excellent critique of the Ranjitsinghi 'Jubilee Book' of 1897. At one time his friends hoped that he would write a book of his cricketing memories, but the idea never came to anything—unfortunately perhaps, because such a book might possibly have served as a corrective to the intensities of 'The Hound of Heaven' and his other mystical poems.

Albert Neilson Hornby, who began his brilliant cricketing career at Harrow, was captain of the Lancashire XI at the time of the match celebrated in Francis Thompson's poem, and Richard Gorton Barlow was its leading professional. They were probably the most famous opening pair in the club's history.

Lancashire in the 1880's: A. N. Hornby middle row, capless; Richard Barlow seated left front row

My Hornby and my Barlow

. . . Barlow was the straight man, the sturdy professional, sober, slow, resourceful and steady; Hornby was the inspired amateur, excitable, dashing, immensely combative and slightly outrageous . . .

The best-remembered lines in Francis Thompson's poem, *As the run-stealers flicker to and fro, to and fro,* draw their inspiration from Hornby's diabolical *penchant* for running short runs, which kept spectators (and his unfortunate partners) in a fever of mingled delight and terror . . .

The run-stealing of Hornby and Barlow was not that smooth, well-oiled machine as perfected by Hobbs and Rhodes and afterwards by Hobbs and Sutcliffe. The secret of this technique, Wilfred Rhodes explained, as always with a straight face: 'When we're comin', we say Yes, and when we're staying, we say No . . . o'. It would be over-simplifying to say that the Hornby and Barlow method was just the opposite. It was much more complicated than that. But sometimes, on a bellow of 'Come on, Dick!', both batsmen would dash madly up the pitch and just as madly back again, with the result that a demented fieldsman would hurl the ball over the wicket-keeper's head for four overthrows. At another time, Hornby would solemnly intone: 'Stay there, Dick', and those two wicked batsmen would slip along the length of the pitch as swiftly and silently as goldfish darting along the side of a tank. But you never knew; you never really could tell . . .

Though famous as a run-stealer, Hornby was entitled to the greatest respect as a punishing run-getter. What was remarkable was not so much his tip-and-run tactics as his persistent, hard and relentless driving. He was a hitter, but never a mere hitter . . . in his best years he was good enough to be a serious rival to W.G. . . .

Richard Gorton Barlow, it need hardly be insisted, was different and complementary, particularly in his humour. Whereas Hornby's humour was gay and boisterous, even obstreperous, Barlow's, unlike the climate of his native Bolton, was very dry. He would report with solemn face the observation alleged to have been made by an Old Trafford spectator: 'I'm glad to see t'back of 'Ornby; he's never happy till he's got Barlow run out.'

A. A. Thomson: From *Odd Men In: A Gallery of Cricket Eccentrics*, 1958

Lancashire heroes

Soon I reached the inn where we were all staying. In the bar the Lancashire cricketers had already come back from the match. There was Harry Dean, a hero of my boyhood, now entering on his last years in the field. I had seen him through many summers bowling for Lancashire in the pomp of Maclaren's day, a willing horse and a Lancashire lad from the richest soil. He wore blue serge and a watch-chain across his waistcoat, and strong boots. The old professional cricketers did not go to the cinema theatres in the evenings after a long day's play; they sat in bar-parlours and talked cricket. Or you would see them walking slowly and gravely along the streets, two by two, hands in pockets, and smoking their pipes. There was also 'Lol' Cook, bosom friend of Dean, and he was a portly little man whose head hung on one side in a sort of patient acquiescence to a world that was always expecting him to bowl against the wind and would so seldom see eye to eye with him in appeals for leg before wicket. Harry Dean spoke with a deliberate accent, the purest Lancashire, and by his use of certain words and cadences revealed that he had once on a time attended Sunday School and had escaped the advancing blight of industrialism and half-education. He would utter audible capital letters when he extolled the great cricketers of the time of his apprenticeship. 'The reason why we young 'uns learned t'Principles was that we pla-ayed with Wise Men. It were an Education to bat wi' Maister Spooner'— (Harry, by the way, was usually number ten in the order of the innings, and his one and only stroke was an elegant but unproductive forward push, usually straight back to the bowler)—'aye, it were an Education. And Maister Maclaren were a Great Captain, and once at Kennington Oval he coom in dressing-room before start of match and said, "Harry, I've lost toss, so put on three pairs of socks. You'll open at Pavilion end and you'll be bowlin' at half-past six, if I'm not mistaken, because that bloody villain, Sam Apted, has made one of his Shirt Front Wickets." And, by gum, Maister Maclaren were reight; Ah were. Ah bowled mi left toe-nail raw that day and Tom Hayward made two 'undred fit for Buckingham

Palace. Hey, bah gum, and that was the day when Jimmy 'Eap come back in team after 'e'd been dropped . . .'

James Heap was a slow left-hand spinner with a charming action, a little jump, right hand pointing to heaven, side to batsman, then a 'swing-through' of easeful rhythm. On a 'sticky' wicket he could bowl as dangerously as Rhodes himself; but his misfortune was lumbago. For weeks in dry weather, and on cruel hard wickets, he would slave away spinless and harmless. Then the weather would break; he would hear the rain in the night and chuckle. But alas! to quote his own account of the tragedy—'in t'mornin', Maister Maclaren coom into t'dressin'-room, and says, "At last, Jimmy, you've got your 'sticky' wicket! I'll put you on right away—and it's a real 'glue-pot' already, and made for you lad!"' But, continued Heap, 'Ah 'as to tell 'im 'Ah'm sorry, Maister Maclaren, but Ah can 'ardly stand oop this mornin'—lumbago's coom back.'

Neville Cardus: From *Second Innings*

Beginnings of the Australian menace

The Australians brought to our Victorian pastime a terrible realism and cunning. After all, there had been in the vigour and wit of Grace and Hornby and the other squires and yeomen a certain overgrown schoolboy gusto and licence at times to jape and play the fool. But these Australians were cricketers who had come quickly to rare skill in a country with no cant at all in sport, no 'traditions' and what not. They were not hampered by old custom; during the English tour of 1876–77 the Englishmen had to bat on a rough wicket at Sydney and next day the Australians rolled and heavily watered a new pitch for *their* first innings. As time went on they conformed to a more equitable legality; but they continued to see things with fresh eyes, and allowed no stiffening of technical or strategical procedure through precedence. They set different positions in field. During a period when the slow of foot and the unsure of finger were hidden away at square-leg and mid-on, the Australians made these positions hostile and important. On 'sticky' wickets mid-on intimidated the batsmen only seven yards away from the bat. Absit omen!—or . . . Mene, Mene, Tekel, Upharsin. Blackham the wicket-keeper dispensed with a long-stop. This embryo leg-trap snapped up catches sent by reflex-action from the breakbacks of Spofforth, who directed his attack on the off and middle stumps.

Spofforth was called the 'Demon' bowler when he bowled fast in 1878. But in 1882 he had changed his method. Lord Harris, who could speak from severe experience, had recorded that Spofforth was very fast before he came to England, 'but he soon found that on our softer wickets he could "do" so much that, instead of bowling fast with an occasional "judgment" ball, as he called it, he changed to bowling the medium-paced ball as a rule, with an occasional fast one, and so became one of the best bowlers ever seen; in my opinion the best I have ever played'.

Old men who knew him and experienced him on the field of play, agree that Spofforth's best ball broke back. Now the great ball of modern cricket . . . is the one that pitches on the leg stump and 'whips away' towards the off, keeping close to the bat. Most contemporary cricketers will not doubt that the ball which 'leaves the bat' as it breaks away is more difficult to play than the off break. There are known strokes which may be more or less trusted to counter the off-break (no matter under what l.b.w. rule); this ball comes inward to the bat and can be hit or pushed 'with the spin'. No stroke has yet been devised that can safely be exploited against the quick ball that breaks away after pitching on the 'blind' spot. That is why S. F. Barnes was probably a greater bowler technically than Spofforth. I have found no evidence that Spofforth 'ran' the ball away from the bat. But it is not possible to account for the prowess of Spofforth by an analysis of his technique. A terrific personal force possessed him— not so Barnes, who often was sulky and depressed or indifferent, an ordinary mortal visited by the moods of small men. A dynamo of hostility worked ceaselessly in Spofforth; he got on the nerves of his opponents; he had the evil eye; he was tall and angular and satanic of aspect. Spofforth was Australia's spear-head from 1870 to 1886; and it is significant that Australia won nine Test Matches to England's eight from 1878 to 1886, then lost 10 out of 11. There were reasons other than cricket to account for the sudden eclipse; the Australians quarrelled in their own country between themselves. And too long they lagged behind in scientific batsman-ship. There was the stone-waller, Bannerman, true; on the whole, there was an excess of offence and not enough defence. Two immortal bowlers kept the lustre aglow in the doldrum years, Turner and Ferris who in one English summer of 'sticky' pitches took together 534 wickets.

In 1891–1892, W. G. Grace again went to Australia, captain of Lord Sheffield's team. Strong though his forces were, he had to bow to defeat in two out of three Test matches. Bannerman was the spinal column of Australia—three and three-quarters of an hour for 45; four hours for 41; and seven and a half hours for 91. And the beautiful hitter J. J. Lyons was there, too; this was the authentic Australian balance of obstinacy and aggression. By the time Australia celebrates in Test matches her 21st year, from 1878 to 1899, she has given to the game batsmen whose names are fit to be pronounced with any of ours: Giffen, Darling, Noble, Trumper, Hill, and Gregory, Armstrong, Trumble, Worrall, Saunders, Trott . . .

There has always been a certain dourness about Australian cricket, an unashamed will-to-power, with no 'may the best side win' nonsense. Even the brilliant Victor Trumper was an Ironside in Cavalier's colours, his bat a conquering sword, not a lance in a tournament . . .

Neville Cardus: From *English Cricket*, 1945

A poet-cricketer and war

When the woeful hunting of War is let loose, cricket cannot escape the prevailing fate of all pleasant things, and its charm is even less recoverable at such times than that of things less passionately adored. 'The Greater Game' appals this one, not merely driving it from its field but making it hard to read of or talk about. I have lately, in the fourth year of the Greater War, glanced through some of Wisden's scores of important matches, but could not bring myself to do this until now, and even now the figures and the narrative mocked me. They had a dead look. This was not a new experience. In the trenches in May 1916, I remembered that the cricket season should have just begun, but the thought died in me almost as soon as it was born. The essence of cricket is subtle, and I did not feel under that burden of destruction and vast decision that its complex sources would ever be well re-created. A few days later a sergeant of my platoon, who had already made me more than usually diffident over my hopes of being of any use, mentioned cricket, and, leaning against the sandbags, six feet of him, gazed cheerfully, carelessly into space. I asked him, as he intended I should, what exactly he used to do as a cricketer; and he got started on that. His highest score, it came out, was 173. But as usual he rather prided himself on being a bowler, though I got no details of corresponding successes in that branch. Naturally he carried himself with a certain pride. But I fear he did not survive the next battle. After this I seldom heard any cricketana, though so many had had the game by heart, throughout the war. In the home camp towards the end a few of us once got out the bat and ball. But what did it signify? Even when the guns had ceased to fire, I could not come back to cricket for a season or two; and I think cricket itself did not come back all at once. It had been dismayed; it did not guess in the golden days at things like world wars, or that the score-books should be splashed with the blood of the quiet men its votaries.

Edmund Blunden: From *Cricket Country*, 1944

A time will come

A Time will come, a time will come,
(Though the world will never be quite the same)
When the people sit in the summer sun,
Watching, watching the beautiful game.

A time will come, a time will come,
With fifteen stars in a green heaven,
Two will be batting, and two to judge,
And round about them the fair Eleven.

A time will come, a time will come,
When the people sit with a peaceful heart,
Watching the beautiful, beautiful game,
That is battle and service and sport and art.

A time will come, a time will come,
When the crowds will gaze on the game and the green,
Soberly watching the beautiful game,
Orderly, decent, calm, serene.

The easy figures go out and in,
The click of the bat sounds clear and well,
And over the studying, critical crowds
Cricket will cast her witching spell.

Yet a time will come, a time will come,
Come to us all as we watch and seem
To be heart and soul in the beautiful game,
When we shall remember and wistfully dream—

Dream of the boys who never were here,
Born in the days of evil chance,
Who never knew sport or easy days,
But played their game in the fields of France.

Arnold Wall

Arnold Wall (born c. 1870) was a Cambridge man who became Professor of English Literature at Canterbury, New Zealand. The poem was written during the First World War.

The air is hushed

The air is hushed; but thoughts that keep
Patrol above the aerodrome,
Circling the treadmill toils of sleep,
Light on the cricket-ground at home.

I seek again the ordered square,
The outfield seared in August heat
And where the measured turf shows bare
Scarred by the plunging bowlers' feet.

And see the flashing wand awake
The flickering forms that start and run
And catch the rumbling taunts that take
The pleasured air when play is done.

But all is altered; ragwort reigns
Unchallenged in the tarnished maze;
The nets lie rotting in the rains,
The benches gone to make a blaze.

And in the littered dressing-room
A boy stares through the broken door,
Like one who breaks a royal tomb,
At bats and pads strewn on the floor.

And all the players—where are they?
Earthwide they wander quick and slain,
And those who shall return to play
Shall scan the scorebook all in vain.

R. W. Moore

R. W. Moore (1906–1953) was Headmaster of Harrow from 1942 until the year of his death. The poem comes from Trophy for an Unknown Soldier, *1952.*

Can it be cricket ?

Cricket is played by only one person for every three who play football, and watched by only one man for every three who watch football. There are more lawn tennis players, and more swimmers, than cricket players among the population.

Yet it is through cricket that our love of games has become known to the world, for cricket is the characteristically British game which has failed to attract any other than the English-speaking nations. Cricket on the village green on a hot summer's day; county cricket at Lord's; and the international contest every third year with Australia for 'The Ashes' —these recall Britain to mind, not because they are a majority interest, but because they represent something which is to be found only in Britain. Cricket is a slow, ceremonious, long-lasting game with rigid rules, rigidly kept. Spectators in the stands or the pavilion, or lolling on the grass at the side of the green, may applaud, or exclaim, but unlike the spectators at many other games, they seldom if ever cheer or shout approval, boo or hiss a failure, or query the decision of the umpire. The rigid formality of this slow-moving game, combined with the intensely serious interest in it of the spectators, the nicety with which the performance of each player is weighed and evaluated, and the utter failure of intense partisanship to affect judgment, make a cricket game which will always puzzle and fascinate foreign visitors.

From *Britain and Her People*, 'The British—Their Character and Life' by H. D. Wilcock, 1951.

Contrast, 1858!

The match of matches for a startling and unexpected finish was West Gloucestershire v. Redland, at Rodway Hill, on 28 July 1858. With the exception of Fred, all the members of the family, uncle included, were playing, and a good match was expected. We were on the ground practising before the Redland turned up, and had a fair number of spectators even at that early hour. One onlooker, who had been drinking rather freely, lay full-length unpleasantly close to where we were playing, and all our persuasions to get him to move further were unavailing. When the Redland eleven arrived, an attempt was made to clear the ground, but our noisy critic resented, and my father, much against his will, had to resort to force of arms. Calling up my brother Alfred, who had a fair reputation as a boxer, he ordered him to remove the obstinate individual; he did not seem to object, and the unusual sight of a fight *before* a cricket match was witnessed. Two minutes proved that Alfred had a very easy undertaking, and he dealt very lightly with his opponent who had the sense, or feeling, to cry 'Enough', and left the field altogether. The little preliminary excitement added to the interest of the match, and a keen and enjoyable one it became.

Redland scored 51 first innings, 116 second. West Gloucestershire scored 67 first, and were 84 in the second for five wickets, with about an hour remaining for play, when our friend of the morning turned up again. This time he brought his friends with him, who asserted that he had been unfairly treated. It seemed absurd that a cricket match should be delayed a second time for so small a matter; but there was no alternative. Alfred had a tougher task this time; but, rising to the occasion, he polished off his opponent in an artistic and satisfactory manner.

That did not satisfy him or his friends; for they betook themselves to a convenient heap of stones, and a free-fight ensued. For a little while the West Gloucestershire and Redland, fighting side by side, had rather the worst of the contest; but, charging shoulder to shoulder with stumps and bats, they drove the crowd from the heap of stones, and assumed the offensive. A lively state of affairs prevailed the next half-hour. In the meantime my father had ridden off hurriedly to the nearest magistrate, who returned with him, and threatened to read the Riot Act if they did not disperse. Fortunately for the reputation of the two clubs and the villagers, so extreme a measure was unnecessary, and the opposition collapsed; but the match had to be abandoned.

W. G. Grace: From *Cricket*

Contrast: Lord's, 1950

Jubilant scenes at Lord's, headquarters of English cricket, yesterday followed the West Indies' victory in the second Test Match. It was their first win over England in this country.

Almost before the England second innings had ended scores of West Indian spectators rose to their feet, shouting, cheering and waving. Their dark faces were wreathed in delighted smiles.

In the next second after the usual grab for stumps and bails by the players West Indies supporters ran across the ground from a corner at the Nursery End. At the same time members of the ground staff darted out from the Tavern side and barred their route across the wicket with posts and ropes.

Undaunted, the enthusiasts ran after their team, which was walking back to the pavilion. They caught up with them, shook their hands, arms and fingers and patted them on the back.

To escape, the team ran to the dressing-rooms. Extra police who were drafted into the ground, cordoned a wide circle surrounding the Test wicket.

In the next minute the invading spectators formed in a group, and led by a guitarist, broke out into a rhythmic calypso . . . extolling the great achievement of their team . . .

When they all had reached their seats they were warmly applauded. The spell was broken. The crowds gathered their coats and hampers and left.

The same exultant party later continued its celebration down St John's Wood Road and out of sight. Then Lord's, the green arena deserted, once more returned to its characteristic calm and dignity.

E. W. Swanton: From his report in the *Daily Telegraph*, 30 June 1950

The Victory Calypso: Lord's, 1950

Cricket, lovely cricket,
At Lord's where I saw it;
Cricket, lovely cricket,
At Lord's where I saw it;
Yardley tried his best
But Goddard won the test.
They gave the crowd plenty fun;
Second Test and West Indies won.
Chorus: With those two little pals of mine
            Ramadhin and Valentine.

The King was there well attired,
So they started with Rae and Stollmeyer;
Stolly was hitting balls around the boundary,
But Wardle stopped him at twenty.
Rae had confidence,
So he put up a strong defence;
He saw the King was waiting to see,
So he gave him a century.
Chorus: With those two little pals of mine
            Ramadhin and Valentine.

West Indies first innings total was three-twenty-six
Just as usual.
When Bedser bowled Christiani
The whole thing collapsed quite easily,
England then went on,
And made one-hundred-fifty-one;
West Indies then had two-twenty lead,
And Goddard said, 'That's nice indeed'.
Chorus: With those two little pals of mine
            Ramadhin and Valentine.

Yardley wasn't broken-hearted
When the second innings started;
Jenkins was like a target
Getting the first five into his basket.
But Gomez broke him down,
While Walcott licked them around;
He was not out for one-hundred and sixty-eight,
Leaving Yardley to contemplate.
Chorus: The bowling was super-fine,
          With those two little pals of mine
          Ramadhin and Valentine.

West Indies were feeling homely,
Their audience had them happy.
When Washbrook's century had ended,
West Indies' voices all blended.
Hats went in the air.
They jumped and shouted without fear;
So at Lord's was the scenery
Bound to go down in history.
Chorus: After all was said and done,
          Second Test and West Indies won!

Egbert Moore (Lord Beginner)

An Australian remembers

There were those happy summers when I lay on The Hill in the uncut grass, sipped lemonade and watched with other small boys the cricket on the sun-burned field below known as the Sydney Cricket Ground. All around us men would eat pies of a brand as notorious as any thrown in Keystone Cop farces, and swig their bottled beer and occasionally trudge up the tracks they had worn in The Hill to the bar tucked under the big scoreboard which Englishmen think is more informative than a tax-return.

Most of the time the Hillites would chatter noisily and barrack, and one voice, coarse and incisive like the gravel-tones of Louis Armstrong, would periodically holler above the rest. Even the flannelled figures below would smile then. We would all wait for the voice's next shout with a mixture of amused expectation and awe.

Big Bill O'Reilly, adored up there on The Hill, would move splay-footed up the crease and wheel his heavy arm over in his characteristically defiant style; nimble Clarrie Grimmett would flip leg-breaks up towards the tiny, twinkling, often pained feet of Stan McCabe, each enjoying the other's skill; and Bradman would stride in to bat and soon the crowd on

'The Hill', *Sydney*

The Hill would start to multiply as men left their offices to attend funerals of grandmothers long since dead.

There were the breath-taking tensions of Test Matches; Ken Farnes and Gubby Allen unleashing high-kicking deliveries; and the same 'Tiger' Bill O'Reilly smacking Hedley Verity up into the crowded grandstand to the left of The Hill. A wee Tasmanian, Jackie Badcock, one of the first of his island to play for Australia, showed his special type of hook, and a dashing Victorian, Ross Gregory, his lovely driving. There were the inter-state matches, with a wizard called Don Tallon lashing away the bails and turning his appeals to square-leg, and the comparison of Bert Oldfield, neat and unhurried with flowing hands, swift as a mongoose.

I would watch all day in the sun, and then sprint out of the ground and up over the slope to the back streets of Paddington, the suburb where Victor Trumper rehearsed in the local district team for Test heroics, to try to imitate strokes seen that day, before the darkness came. The wicket was chalked on a wall, the pitch uneven bitumen, and hits over the fence were 'six and out', and the criticism of S.P. bookmaker's runners substituted for that dominating voice on The Hill.

I had caught the bug. I had joined a privileged group. This kind of initiation, with countless variations, has come to millions all over the world who now enjoy the capacity to watch cricket. When somebody told me that a man once died from excitement at a cricket match and another spectator gnawed the handle of his umbrella in a nervous spasm, it was hardly a shock. It seemed a pleasing way to die. Now, as I am saddened because I did not know at the time that the rough and friendly voice which sounded above the others during my apprenticeship as a cricket spectator was Stephen Harold Gascoigne, perhaps the most celebrated of all Australians who have watched cricket. On The Hill they called him Yabba.

Yabba was a hawker who sold rabbits from a battered two-wheeled cart around the slums of Sydney. He became more famous than many of the cricketers he chided, a horny-handed rebel who could match his press notices with any film star. He would hold court on The Hill, standing or sprawled on the grass, with a comical, earthy wit, a great clown's sense of timing, and an uninhibited vocabulary which owed a lot of its striking power to a term he had served as a soldier in the South African War.

He had a vast appetite for life, and he always seemed able to enjoy the antics of cricketers, however dull the play. His confidence was immense, and long before he died in 1942, at the age of sixty-four, he habitually referred to himself as 'The One and Only'. He could skin a rabbit in less time than it takes Ray Lindwall to run up to the bowling crease.

Yabba's kingdom was The Hill and he ruled over it with a touch which enriched the business of spectatorship and left cricket freshly stocked with jokes. Many of them have been drained of their humour now through repetition, or the lack of a voice like Yabba's with which to deliver them . . .

It was men like Yabba, the son of a storekeeper who migrated from Oxford to settle in Australia, who established Patsy Hendren as an idol and clinched Douglas Jardine's unpopularity. They were delighted with Hendren's fielding in the outfield so close to them at the foot of The Hill. He had the habit of jumping the fence among them or swig their beer after the fall of a wicket. They disliked Jardine's Harlequin cap, with its hint of class distinctions, and they laughed at Jardine's stiff-legged running when he was forced to chase a ball to the outfield.

'Mind your stays, old man!' Yabba would call at him, nasal-accented, mocking the English Public School prototype. The apparently hurt, humourless way with which Jardine took these cracks convinced Hillites they were right to chide him so mercilessly. The fervour men like Yabba put into their spectatorship contributed heavily to the Bodyline crisis.

Since that delightful beginning on The Hill there have been many wonderful moments as a sun-bemused spectator on the Sydney Ground: Lindsay Hassett's century in each innings against Tiger Bill at his prime; Colin McCool's slip catch to dismiss Bradman in McCool's first-class début; Len Hutton's incredible 39, superior to most centuries; the impact of Doug Wright's run-up at the first sight of him bowling; Alec Bedser's remarkable determination, still unquenched when Bradman or Barnes had scored double hundreds; Vinoo Mankad's driving or bowling out of a curled left hand up towards Miller's floppy hair.

But the joys of watching cricket are happily not confined to one ground . . . I remember my first trip to Lord's. I was disappointed. Accommodation in the shapeless stands was hard to find at big matches after the vast spaces of The Hill and the towering grandstands of Melbourne Cricket Ground. The scoreboard was so unrevealing it was necessary to undertake a strange ritual common to all English cricket spectators: buy a scorecard. People schooled in Yabba's classes, where money is for beer and meat pies, don't take easily to spending money on bits of paper . . . However, if Lord's was slow in winning appreciation, the joys of Hove and Chesterfield and the hundreds of village pitches—Bray tops my popularity poll—was immediate. Old Trafford weaved a particular spell because of the thick-accented wit and the surprise of discovering that those around you really are as unrelentingly partisan and intractable as the legend says. If Yabba had got among that lot the exchanges would have scorched dry even the dampest Manchester pitch. But who would have won?

It was at Old Trafford that a collector's item for cricket spectators occurred when Dick Pollard hit Sid Barnes off his spot a few yards from the wicket. And the story goes it was at Old Trafford, too, that a spectator, obviously from the south, returned to his seat after lunch to find his hat on the grass under the bench and his place occupied by the large backside of a Lancashireman. 'I say, old chap, that's my seat you're in', he said, in well-bred tones. Repeated challenges left the Lancashireman's backside undisturbed, but finally moved him to comment: 'Oop here, 'tis rears wat counts, not 'ats,' he said.

Yabba would have enjoyed that ground more than any other cricket field in England, I think, if not its rain . . . But it would be risky to speculate what he would have made out of the Eton and Harrow Match, for there is nothing like it in the wide canvas of cricket watching. How would Yabba, who jibed at a man because of his coloured cap, have taken to fellow spectators in top-hats who drink champagne, eat salmon and chicken wings, and stage a parade around the pitch at the intervals, and retire for refreshment to their own exclusive club tents? To less aggressive onlookers it is none the less richly intriguing to watch for the aged dowagers who venture on to the hallowed Lord's turf in wheel-chairs rather than miss the tea adjournment parade . . .

The Yabba tradition has gone, they say, and with him the age of talkative spectatorship, almost as if cricket watchers have tired of scholarly arguments among critics on which country's crowds are the most voluble and witty. The Hill would be poorer if that were true, but one suspects it is but a phase, a pause while the boisterous take breath—or replenish their stocks of pies and wait for the beer to take effect.

Jack Pollard: From *The Hill 'Down Under'*, 1962

Shall we join the ladies ?

Yes, please do, but first of all perhaps we'd better tell you something about ourselves. Did you know, for instance, that records show that women have been playing cricket for 216 years? That it was a woman who first bowled round arm, which eventually became the bowling action with which we are now all familiar? And that throughout the years women have had a considerable impact on the game, among them Christina Willes, the round-arm bowler; the redoubtable Mrs Grace, mother of W.G. and E.M.; Elizabeth Ann Burrell, who 'got more notches in the first and second innings than any Lady in the game', so that the eighth Duke of Hamilton fell in love with her on the spot? This particular game was played at the Oaks in Surrey in 1778.

But what of cricket as played by women today? The Women's Cricket Association, founded in 1926, is the governing body of the game in Great Britain—the M.C.C., as it were, of women's cricket. For ease of organization the country is divided into five territories, North, South, East, West and Midlands. We abide by the M.C.C. Laws of Cricket with one exception; we use a 5-oz, ball, ½ oz. lighter than the men. Our equipment is the same as that used by the men but adapted to our height and strength . . .

Progress for the talented player is ensured through promotion from her club to county team and thence to her territory and England.

There are no professionals in women's cricket.

We owe a great deal to our men colleagues in clubs, and individually, who have helped and encouraged us over the years. The M.C.C. have contributed to our Tour Funds and granted us practice facilities at Lord's; many of our matches are played on grounds loaned by men's county clubs and ordinary clubs; although we have our own official panel of coaches and umpires, we have been coached by men cricketers, some of them with famous names. We should like to stress that we do not try, and have never tried, to beat the men at their own game. We play merely for the enjoyment of playing. No woman will ever be able to bowl as fast as Freddie Trueman or throw as far as Norman O'Neill, but we have our women Truemans and O'Neills . . .

Mary Duggan, 1962

Mary Duggan, all-rounder (Middlesex, South and England), toured Australia and New Zealand in 1948–49, and again, as captain, in 1957–58.

To John Berry Hobbs on his Seventieth Birthday
16 December 1952

There falls across this one December day
The light remembered from those suns of June
That you reflected, in the summer play
Of perfect strokes across the afternoon.

No yeoman ever walked his household land
More sure of step or more secure of lease
Than you, accustomed and unhurried, trod
Your small, yet mighty, manor of the crease.

The game the Wealden rustics handed down
Through growing skill became, in you, a part
Of sense; and ripened to a style that showed
Their country sport matured to balanced art.

There was a wisdom so informed your bat
To understanding of the bowler's trade
That each resource of strength or skill he used
Seemed but the context of the stroke you played.

The Master: records prove the title good:
Yet figures fail you, for they cannot say
How many men whose names you never knew
Are proud to tell their sons they saw you play.

They share the sunlight of your summer day
Of thirty years; and they, with you, recall
How, through those well-wrought centuries, your hand
Reshaped the history of bat and ball.

John Arlott

*Sir John Berry Hobbs (Surrey and England) was born at Cambridge in 1882
and died in 1963. He was undoubtedly one of the greatest of all batsmen.
Between 1905 and 1934 he scored 61,237 runs (average 50.65), including
197 centuries. He was 40 when he scored his hundredth century, and went on
to score a further 97, at an age when many cricketers have retired. His
opening partnerships with several fine batsmen, including T. Hayward and
Andy Sandham for Surrey, and Wilfred Rhodes and Herbert Sutcliffe for
England, enabled him to achieve no less than 166 century first-wicket stands
during his 1,315 innings in first-class cricket. In the 1925 season he scored
16 centuries—a record until Denis Compton scored 18 centuries in 1947. In
the same season Hobbs equalled and then beat W. G. Grace's record of 126
centuries in the same match against Somerset at Taunton. He was knighted
for his services to cricket in the 1953 Coronation Honours List.*

Some cricketing yarns

. . . most cricketers have their favourite cricket stories, and I would like to tell you of *my* favourite three . . . I don't pretend they are new—like some wines, they tend to improve with age—and, so far as I have been able to check, two of them are true. Which one is not, I will leave the reader to guess for himself.

The first story is one Gilbert Harding used to tell about himself. As a schoolboy he hated cricket and it appears that even then he was extremely short-sighted and unathletic, and had no idea how to catch a ball, let alone hold a bat. So eventually the headmaster excused him playing, as it was such agony for him and for those playing with him. He was allowed to go for walks instead. But this did not please the keen young cricket master, just down from Oxford. He hated the idea of someone *not* playing cricket and decided to get his own back on Gilbert—or so he thought. Accordingly, when the teams were pinned up on the board for the annual Masters v. School match, it was noticed that one of the umpires selected by this master was Gilbert!

Naturally enough he was furious. But there was nothing he could do about it. He had only been excused *playing*. So on the morning of the match there he was in a white coat, determined to get his revenge. The opportunity soon came. The masters batted first and the keen young master went in first and began to hit the boys' bowling all over the field. The score mounted rapidly and he was soon in the nineties with everyone waiting to applaud the inevitable century. But then a boy, who was bowling from the end at which Gilbert was umpire, bowled a ball which struck the master high up on the thigh. The boy immediately let out a 'How's that?' and then tried to stifle the appeal; but before he could do so, up went Gilbert's finger and, pointing towards the pavilion he glared at the master and said, 'Out!' The master looked livid but he had to go, and as he passed Gilbert he muttered through clenched teeth, 'Harding you were *not* paying attention. I wasn't out.' To which Gilbert, with great relish, replied, 'On the contrary, sir, I *was* paying attention and you weren't out!'

My second story concerns an umpiring incident in a village cricket match. The visiting team was batting and one of the batsmen hit a ball hard on to his pads. There was a loud and immediate appeal for l.b.w. and up went the home umpire's finger. The batsman was very angry, and as he passed the umpire he said, 'I hit that one hard. I wasn't out.' 'Oh yes you were,' said the umpire, 'and if you don't believe me look in next Thursday's—*Gazette*' (naming the local paper). '*You* look,' replied the batsman. 'I'm the editor.'

And thirdly—almost inevitably—one of the many stories about Freddie Trueman. Each year at the beginning of the season Yorkshire play, or used to play, some one-day matches against clubs around the county. The idea was to give the team some practice out in the middle before starting their championship matches. One year they were playing against a club just outside York. Yorkshire fielded first and Freddie Trueman soon got among the wickets, bowling with surprising speed and ferocity for so early in the season. He had taken the first five wickets and the next batsman emerged from the pavilion. He was an upright military figure, with bristling white moustache and an old-fashioned 'I Zingari' cap on his head, complete with button on the top. The sleeves of his cream silk shirt were buttoned down to the wrist and he had on a pair of those skeleton pads which used to be fashionable in the days of W.G. He was an imposing figure, but understandably enough he looked a trifle apprehensive at what he was about to face. The Yorkshire captain saw him coming and, realizing the county were doing a bit too well, went up to Freddie and said: 'This is Brigadier X. He is an important member of the county. Let him get a few.' So Freddie, in his most affable and friendly manner went up to the brigadier as he approached the wicket and said: 'Good morning, Brigadier. With my first ball I will give you one to get off the mark.' The brigadier looked greatly relieved, but his expression soon changed as Freddie went on: 'Aye, and with my second I'll pin you against flippin' sightscreen!'

Brian Johnston, M.C.: From *Three of the Best*

A grand old man in Hollywood

You will remember Sir Aubrey Smith, the tall, handsome Englishman who went into films and, late in life, became the uncrowned king of Hollywood. Even Hollywood is not wrong about everything, and when it came to regard Sir Aubrey as its ideal of a fine old English gentleman it showed more than usual intelligence. Long before that time, though few can recall it now, he had been C. A. Smith, of Cambridge University, Sussex and England, and captain of the first touring side in South Africa. He was a slow bowler—slow to the point of slow motion who used to start his run about mid-off and then, as though by after-thought, bowled round the wicket. That is why they called him 'Round-the-Corner' Smith and his house in Hollywood was christened *Round the Corner*. In the film colony he ran his own cricket team, and he ran it as strictly as Lord Hawke or Lord Harris would have done. He was a stickler, as you may imagine, for etiquette and insisted on the correct interpretation of cricket's laws, both social and sporting, on all occasions. As he grew older, he grew stricter; as he grew older, too, his eyesight grew sketchier and one day in the field he committed the enormity, so hard to forgive in others, of dropping a slip catch. Instantly he stopped the game and signalled for his butler, who walked ceremoniously across the ground and bowed low.

'Bring me my spectacles,' ordered Sir Aubrey.

Slowly the butler returned to the outer world and once more appeared, bearing a pair of spectacles (in case) on a silver salver. Sir Aubrey put on his spectacles and signalled to the umpires permission to resume action. The bowler bowled, the batsman snicked, the ball shot into Sir Aubrey's hands and shot out again. There was an almost interminable pause. Finally a loud complaint arose to heaven. 'Egad,' exclaimed Sir Aubrey, 'the dam' fool brought my reading glasses.'

A. A. Thomson: From *Some Eccentric Matches*

Ninth wicket

The bowling looks exceptionally sound,
The wicket seems unusually worn,
The balls fly up or run along the ground;
I rather wish that I had not been born.
I have been sitting here since two o'clock;
My pads are both inelegant and hot;
I do not want what people call my 'knock',
And this pavilion is a sultry spot.
I shall not win one clap or word of praise,
I know that I shall bat like a baboon;
And I can think of many better ways
In which to spend a summer afternoon.
I might be swimming in a crystal pool;
I might be wooing some delicious dame;
I might be drinking something long and cool—
I can't imagine why I play this game.

Why is the wicket seven miles away,
And why have I to walk to it alone?
I hope that Bottle's bat will drive to-day—
I ought to buy a weapon of my own.
I wonder if this walk will ever cease;
They should provide a motor-car or crane
To drop the batsman on the popping-crease
And when he's out, convey him back again.
Is it a dream? Can this be truly me,
Alone and friendless in a waste of grass?
The fielding side are sniggering, I see,
And long-leg sort of shudders as I pass.
How very small and funny I must look!
I only hope that no one knows my name
I might be in a hammock with a book—
I can't imagine why I play this game.

Well, here we are. We feel a little ill.
What is this pedant of an umpire at?
Middle and off, or centre—what you will;
It cannot matter where I park the bat.
I look around me in a knowing way
To show that I am not to be cajoled;
I shall play forward gracefully and pray . . .
I have played forward and I am not bowled.
I do not like the wicket-keeper's face,
And why are all the fielders crowding round?
The bowler makes an imbecile grimace,
And mid-off makes a silly whistling sound.
These innuendoes I could do without;
They mean to say the ball defied the bat,
They indicate that I was nearly out;
Well, darn their impudence! I know all that.
Why am I standing in this comic pose,
Hemmed in by men that I should like to maim?
I might be lying in a punt with Rose—
I can't imagine why I play this game.

And there are people sitting over there
Who fondly hope that I shall make a run;
They cannot guess how blinding is the glare;
They do not know the ball is like a bun.
But courage, heart! We have survived a ball;
I pat the pitch to show that it is bad;
We are not such a rabbit after all;
Now we shall show them what is what, my lad!
The second ball is very, very swift;
It breaks and stands up steeply in the air;
It looks at me, and I could swear it sniffed;
I gesture at it, but it is not there.
Ah, what a ball! Mind you, I do not say
That Bradman, Hobbs, and Ranji in his prime,
Rolled into one, and that one on his day,
Might not have got a bat to it in time . . .
But long-stop's looking for my middle stump,
And I am walking in a world of shame;
My captain has addressed me as a chump—
I can't imagine why I play this game.

A. P. Herbert
(dedicated to the Lord's Taverners)

The Glory of Uncle Sid

Uncle Sid's story . . . began in the South African War. As a private soldier he had earned a reputation for silence, cunning and strength. His talent for cricket, learned on the molehills of Sheepscombe, also endowed him with special privileges. Quite soon he was chosen to play for the Army and was being fed on the choicest rations. The hell-bent technique of his village game worked havoc among the officers. On a flat pitch at last, with a scorched dry wicket, after the hillocks and cow-dung of home, he was projected straightway into regions of greatness and broke records and nerves galore. His murderous bowling reduced heroes to panic; they just waved him good-bye and ran; and when he came in to bat men covered their heads and retired piecemeal to the boundaries. I can picture that squat little whizzing man knocking the cricket ball out of the ground, his face congested with brick-red fury, his shoulders bursting out of his braces. I can see him crouch for the next delivery, then spin on his short bowed legs, and clout it again half-way to Johannesburg while he heard far-off Sheepscombe cheer. In an old Transvaal newspaper, hoarded by my Mother, I once found a score-card which went something like this:

Army v. Transvaal, Pretoria, 1899

Army

Col. 'Tigger' Ffoukes-Wyte	1
Brig. Gen. Fletcher	0
Maj. T. W. G. Staggerton-Hake	12
Capt. V. O. Spillingham	0
Major Lyle (not)	31
Pte S. Light (not)	126
Extras	7
Total (for 4 dec.)	177

Transvaal   21 all out (Pte S. Light 7 for 5)

This was probably the peak of Uncle Sid's glory, the time he would most wish to remember.

Laurie Lee: From *Cider with Rosie*, 1959

Pride of the village

A new grave meets the hastiest passer's eye
It's reared so high, it lacks not some white wreath;
Old ones are not so so noticed; low they lie
And lower still the equal grass forgets
The bones beneath.

His now, a modest hillock it must be,
The wooden cross scarce tells such as pass by
The painted name; beneath the chestnut tree
Sleep centuries of such glories and regrets.
But I can tell you, boys who that way run
With bat and ball down to the calm smooth leas,
Your village story's somewhere bright with one
To whom all looked with an approving joy
In hours like these.
Cricket to us, like you, was more than play,
It was worship in the summer sun,
And when Tom Fletcher in the month of May
Went to the field, the feet of many a boy
Scarce pressed the buttercups; then we stood there
Rapt, as he took the bat and lit day's close,
Gliding and glancing, guiding fine or square
The subtlest bowls, and smoothing, as wave-wise
Rough-hurled they rose,
With a sweet sureness; his especial ease
Did what huge sinews could not; to a hair
His grey eyes measured, and from the far trees
Old watchers lobbed the ball with merry cries.

And when the whitened creases marked the match,
Though shaking hands and pipes gone out revealed
The hour's impress and burden, and the catch
Or stumps askew meant it was Tom's turn next,
He walked a field
Modest, and small, and seldom failed to raise
Our score and spirits, great delight to watch;
And where old souls broke chuckling forth in praise
Round the ale booth, Tom's cricket was the text.

Summers slipt out of sight; next summer—hush!
The winter came between, and Tom was ill,
And worse, and with the spring's sweet rosy flush,
His face was flushed with perilous rose; he stayed
Indoors, and still
We hoped; but elders said, 'Tom's going home'.
The brake took cricketers by inn and bush,
But Tom not there! What team could leave out Tom?

He took his last short walk, a trembling shade.
And 'short and sweet', he said, for his tombstone
Would be the word; but paint and wood decay,
And since he died the wind of war has blown
His companions far beyond the green
Where many a day
He made his poems out of bat and ball.
Some few may yet be left who all alone
Can tell you, boys, who run at cricket's call,
What a low hillock by your path may mean.

Edmund Blunden

Southgate Cricket Ground 1952

The honest batsman

No, I didn't lift my head a single fraction.
My left elbow—it was well and truly bent.
Yes, I played right down the line,
And the ball had lost its shine,
So it didn't swerve to any great extent.
No, the wicket isn't green, nor is it sticky,
It's as true as any wicket well could be;
Yes, conditions are so nice,
They're a batsman's paradise,
But a paradise soon lost—alas—for me.

No, the ball was not a bouncer nor a bumper;
No, it didn't turn an inch from off or leg;
No, it wasn't sheer bad luck
That I'm back here for a duck,
So please spare me your condolences, I beg.
No, it wasn't a leg-cutter or a yorker;
No, it didn't turn, or twist, or sway, or swing;
It just pleaded to be hit,
Why I'm out, I must admit—
IS BECAUSE I WENT AND MISSED
　　　　　THE RUDDY THING ! ! !

Cardew Robinson

Poem

Flowing together by devious channels
From farm and brickyard, forest and dene,
Thirteen men in glittering flannels
Move to their stations out on the green.

Long-limbed Waggoner, stern, unbudging,
Stands like a rock behind the bails.
Dairyman umpire, gravely judging,
Spares no thought for his milking-pails.

Bricklayer bowls, a perfect length,
Grocery snicks and sneaks a run.
Law, swiping with all his strength,
Is caught by Chemist at mid-on.

Two to the boundary, a four and a six,
Put the spectators in fear of their lives:
Shepherd the slogger is up to his tricks,
Blithely unwary of weans and wives.

Lord of the manor makes thirty-four.
Parson contributes, smooth and trim,
A cautious twelve to the mounting score:
Leg-before-wicket disposes of him.

Patient, dramatic, serious, genial,
From over to over the game goes on,
Weaving a pattern of hardy perennial
Civilization under the sun.

Gerald Bullett

Village cricket

. . . Broiling afternoon . . . deck-chairs under the spreading . . . the muted
coo of pigeons in the immemorial . . . delicate tracery etched against blue
. . . gently undulating emerald velvet sward . . . cucumber sandwiches . . .
distant tinkle of ice in lemonade jug . . . satisfying clunk of pad against
willow . . . distant click of curate's false . . . 'Oh, well played, Ronald!
. . . Run, Doctor, run!' . . . Doctor's reflexes not what they were . . . short
single . . . hair's breadth . . . flutter of applause . . . soporific hum of bees
in . . . white figures moving in ancient ritual against time-honoured back-
cloth . . . part and parcel of cherished national heritage . . . warp and woof
of very fabric . . . Ronald caught in gully by bounder who looks as though
he ought to be wearing braces, black trousers and snake-fastener belt . . .
'Nice little knock, Ronald!' . . . helped us into double figures, anyway . . .
22 for three . . . not bad . . . not bad at all . . . clatter of crockery . . .
drowsy murmur . . . shadows imperceptibly . . . smell of freshly cropped
. . . democracy in action . . . squire and labourer toiling side by side for the
common . . . glorious uncertainty . . . all sorts and conditions of men . . .
regardless of race, colour, or . . . young thingummy-bob in next . . . all
pimples and Brylcreem . . . hopeless . . . notice out of corner of eye Mrs
Bisset struggling with tea-urn . . . ought to help her . . . magnificent figure
of a woman . . . summer dress certainly shows off her . . . Wonder what she
ever saw in old . . . hypnotic drone . . . stray dog . . . harsh cawing of rooks
high in . . . six by young whatsisname . . . sheer fluke . . . plumb through
Granny Murchison's lavatory again . . . enthusiastic ripple and sporadic

. . . distant tinkle of broken glass . . . hypnotic click of knitting . . .
satisfying clunk of bat meeting . . . crimson orb setting in . . . wonderful
cloud effects . . . just like galleons . . . shadow of church spire imperceptibly . . . white figures moving like ghosts in ancient . . . where else but in
England would you . . .

Peter Sellers and Peter Munro Smith

Cricket in Cumberland

Let me describe the field:
Its size, a double acre; walled
Along the north by a schoolyard,
West by a hedge and orchards; tarred
Wood railings on the east to fence
The grass from the station shunting lines,
That crook like a defensive ditch
Below the ramparts of the church;
And south, the butter meadows, yellow
As fat and bumpy as a pillow,
Rumpling down the mile or more
That slopes to the wide Cumbrian shore,
With not a brick to lift a ban
Between the eye and the Isle of Man.
A common sort of field you'll say:
You'd find a dozen any day
In any northern town, a sour
Flat landscape shaped with weed and wire,
And nettle clump and ragwort thicket—
But this field is put by for cricket.
Here among the grass and plantains
Molehills matter more than mountains,
And generations watch the score
Closer than toss of peace or war.
Here, in matches won and lost,
The town hoards an heroic past,
And legendary bowlers tie
The child's dream in the father's lie.
This is no Wisdom pitch; no place
For classic cuts and Newbolt's verse,
But the luck of the league, stiff and stark
With animosity of dark
In-grown village and mining town,
When evening smoke-light drizzles down,
And the fist is tight in the trouser pocket,

And the heart turns black for the want of a wicket.
Or knock-out cricket, brisk as a bird,
Twenty overs and league men barred—
Heels in the popping crease, crouch and clout,
And the crowd half-codding the batsmen out.
Over the thorn and elder hedge
The sunlight floods, but leaves a ledge
Of shadow where the old men sit,
Dozing their pipes out. Frays of light
Seam a blue serge suit; gnats swarm,
And swallows dip round the bowler's arm.
Here in a small-town game is seen
The long-linked dance of the village green:
Wishing well and maypole ring,
Mumming and ritual of spring.

Norman Nicholson, 1950

High-lights of a village cricket match

. . . At the other end the fast bowler pounded away grimly until an
unfortunate accident occurred. Mr Southcott had been treating with
apologetic contempt those of his deliveries which came within reach, and
the blacksmith's temper had been rising for some time. An urchin had
shouted, 'Take him orf!' and the other urchins, for whom Mr Southcott
was by now a firmly established deity, had screamed with delight. The
captain had held one or two ominous consultations with the wicket-
keeper and other advisers, and the blacksmith knew that his dismissal was
at hand unless he produced a supreme effort.

It was the last ball of the over. He halted at the wicket before going
back for his run, glared at Mr Harcourt, who had been driven out to
umpire by his colleagues—greatly to the regret of Mr Bason, the landlord of
'The Shoes'—glared at Mr Southcott, took another reef in his belt, shook
out another inch in his braces, spat on his hand, swung his arm three or
four times in a meditative sort of way, grasped the ball tightly in his
colossal palm, and then turned smartly about and marched off like a
Pomeranian grenadier and vanished over the brow of the hill. Mr Southcott, during these proceedings, leant elegantly upon his bat and admired
the view. At last, after a long stillness, the ground shook, the grasses
waved violently, small birds arose with shrill clamours, a loud puffing
sound alarmed the butterflies, and the blacksmith, looking more like Venus
Anadyomene than ever, came thundering over the crest. The world held
its breath. Among the spectators conversation was suddenly hushed. Even
the urchins, understanding somehow that they were assisting at a crisis in
affairs, were silent for a moment as the mighty figure swept up to the

crease. It was the charge of Von Bredow's Dragoons at Gravelotte over again.

But alas for human ambitions! Mr Harcourt, swaying slightly from leg to leg, had understood the menacing glare of the bowler, had marked the preparation for titanic effort, and, for he was not a poet for nothing, knew exactly what was going on. Mr Harcourt sober had a very pleasant sense of humour, but Mr Harcourt rather drunk was a perfect demon of impishness. Sober, he occasionally resisted a temptation to try to be funny. Rather drunk, never. As the giant whirlwind of vulcanic energy rushed past him to the crease, Mr Harcourt, quivering with excitement and internal laughter, and wobbling uncertainly upon his pins, took a deep breath and bellowed, 'No ball!'

It was too late for the unfortunate bowler to stop himself. The ball flew out of his hand like a bullet and hit third-slip, who was not looking, full pitch on the knee-cap. With a yell of agony third-slip began hopping about like a stork until he tripped over a tussock of grass and fell on his face in a bed of nettles, from which he sprang up again with another drum-splitting yell. The blacksmith himself was flung forward by his own irresistible momentum, startled out of his wits by Mr Harcourt's bellow in his ear, and thrown off his balance by his desperate effort to prevent himself from delivering the ball, and the result was that his gigantic feet got mixed up among each other and he fell heavily in the centre of the wicket, knocking up a cloud of dust and dandelion-seed and twisting his ankle. Rooks by hundreds rose in protest from the vicarage cedars. The urchins howled like intoxicated banshees. The gaffers gaped. Mr Southcott gazed at the heavens. Mr Harcourt did not think the world had ever been, or could ever be again, quite such a capital place, even though he had laughed internally so much that he had got hiccups . . .

* * * * *

The scores were level and there was one wicket to fall. The last man in was the blacksmith, leaning heavily upon the shoulder of the baker, who was going to run for him, and limping as if in great pain. He took guard and looked round savagely. He was clearly still in a great rage.

The first ball he received he lashed at wildly and hit straight up in the air to an enormous height. It went up and up and up, until it became difficult to focus it properly against the deep, cloudless blue of the sky, and it carried with it the hopes and fears of an English village. Up and up it went, and then at the top it seemed to hang motionless in the air, poised like a hawk, fighting, as it were, an heroic but forlorn battle against the chief invention of Sir Isaac Newton, and then it began its slow descent.

In the meanwhile things were happening below, on the terrestrial sphere. Indeed, the situation was rapidly becoming what the French call *mouvementé*. In the first place the blacksmith forgot his sprained ankle and set out at a capital rate for the other end, roaring in a great voice as he went, 'Come on, Joe!' The baker, who was running on behalf of the invalid, also set out, and he also roared, 'Come on, Joe!' and side by side, like a pair of high-stepping hackneys, the pair cantered along. From the other end Joe set out on his mission, and he roared, 'Come on, Bill!' So all three came on. And everything would have been all right, so far as the running was concerned, had it not been for the fact that Joe, very naturally, ran with his head thrown back and his eyes goggling at the hawk-like cricket ball. And this in itself would not have mattered if it had not been for the fact that the blacksmith and the baker, also very naturally, ran with their heads turned not only upwards but also backwards as well, so that they too gazed at the ball, with an alarming sort of squint and truly terrific kink in their necks. Half-way down the pitch the three met with a magnificent clang, reminiscent of early, happy days in the tournament-ring at Ashby-de-la-Zouch, and the hopes of the village fell with the resounding fall of their three champions.

But what of the fielding side? Things were not so well with them. If there was doubt and confusion among the warriors of Fordenden, there was also uncertainty and disorganization among the ranks of the invaders. Their main trouble was the excessive concentration of their forces in the neighbourhood of the wicket. Napoleon laid it down that it was impossible to have too many men upon a battlefield, and he used to do everything in his power to call up every available man for a battle. Mr Hodge, after a swift glance at the ascending ball and a swift glance at the disposition of his troops, disagreed profoundly with the Emperor's dictum. He had too many men, far too many. And all except the youth in the blue silk jumper, and the mighty Boone, were moving towards strategical positions underneath the ball, and not one of them appeared to be aware that any of the others existed. Boone had not moved because he was more or less in the right place, but then Boone was not likely to bring off the catch . . . Major Hawker, shouting 'Mine, mine!' in a magnificently self-confident voice, was coming up from the bowler's end like a battle-cruiser. Mr Harcourt had obviously lost sight of the ball altogether, if indeed he had ever seen it, for he was running round and round Boone and giggling foolishly. Livingstone and Southcott, the two cracks, were approaching competently. Either of them would catch it easily. Mr Hodge had only to choose between them, and, coming to a swift decision, he yelled above the din, 'Yours, Livingstone!' Southcott, disciplined cricketer, stopped dead. Then Mr Hodge made a fatal mistake. He remembered Livingstone's two missed sitters, and he reversed his decision and roared, 'Yours, Bobby!' Mr Southcott obediently started again while Livingstone, who had not heard the second order, went straight on. Captain Hodge had restored the *status quo*.

In the meantime the professor of ballistics had made a lightning calculation of angles, velocities, density of the air, barometer readings and temperatures, and had arrived at the conclusion that the critical point, the spot which ought to be marked in the photographs with an X, was one yard to the north-east of Boone, and he proceeded to take up station there, colliding on the way with Donald and knocking him over. A moment later Bobby Southcott came racing up and tripped over the recumbent Donald and was shot head first into the Abraham-like bosom of Boone. Boone stepped back a yard under the impact and came down with his spiked boot, surmounted by a good eighteen stone of flesh and blood, upon the professor's toe. Almost simultaneously the portly wicket-keeper, whose movements were a positive triumph of the spirit over the body bumped the professor from behind. The learned man was thus neatly sandwiched between Tweedledum and Tweedledee, and the sandwich was instantly converted into a ragout by Livingstone, who made up for his lack of extra weight—for he was always in perfect training—by his extra momentum. And all the time Mr Shakespeare Pollock hovered alertly upon the outskirts like a rugby scrum-half, screaming American University cries in a piercingly high tenor voice.

At last the ball came down. To Mr Hodge it seemed a long time before the invention of Sir Isaac Newton finally triumphed. And it was a striking testimony to the mathematical and ballistical skill of the professor that the ball landed with a sharp report upon the top of his head. Thence it leaped up into the air a foot or so, cannoned on to Boone's head, and then trickled slowly down the colossal expanse of the wicket-keeper's back, bouncing slightly as it reached the massive lower portions. It was only a foot from the ground when Mr Shakespeare Pollock sprang into the vortex with a last ear-splitting howl of victory and grabbed it off the seat of the wicket-keeper's trousers. The match was a tie. And hardly anyone on the field knew it except Mr Hodge, the youth in the blue jumper, and Mr Pollock himself. For the two batsmen and the runner, un-daunted to the last, had picked themselves up and were bent on completing the single that was to give Fordenden the crown of victory. Unfortunately, dazed with their falls, with excitement, and with the noise, they all three ran for the same wicket, simultaneously realized their error, and all three turned and ran for the other—the blacksmith, ankle and all, leading by a yard, so that they looked like pictures of the Russian troika. But their effort was in vain, for Mr Pollock had grabbed the ball and the match was a tie . . .

A. G. Macdonnel: From *England, Their England*, 1933

The Song of the Pitch

Oh, take me to a cricket ground,
    to hear the cricket's call,
The soothing sentimental sound
    As bat belabours ball,
The thunder of a swelling score,
    The rich unearthly rent,
Fuller and fiercer than a four,
    Of sixes heaven-bent;
The sudden song as second slip
    Concedes a finger nail,
The gentle lapping of a grip,
    The brushing of a bail.
How fervently I love the sound
    Of pad-enshrouded feet,
Boldly and boisterously bound
    For their white-walled retreat.
But more than all I love to hear
    The male magnificat,
The joyous paean, thick or clear,
    The clarion call, 'HAAAAA-AT?'

Daniel Pettiward 'Truly Rural', 1939

Farewell to a fast bowler

He has some rare statistics to contemplate—and he has always cherished his figures—such as taking 2,304 wickets; only fifteen other bowlers in the history of cricket—but no one of his pace—can lay claim to more. He bowled over twenty thousand overs; which is a huge labour for a fast bowler. He stands above all others in taking 307 wickets in Test Matches, (and he played in only 67 so he averaged four-and-a-half wickets a match). His average—21.57 in Tests, 18.29 in all cricket—is the more striking for the fact that he bowled so frequently to an attacking field, often without a third man or long leg, so that the ball edged through the slips or the short legs usually went for four. He scored some 9,000 runs, including three centuries of which he was inordinately proud: made 438 catches, most of them at short leg where he fielded with remarkable alertness and a balance which could justifiably be called graceful, even at intervals of bowling at top speed in exhausting conditions.

    Other cricketers have ceased to play first-class cricket and continued smoothly in or near it in the leagues, as coaches, or umpires. Fred Trueman could not do that because he was never simply a cricketer; he was purely— in method, mind and heart—a fast bowler; and he could never be less

F. S. Trueman in his pomp

than that. For that reason he could never be a fast-medium or medium-pace bowler. There is little doubt that his experience, skill and accuracy would have enabled him to play for another three or four seasons as a capable county stock bowler. With the years his pace did, indeed, deteriorate to fast medium; but that was, in fact, deterioration, not a compromise nor a deliberate adjustment. He was never content to be less than the fastest bowler he could be; fast-medium was not for him a technical change, but a defeat. So when at length the fact was borne in upon him that he was no longer fast, he went away.

If he had done anything else he would have destroyed an image which, even at his wildest, he had religiously maintained. There were occasions in the later years when, not as a gesture or a threat, but from need to express the self he believed in, he dug in a bouncer which was as mild as it was predictable. It had its own particular nostalgic dignity, but a deeper pathos; for batsmen then treated it lightly who would have taken hasty evasive action in the days of his high pace.

When he ceased to be a fast bowler a life ended. No doubt there was, and will be a life of a person by the name of Frederick Sewards Trueman who is not a fast bowler; but that is a separate man, almost a stranger to Fred the fast bowler. This other man will not roll truculently up from short-leg, cap crumpled on head, to snatch a thrown cricket ball out of the air. He will not, having now caught his audience, set off, shoulders and arms heavy with threat, thick legs unhurriedly purposeful, to a distant mark. He will not, ringed by a tensely silent crowd, come rocking aggressively to bowl faster—in his faith—than anyone else in the world. He will not make a threateningly propelled cricket ball cut curves in the air and angles from the pitch almost as sharp as those of his reminiscence. He will not blast out the finest batsmen of his time to a figure beyond all others. He will not lard the earth with his sweat, nor curse flukers and edgers with lurid oaths, nor damn authority. He will not shock the cricket world into half-delighted, half-awed repetition of his ribaldry. Fred did that: Fred, the fast bowler who is now cricket history—a complete chapter of it.

John Arlott: From *Fred: Portrait of a Fast Bowler*, 1971

The old cricketer

He sits alone to watch the men
At cricket on the village green;
And savours calmly, once again,
The life-remembered, quiet scene
That, to his ageing sight, grows dim;
And then he sees, with clearer eye,
That these men's fathers play with him,
Their fathers' fathers standing by.
He leaps once more, with eager spring,
To catch the brief-glimpsed, flying ball,
And quickens to its sudden sting:
The brightness dies: the old eyes gall:
They see, but do not understand,
A pursed, rheumatic, useless hand.

John Arlott

Players of my time

Fred Trueman

Trevor Bailey

The Barnacle was one of the greatest all-rounders of all time. He was a cricketer of character, of grit, of independence, of determination. He was proud to be an England cricketer. He hated to lose any game, but most of all he hated to lose when he was playing for England.

In fact I just don't know how Trevor Bailey came to be born anywhere other than in Yorkshire!

As a batsman he could make strong men weep and nowhere did he infuriate the opposition—and their supporters—by his stubbornness more than in Australia. It was there that they named him 'Barnacle' for the most obvious of reasons. And it was there (through sheer perversity, I'm absolutely certain) that he, of all people, hit the first six in a Test Match in which an Aussie businessman had offered £100 for the first man to do it. The chap who had offered the hundred quid was so outraged that Trevor had won it that he did his best to get out of paying.

'Boyle', elongated into 'The Boyle', is another name he has picked up along the way of his career but in quite a different fashion. He was a soccer, as well as a cricket Blue at Cambridge, and it was while playing in a tour match in Switzerland that the forward-line heard their names announced with such excruciating mispronunciation that they memorized them and brought them home. 'Boyly' so delighted Douglas Insole that he passed it around and no one uses it more frequently or with more impish delight than Brian Johnston who specializes in nick-names for everyone he encounters.

Trevor himself has always had a tremendous sense of humour and few things appealed to it more than goading the opposition into a frenzy of frustration. That forward lunge has reduced great bowlers in all parts of the world to tears of impotent fury. Yet it has characterized many valuable innings for England in his 61 Tests, which brought him 2,290 runs and 132 wickets, while his splendid close-to-the-wicket fielding earned him 32 Test catches.

Like all top class bowlers he studied opposition batsmen closely, working out his own theories and standing by them. Probably his outstanding Test bowling performance came at Kingston in the last Test of the 1953–54 tour to the West Indies. His first innings seven for 34 gave England a nine-wickets win to square the series when we had been two down after the first two. Then he went out and opened the England innings with Len Hutton!

But somehow he always saved his grittiest batting for the Australians and how they loved to hate him!

He was a fine tourist and went out of his way to try to help anyone with any kind of problem. We toured together, batted together, bowled together, and now we work together on Radio 3's Test Match Special and that gives me just as much pleasure as all my many associations with him as a player.

But I just can't work it out . . . *how* did he come to be born outside Yorkshire? I didn't think they made 'em like 'Boyle' anywhere else.

Trevor Edward Bailey (1923–   )

Cambridge University 1947–48; Essex 1946–67 (captain 1961–66).
England in England 1949 to 1951, 1953 to 1958; in Australia 1950–51, 1954–55, 1958–59; in South Africa 1956–57; in West Indies 1953–54; in New Zealand 1950–51, 1954–55.

Test Record

	Ins	NO	HS	Runs	Av.	100s
Batting	91	14	134*	2,290	29·74	1

Highest score   134 not out v. New Zealand (Christchurch) 1950–51
Matches   61
Bowling   132 wickets at 29·21
Best bowling   7 for 34 v. West Indies (Kingston) 1953–54

Career Figures

	Ins	NO	HS	Runs	Av.	100s
Batting	1072	215	205	28,642	33·42	28

1,000 runs in a season   17 times
Bowling   2,082 wickets at 23·13
100 wickets in a season   9 times
Catches   425

England's premier all-rounder throughout his Test career. No more determined batsman ever played Test cricket, and his dour method attracted slow-scoring records and slow-handclapping. Considerable fast-medium bowler and superb fieldsman close to the wicket. Cricket journalist and BBC broadcaster.

Ken Barrington

The man who came to be known as 'The Run Machine' went to The Oval as a leg-spin bowler in the first place and later in his career, especially in Tests, he took some very useful wickets. He wasn't the worst of slip-fielders, either.

But it is as a maker of runs that Ken Barrington will be remembered.

His philosophy in Test cricket was quite simple: he believed that the longer he occupied the crease, the more the runs would come. He loved playing for England. He worked hard at it—and at making centuries for his country. In fact Wally Grout once said that when Ken walked out to bat one could see a Union Jack waving behind him. It was a tribute I particularly liked because I, too, have always been a very proud Englishman.

For some reason which I have never worked out (because I'm a damn sight better-looking than he could ever be) we were often mistaken for each other on tour. It became a bit of a laugh because when he was mistaken for me, Kenny would occasionally let it go on by trying to put on a Yorkshire accent. It must have sounded like hell. Once, when we arrived in Wellington, New Zealand, Ken found a wheelchair and pushed me round the airport in it which caused one of the locals to say, 'How nice to see that chap being looked after by his brother.'

Brother indeed. He'd always be in my Ugly XI!

He'd also always be in my England XI, too, because he was a great run-maker and a great bloke to tour with. He loved a joke, a tale, a laugh. As a batsman he no doubt gave the impression of being a dour sort of individual.

Far, far from it. One of his favourite roles in India, for example, was to stand at the crease with the heel of the left foot on the ground, toe pointing upwards, caricaturing one of the pukka sahibs of yesteryear. The Indian crowds recognized at once what he was doing and they were in stitches.

At the time when he was being heavily criticized as a slow-scorer, he began to pace an innings—perhaps 'organize' it is a better way of putting it—so that he reached his century with a straight six back over the bowler's head. Now that takes a bit of doing. Only great players *can* work it out like that, and Ken did it on more than one occasion and in more than one country.

He was probably the last of that long line of England middle-order batsmen of the highest class.

Kenneth Frank Barrington (1930– 1981)

Surrey 1953–68.
England in England 1955, 1959 to 1968; in Australia 1962–63, 1965–66; in West Indies 1959–60, 1967–68; in New Zealand 1962–63; in India 1961–62, 1963–64; in Pakistan 1961–62; in South Africa 1964–65.

Test Record

	Ins	*NO*	*HS*	*Runs*	*Av.*	*100s*
Batting	131	15	256	6,806	58·67	20

Highest score   256 v. Australia (Old Trafford) 1964
Matches   82
Bowling   29 wickets at 44·82

Career Figures

	Ins	*NO*	*HS*	*Runs*	*Av.*	*100s*
Batting	831	136	256	31,714	45·63	76

1,000 runs in a season   15 times
Bowling   273 wickets at 32·61
Catches   511

Dedicated, conscientious cricketer whose health suffered from his intensity of application. Strong back-foot batsman, safe fielder, and occasional leg-spin bowler. Now an England selector and manager of MCC in India, Sri Lanka, and Australia in 1976–77.

Alec Bedser

After the war, in the late forties and through into the fifties, 'Big Al', or 'The Big Fella', carried England's opening attack, even though he was himself a medium-fast rather than a genuinely fast bowler.

And even that came by the toss of a coin. When he and his twin, Eric, joined the Surrey staff it was plain that there wasn't going to be much future for *two* medium-fast seam bowlers so they tossed to see who would carry on with the style they both knew, and who would turn his attention to batting and off-spinning.

The extraordinary thing about Alec was that he bowled an *in*-swinger with a very sideways-on action, which is the hallmark of the *out*-swinger. Perhaps Don Bradman couldn't really believe it—look at the number of times he was caught by Len Hutton at leg-slip! Later, Alec, who was always willing to experiment with different types of delivery, developed probably the most devastating leg-cutter in the history of the game. I remember him bowling Graeme Hole round his legs for a duck when he opened in the First Test at Trent Bridge in 1953, and Hole simply gaped in disbelief. He just couldn't believe it had happened.

Alec is, of course, a big man and his hands are huge. The Surrey players used to say that that particular ball was like a very fast leg-break and it was when you saw the ball disappear into those massive hands that you began to get some idea how he could perform such remarkable tricks with it.

He wasn't exactly a slouch with the bat. After all, he made 79 against Australia at Headingley in 1948 after going in as night watchman. But he was No. 11 when he came in to bat in his Benefit game at The Oval a few years later. I was in the RAF at the time and Alec wrote to my C.O. to ask if I could be released to play for Yorkshire in that match and then he came in . . . on a hat-trick. I started to push the field back to give him the courtesy one-off-the-mark but he said, 'No, No, Fred. Go for your hat-trick.' I thought about it, then gave him the long half-volley which he hit for two. That was fair enough, but I began to regret it when he and Jim Laker put on about 90 for the last wicket!

In my first Test Match—against the Indians at Headingley—he gave me a simple piece of advice which I have always believed was as good as any I have ever received. I was a bit tense and he said, 'Don't worry about it. Treat it just as another match.'

Come to think about it, if all Tests had gone like that they wouldn't

take up so much time. Remember that second-innings scoreboard: 'India, o for 4'? It was good advice, just the same, from a great bowler— one of the all-time greats.

Alec Victor Bedser, O.B.E. (1918–　　)

Surrey 1939–60.
England in England 1946 to 1955; in Australia 1946–47, 1950–51, 1954–55; in South Africa 1948–49; in New Zealand 1946–47, 1950–51.

Test Record

	Ins	NO	HS	Runs	Av.	100s
Batting	71	15	79	714	12·75	o

Highest score　79 v. Australia (Leeds) 1948
Matches　51
Bowling　236 wickets at 24·89
Best bowling　7 for 44 (14 for 99 in match) v. Australia (Trent Bridge) 1953

Career Figures

	Ins	NO	HS	Runs	Av.	100s
Batting	576	181	126	5,735	14·51	1

Bowling　1,924 wickets at 20·41
100 wickets in a season　11 times
Catches　290

Backbone of England bowling from post-war resumption of Tests until discarded in 1954–55 series in Australia. Among elite of fast-medium bowlers. Helped Surrey to seven successive County Championships from 1952. Loyal, dedicated, seemingly-always-fit professional. Test selector since 1962, latterly chairman. Assistant manager and manager of M.C.C. sides abroad. Younger of twins.

Richie Benaud

Richie Benaud was the most successful of the post-war Australian captains and no Englishman would complain about that. He was an extremely shrewd and thoughtful leader and his belligerence was expressed in the way he handled his forces, not through the agency of his powers of invective! He was always an *aggressive* captain because he believed in attacking, but his methods were not simply *oppressive*.

Like most leg-spinners he had to serve a long apprenticeship and that took him into his late twenties before he became a real force in international cricket but the long years of 'grooving' his bowling were not wasted. In 1975, he played in a club centenary match in this country at pretty short notice. He hadn't bowled a leg-spinner in anger since goodness-knows-when—but in his first over he 'dropped' all six right on the mark, and spun 'em, too.

His early tours of England were not exactly the best years of his life in the bowling sense, yet he ended his career as the highest Australian wicket-taker—248 at 27.03. Perhaps his best-remembered Test in this country was the 1961 game at Old Trafford when, bowling into the rough at the other end, he took six second-innings wickets for 70 to bowl out England when, at 150 for two, they had looked pretty sure of victory themselves. Brian Close will remember that game, of course, because he was (and has been ever since) pilloried for getting caught lapping Benaud. Not only has Close, who isn't exactly daft when it comes to tactics, always insisted that his approach was the right one, but Richie Benaud has always backed up this view.

Richie is a member of a cricketing family, with his father and a brother both playing first-class cricket for New South Wales, so his pedigree was always right. He learned his trade bowling by himself in a barn—but in his imagination bowling against a whole galaxy of overseas stars. It is perhaps a little odd that the chief opponent of these dream sequences was Laurie Fishlock, the Surrey batsman, not perhaps the best-known of the 1946–47 side who in his *one* Test didn't make much of a splash. Perhaps, as an impressionable teenager, he had seen Laurie make runs in a State Match; I must ask him some time.

At Lord's, in 1956, I had Richie caught behind first ball, and he was given not out. He went on to score 97 (batting at No. 8) which proved absolutely decisive and, to a major degree, was responsible for Australia winning the Test. Some years later, in South Africa, he told me the ball

went off the edge of the bat, flicked his shirt and went to Godfrey Evans, but Richie, by immediately rubbing the arm where the ball had brushed his shirt, got the decision. Oh, yes! He was a great Australian!

Richie Benaud, O.B.E. (1930–   )

New South Wales 1948–64 (captain 1958–63).
Australia in Australia 1951–52, 1952–53, 1954–55, 1958–59 (captain), 1960–61 (captain), 1962–63 (captain), 1963–64 (captain one Test); in England 1953, 1956, 1961 (captain); in South Africa 1957–58; in West Indies 1954–55; in India 1956–57, 1959–60 (captain); in Pakistan 1956–57, 1959–60 (captain).

Test Record

	Ins	NO	HS	Runs	Av.	100s
Batting	97	7	122	2,201	24·45	3
Highest score	122 v. South Africa (Johannesburg) 1957–58					
Matches	63					
Bowling	248 wickets at 27·03					
Best bowling	7 for 72 v. India (Madras) 1956–57					

Career Figures

	Ins	NO	HS	Runs	Av.	100s
Batting	359	44	187	11,432	36·29	23
Bowling	935 wickets at 24·80					

Test debut at 21, but not established until 1957–58, six years later. Accurate leg-spin bowler with aggressive variety. Fine close fieldsman and hard-hitting middle-order batsman. Made his greatest mark as a captain, his successful record the product of shrewd strategies and the power to inspire his players. Cricket journalist and BBC broadcaster.

Denis Compton

Like Sobers, Denis Compton was one of the great *instinctive* cricketers, one of the greatest of all time.

He differed from Len Hutton his contemporary in the English side in just about every way and yet both were among the finest batsmen this country has ever produced. He did not rely, like Hutton, on perfect balance but on razor-sharp reflexes and a gift for improvization which was quite marvellous to see.

He went further down the wicket to bowlers than anyone I have ever seen; he even went down the pitch to Lindwall! And Ray didn't like that at all. But that, of course, meant less than nothing to Compton. He had no respect whatsoever for reputations. He would take a century off Lindwall and Miller without ruffling a hair of that much-advertised head, then get out to a rhubarb bowler who had been brought over to play in the county matches. He was the *cheekiest* batsman I ever saw, again something which was related to his refusal to be impressed by reputations.

He still holds the record for most centuries in a season—18 of them in that golden summer of 1947 when everyone was busy forgetting about the war, and Denis Compton and Bill Edrich are said to have scored 3,000 runs apiece, downed 6,000 pints and crammed 12,000 nights out into the year!

Those who saw him go down the pitch, fall and then still sweep the ball for four while sitting on his backside still marvel at the shot. But everyone who saw Denis Compton in his prime can recall at least one shot which really defied description but which lives on in the memory.

The two greatest innings *I* saw him play were his 133 at Port of Spain, Trinidad, in 1954, and one for the International Cavaliers in the late fifties. The second of these—all right, it was a charity match, a deliberately contrived crowd-pleaser, but what an exhibition of hitting! The other was in a game where lots of people got runs . . . Weekes 206, Worrell 167, Walcott 124 and in the England innings, May 135 and Graveney 92. Now there's a pretty fair collection of stroke-makers for you, but Compton's 133 still conjures up for me the recollection of an incredible exhibition of batting.

He loved his public image—the gay cavalier of cricket, the international playboy and he lived up to it. He used to sleep in his own particular spot in every dressing-room, taking no interest at all in what was happening out in the middle—until someone woke him up to bat.

Then, without any kind of mental preparation at all, out he would go and ENTERTAIN. That, I think, is the key word when you think about Denis. He was, above everything else, an entertainer. There aren't too many of them today.

But I think that, in his heyday, he could have picked up his bat at any time, in any place, on just about any kind of wicket if he was feeling like it and without any practice at all make a century.

That is cricketing genius.

Denis Charles Scott Compton, C.B.E. (1918–)

Middlesex 1936–58 (joint-captain 1951–52).
England in England 1937 to 1956; in Australia 1946–47, 1950–51, 1954–55; in South Africa 1948–49, 1956–57; in West Indies 1953–54; in New Zealand 1946–47, 1950–51.

Test Record

	Ins	NO	HS	Runs	Av.	100s
Batting	131	15	278	5,807	50·06	17
Highest score	278 v. Pakistan (Trent Bridge) 1954					
Matches	78					
Bowling	25 wickets at 56·40					
Best bowling	5 for 70 v. South Africa (Cape Town) 1948–49					

Career Figures

	Ins	NO	HS	Runs	Av.	100s
Batting	839	88	300	38,942	51·85	123
1,000 runs in a season	17 times (3 overseas)					
Bowling	620 wickets at 32·28					
Catches	416					

English romantic sporting hero, a batsman with all the strokes and a willingness to entertain. Took on the best bowlers from all countries and won more battles than he lost. Famed for his sweep stroke; only pronounced weakness was his uncertainty in running between wickets. Irregular left-arm slow spin bowler. Cricket journalist and occasional broadcaster.

Colin Cowdrey

Michael Colin Cowdrey is one of the interesting line of cricketers who were born abroad but who captained England. In fact he had the captaincy given to him, taken away, and then given back, more frequently than any man in history. Dexter, Close, Illingworth, May, all took over from him at one time or another.

Cowdrey was one of the very best of post-war cricketers and achieved more appearances for England than anyone else. When you think about how many runs he scored it might seem a bit strange if I say he never made as many as his great ability suggested he should have done. For me, he should have hit 150 centuries.

Yet let us not forget that besides being one of the best slip-catchers ever (holding more than 100 catches in Test Matches), he is England's heaviest run-scorer in history. His 307 against South Australia at Adelaide is the highest score by an English batsman in Australia and is, incidentally, one of the only two treble centuries I have ever seen scored.

Colin, I always felt, was a natural No. 4—the position which used to be reserved for a side's best stroke-maker before limited-overs cricket made nonsense of batting orders—but he had the ability to bat in any position if he felt like applying himself to it. He really had a prodigious natural talent.

As a captain he had obvious shortcomings. To begin with (and it's quite a handicap) I thought he was too nice a person to *be* a skipper. He was always trying to do the right thing. He wanted to keep everybody happy and you most certainly can't do that if you are going flat out to win Test Matches. He wanted to be a nice guy to everyone, and you can't do that, either.

He would give all he had got to a captain if he himself was not the skipper yet I've known him smile, though entirely without malice, when a captain got himself in a tangle.

At The Oval in 1964, I wanted three to clock up 300 Test wickets and before the game I had been talking to Neil Hawke. He'd said with a grin, 'I wouldn't mind being your 300th, Fred. At least I would go into the record books for evermore.' Little did he know . . .

We'd got into a bit of a state. Australia were climbing away from our first-innings total of 182 and, quite frankly, Ted Dexter didn't know what to do. I hadn't bowled for ages, it seemed, and I heard him talking to Colin about what to do next and then he said he thought he'd put Peter Parfitt on.

Well, Parf, like Hawkie, now lives near me and is a good mate of mine, but the thought of him bowling in a Test Match when I was raring to go was a bit too much. I snatched the ball out of Dexter's hand and said, '*I'm* going to bowl.'

Colin tried his best not to laugh. He dropped his head and walked away, but I knew he was laughing as Dexter stood looking a bit shaken.

The rest is history. After a bit I bowled Ian Redpath and had Garth McKenzie caught first ball—by Colin Cowdrey. And Neil Hawke came in on a hat-trick. He prevented another bit of cricketing folklore being created by stopping my next ball and grinned at me, 'Sorry, Fred.' But eventually I got him—again caught at slip by MCC Cowdrey. So they're *both* in the record books for evermore.

I had a great relationship with Colin (called 'Kipper' because he could sleep anywhere, anytime) but I still think he was too nice a bloke to be captain of a Test side. And if he hadn't been captain—who knows?—he could have got 150 centuries.

Michael Colin Cowdrey, C.B.E. (1932–)

Oxford University 1952–54 (captain 1954); Kent 1950–76 (captain 1957–71). England in England 1955 to 1968, 1971 (captain during all or part of series in 1959 to 1962, 1966, 1968); in Australia 1954–55, 1958–59, 1962–63, 1965–66, 1970–71, 1974–75; in New Zealand 1954–55, 1958–59, 1962–63, 1965–66, 1970–71; in South Africa 1956–57; in West Indies 1959–60 (captain 2 Tests), 1967–68 (captain); in India 1963–64; in Pakistan 1968–69 (captain).

Test Record

	Ins	*NO*	*HS*	*Runs*	*Av.*	*100s*
Batting	188	15	182	7,624	44·06	22
Highest score	182 v. Pakistan (Oval) 1962					
Matches	114					
Bowling	0 wicket for 104					

Career Figures

	Ins	*NO*	*HS*	*Runs*	*Av.*	*100s*
Batting	1,130	134	307	42,719	42·89	107
1,000 runs in a season	27 times (6 overseas)					
Bowling	65 wickets at 51·07					
Catches	638					

Popular, modest, master batsman. Smooth, correct, effortless technique. First and still only player to take part in a hundred Test matches. Approach to batting subject to moods: frustratingly introspective sometimes against even mediocre bowling, yet capable of destroying the best—always in a manner expressive of the highest class. Deft slip fieldsman, neglected leg-spin/googly bowler. Wedded to cricket, and one of its finest representatives.

Alan Davidson

A. K. Davidson was known as 'The Claw' because of the way he clutched, and hung on to, short leg and leg slip catches which would have been impossible to almost everyone else except, perhaps, Tony Lock.

As a left-arm bowler, he had a run-up which was easy, almost effortless, taking very little out of himself. He could swing the ball in, move it away off the seam, or push it straight across the batsman from left-arm over, forcing that eternal guarding of the off stump. As a batsman, he could play to any situation demanded—in full defensive control, or fiercely showing shots of the highest class.

Yet this man of so many talents and so much ability came late on to the Australian Test scene because of the reign of Lindwall, Miller and their great 'assistant', Bill Johnston. Even in the state side of New South Wales he had to queue up behind Lindwall and Miller and that's the sort of thing that happens when you have a very limited amount of first-class cricket played in a country. 'Davo' would certainly have taken many, many more Test wickets than he did (186 at 20.58) if he had been able to play before he did.

He was a 'thinking' bowler, too, and I rather enjoy the memory of out-thinking him (as I believe) on one occasion. I went out to bat on a hat-trick and I asked myself, 'What would I do in Davo's position . . . drop it a bit short and rely on getting an edge or ping in the yorker? I'm Number 9 . . . I'd bowl a yorker at No. 9.' So I played forward. It was the yorker and I stopped it.

He looked at me and said, 'I *knew* you'd play forward. *Why* did I try it?' It wasn't said with a snarl, or any sort of ill-will. Alan wasn't that sort of bloke. It was more a musing sort of remark, an exchange of technical ideas with a fellow practitioner, if you like, rather as a couple of pro golfers, battling with each other for a £5,000 prize, may think out loud to each other: 'I damn-well knew it was a six-iron when I took out my five but there I am, through the back . . .'

Like me, Davidson is a great fan of Rugby League—a man's game for a man's man—and he and I have spent hours talking about the game with Norm O'Neill, another avid fan.

I don't think I have one particular memory of a bowling spell by 'Davo', or one innings, or one catch. He was the sort of player who was *always* doing his job, whatever it was, in a supremely professional way. He was the sort of chap who would never let you down no matter what you asked of him—the complete professional.

Alan Keith Davidson, M.B.E. (1929–   )

New South Wales 1949–63.
Australia in Australia 1954–55, 1958–59, 1960–61, 1962–63; in England 1953, 1956, 1961; in South Africa 1957–58; in India 1956–57, 1959–60; in Pakistan 1956–57, 1959–60.

Test Record

	Ins	NO	HS	Runs	Av.
Batting	61	7	80	1,328	24·59

Highest score	80 v. West Indies (Brisbane) 1960–61
Matches	44
Bowling	186 wickets at 20·58
Best bowling	7 for 93 v. India (Kanpur) 1959–60

Career Figures

	Ins	NO	HS	Runs	Av.	100s
Batting	246	39	129	6,804	32·86	9
Bowling	672 wickets at 20·91					

Clever exponent of new-ball attack, a left-handed all-rounder who ranks with the best. Powerfully built, could hit exceptionally hard as lower middle-order batsman. Brilliant fieldsman, especially at backward short leg. President of the New South Wales Cricket Association.

Godfrey Evans

Godfrey Evans must easily rank amongst England's all-time greats as a wicket-keeper, and until Alan Knott overtook him in the summer of 1976 his figures of 219 victims in 91 Tests placed him far ahead of anyone else in world cricket.

Yet his value to a side lay not only in wicket-keeping of the highest class (and batting which could be wildly exotic or painstakingly dour, as the occasion demanded), but also in his ability to lift a side whose enthusiasm might just be sagging a bit. His catch-phrase, 'We'll be there at the finish', has revived many a flagging spirit. Indeed, it became so much part of a tour that the 1954–55 party to Australia and New Zealand produced a special tie, incorporating the opposition emblems of boomerang and fern and then, with the help of a Roman Catholic priest, they added a Latin translation of Godfrey's rallying-cry.

He was a great tourist. Invariably he won first prize at any fancy-dress party on board ship by togging up as Carmen Miranda, with a borrowed ball-gown and a basket of fruit on his head.

Behind the stumps he was perky to the point of cockiness—and he could afford to be. By standing up to medium-fast bowlers (Alec Bedser is the best example) he gave them a substantial advantage. Batsmen could not move out of their ground to make a good-length ball into a half-volley, and so the medium-fast man was half-a-yard a better bowler. This has been a source of some grief to Alan Knott in recent years because inevitably he has been compared with his distinguished Kent and England predecessor. Knott has never liked standing up to the medium-pacers. Indeed, it was only at The Oval in August 1976, that he at last did it—and that was a private wager with my Test Match Special colleague Brian Johnston!

But Godfrey not only never hesitated to stand up; at times it seemed as though he couldn't wait for the shine to wear off so that he could get to the stumps.

He inspired bowlers with greater confidence in consequence, because you always felt that if a chance were offered it was certain to be taken. And with it all there was the eternal chirpiness, the endless encouraging chat to lift you. On the last session of the hottest day, when you might have had 30 overs on a perfect wicket, you'd hear him saying, 'Come on lads. Let's get a thirst on for tonight.' And somehow you'd pull out a bit extra without really knowing why or how you had managed it.

He holds a Test record for the length of time spent at the wicket without scoring, because that was what a particular situation in Australia required. But one year for Kent he bet his captain £100 that he would score 1,500 runs if given a chance to bat higher up the order. He won.

Perhaps it was this successful bet which led him, in due course, to a role in which he calculates the odds for the bookmakers operating on Test grounds. Godfrey it is who arrives at the commentary box and Press Box at the start of each session with his little chit reading 'West Indies 1–5, England 100–8, draw 7–2'. Still chirpy, still cheerful, still smiling and still, I'm sure, working up a thirst.

Thomas Godfrey Evans, C.B.E. (1920–   )

Kent 1939–59 (one match 1968).
England in England 1946 to 1959; in Australia 1946–47, 1950–51, 1954–55, 1958–59; in New Zealand 1946–47, 1950–51, 1954–55; in West Indies 1947–48, 1953–54; in South Africa 1948–49, 1956–57.

Test Record

	Ins	NO	HS	Runs	Av.	100s
Batting	133	14	104	2,439	20·49	2
Highest score	104 v. West Indies (Old Trafford) 1952					
	104 v. India (Lord's) 1952					
Matches	91					
Wicket-keeping	Ct 173, st. 46—total 219					

Career Figures

	Ins	NO	HS	Runs	Av.	100s
Batting	744	48	144	14,705	21·13	7
1,000 runs in a season	4 times					
Wicket-keeping	Ct 801, st. 239—total 1,040					

First-choice wicketkeeper for England for a dozen years. Effervescent, athletic, a morale-raiser. Spectacular with gloves or bat. Stood up to the stumps for Bedser. Rallied many an innings with cheeky batsmanship. World Test record of 219 victims stood until 1976, when Kent successor Knott passed it.

Tom Graveney

When Australian bowlers first saw Tom Graveney walking out to bat they said, 'He *looks* like a cricketer'. Now that, from an Aussie, is high praise, but one can understand how they felt.

Tom looked poised, relaxed, in control—whatever the situation—whether he was batting at No. 4, 5 or 6. (He batted all over the order in his time.) He had that tall, elegant, willowy figure which always looked relaxed yet at the same time left you in no doubt that there were all kinds of latent power waiting to be let loose.

He was the first of the post-war generation of young batsmen to reach 100 centuries; he made himself into a top-class slip fieldsman; and the effortless timing of his shots earned him the name 'Mr Elegance'.

Timing was the real secret—timing and the balance which dictated the distribution of his weight into the right place at the right time. He never had to belt the ball. He stroked it. And he stroked it with such elegant timing that no obvious effort was called for.

He once scored a century at Scarborough, batting with a runner because he had a groin strain, and he *still* just stroked it about. One four, past extra cover, passed the fieldsman's left hand at such speed that he just stood and joined in the applause of the crowd—and got a *right* blast from the skipper!

Probably the best-innings I saw him play for England was his 164 at The Oval in 1957. He was No. 3 that day—he didn't half move up and down that order! He scored those runs in a total of 412 on a queer sort of wicket that was reddy-brown in colour and the value of the innings was shown when we rolled the West Indies over for 89 and 86 to win by an innings and 237 runs. It was Laker-and-Lock time, of course. I remember it rather well because I only bowled ten overs in the whole game and that didn't happen very often!

Tom was something of a creature of habit. He rigidly got up at the same time each morning (7.30, I think it was) no matter what time he went to bed and at week-ends, at home or on tour, there was one place you could be certain to find him—the golf course. Tom is one of the long line of post-war cricketers who have become low-handicap golfers, men like Ted Dexter, Colin Cowdrey, Brian Close, Arthur Milton, Len Hutton, Denis Compton. He loved his golf and he was an ever-present participant in the many pleasant week-end rounds tourists are invited to join.

On our way to Australia for the 1962–63 tour he was part of the Maryle-

bone Calypso Club which won the captain's talent contest on the ship. The prize was a mixture of brandy and champagne and T. W. Graveney distinguished himself by transforming this into the most magnificent champagne cocktails I've ever tasted. That is perhaps why he now presides over his own pub on the edge of Cheltenham Racecourse.

Thomas William Graveney, O.B.E. (1927–   )

Gloucestershire 1948–60 (captain 1959–60); Worcestershire 1961–70 (captain 1968–70); Queensland 1969–71.
England in England 1951 to 1958, 1962, 1966 to 1969; in Australia 1954–55, 1958–59, 1962–63; in West Indies 1953–54, 1967–68; in New Zealand 1954–55, 1958–59; in India 1951–52; in Pakistan 1968–69.

Test Record

	Ins	*NO*	*HS*	*Runs*	*Av.*	*100s*
Batting	123	13	258	4,882	44·38	11
Highest score	258 v. West Indies (Trent Bridge) 1957					
Matches	79					
Bowling	1 wicket for 167					

Career Figures

	Ins	*NO*	*HS*	*Runs*	*Av.*	*100s*
Batting	1,223	159	258	47,793	44·91	122
1,000 runs in a season	22 times (7 overseas)					
Bowling	80 wickets at 37·96					
Catches	549 (and one stumping)					

Elegant, upstanding batsman, employed by England less often than connoisseurs of style would have wished. Laughter came to him easily. First to make a hundred centuries in solely post-war cricket. Good slip fieldsman; rare leg-spin bowler.

Wally Grout

Wally Grout was very much more than a great wicket-keeper. There was nobody better at encouraging a team of flagging spirits; nobody better at lifting sagging morale; nobody more capable of raising a laugh when there was absolutely nothing in a situation to laugh at.

More than that, he could even make the opposition laugh when *they* were up against it. At Adelaide in 1959, for example, Richie Benaud made a bowling change and suddenly I noticed Wally running about 15 yards down the leg-side and going through the motions of diving another five yards. Then he rolled up his sleeves right to the top and did the same on the off-side as Richie was still setting the field.

I said, 'What's on, Grizzly?' and he said, 'Haven't you seen who's coming on? I'm just getting used to what I'll have to do for the next half-hour.'

The new bowler was Gordon Rorke, who I always thought got away with murder, absolute murder, with both his action and his point of delivery. We reckoned that for most of the time he was . . . er . . . bowling from about 16 yards. No wonder people said he was quick!

(It's another story but against Rorke we were once 14 for two and only two balls had been delivered. Work that one out if you can!)

Wally got his name 'Grizzly' from his growling, gravel-voiced appeal, and we heard quite a lot of that. I've forgotten who first told him he sounded like a grizzly bear but the name stuck.

That liking for the practical joke rebounded once and I remember the occasion well, but not exactly with a smile. I played forward and missed, but my foot hadn't left the ground so there should have been no trouble. Wally, however, swept the ball round and took off the bails, shouting an appeal but in the same breath muttering to me 'It's all right, F.S. Just keeping 'em all on their toes.' To my astonishment and 'Grizzly's' horror the square-leg umpire put his finger up and I had to go.

Wally was really upset. He said, 'Hell, I'm sorry, F.S. I was only kidding and I'll never do that again.'

But he was a great 'keeper and not the world's worst bat, either. His hey-day was in the late fifties and early sixties—three victims in the first innings at Lords in 1961, five in the second; six catches in an innings against South Africa at Johannesburg in 1957–58; a total of 144 victims in only 39 Tests, which puts him way ahead of any Australian rival.

Yet if you ask any world-class cricketer to talk about Wally Grout I am

pretty sure you will find he is remembered just as much for his personality and his sense of humour. To achieve that sort of distinction you have to be at the top long enough to *be* remembered.

Arthur Theodore Wallace Grout (1927–1968)

Queensland 1946–66.
Australia in Australia 1958–59, 1960–61, 1962–63, 1963–64, 1965–66; in England 1961, 1964; in South Africa 1957–58; in India 1959–60, 1964–65; in Pakistan 1959–60, 1964–65; in West Indies 1964–65.

Test Record

	Ins	*NO*	*HS*	*Runs*	*Av.*
Batting	67	8	74	890	15·09
Highest score	74 v. England (Melbourne) 1958–59				
Matches	51				
Wicket-keeping	Ct 163, st. 24—total 187				

Career Figures

	Ins	*NO*	*HS*	*Runs*	*Av.*	*100s*
Batting	253	24	119	5,167	22·56	4
Wicket-keeping	Ct 472, st. 114—total 586					

An outstanding wicketkeeper, with high success ratio of over three victims per Test. Three times took 20 or more wickets in a series. Shares record for most dismissals in Test innings: six. Twice took eight in a match. Game batsman. His premature death was widely lamented.

Wesley Hall

Wes Hall was one of the greatest fast bowlers of all time and possibly *the* greatest the West Indies have produced.

In 1957 I was considerably more impressed by the tall, strong young man I encountered for the first time than some of my colleagues. Perhaps it was that he seemed a bit like me at that time. He had a beautifully balanced, rhythmical run-up and a good delivery-action, and my impressions were certainly confirmed on our 1959–60 tour, when he bowled as quick as anyone I have ever seen. In the Third Test, at Kingston, one or two people who hadn't thought much of him up to that point began to think again, as he took seven for 69 in the first innings.

In the last Test, however, at Trinidad, I noticed for the first time, the terrible state of his boots. One was tied up, round the sole, with a piece of string-like bandage, and both of them looked as though they were likely to fall to pieces at any minute. After the day's play I had a word with him and told him that the fast bowler's two most vital pieces of equipment were his feet and his legs, and urged him to look after them by getting some better boots. So intent was Wes in getting a place in the West Indies side that he had been bowling with blistered feet.

Well, I may have done a disservice to some English batsmen by offering that advice, but I prefer to think it enriched the story of cricket as a whole because there are few better sights than a great fast bowler in full cry.

Despite his ferocity as a bowler, Wes was a really jovial type who loved a story. He was a non-drinker and non-smoker—and like all fast bowlers he took pride in his batting.

The only time I saw him really shattered was at Lord's in 1963 when he got half-way down that long gliding run and then glanced up to see Brian Close advancing yards down the pitch to meet him. He was so startled he tried to pull up and hurt his back and it took all the persuasiveness of his skipper, Frankie Worrell, to convince him that he hadn't seen a vision. A batsman really had had the nerve to walk out to meet him!

In Australia he once damaged himself in another unusual way. Wes wore a medallion round his neck on a chain, and this bounced up, hit him in the eye and caused a hold-up there for running repairs.

But for me, the sight of him snaking in on that beautifully-athletic run when his rhythm was right (which wasn't *always*), remains one of my treasured cricketing memories.

Wesley Winfield Hall (1937–   )

Barbados 1955–67, 1971; Trinidad 1968–70; Queensland 1961–63.
West Indies in West Indies 1959–60, 1961–62, 1964–65, 1967–68; in England 1963, 1966; in Australia 1960–61, 1968–69; in India 1958–59, 1966–67; in Pakistan 1958–59; in New Zealand 1968–69.

Test Record

	Ins	NO	HS	Runs	Av.
Batting	66	14	50*	818	15·73
Highest score	50 not out v. India (Port of Spain) 1961–62				
Matches	48				
Bowling	192 wickets at 26·38				
Best bowling	7 for 69 v. England (Kingston) 1959–60				

Career Figures (to 1969)

	Ins	NO	HS	Runs	Av.
Batting	210	38	102*	2,635	15·31
Bowling	529 wickets at 26·22				

Fast bowler in the classical line: tall, well-built, endowed with amazing reserves of stamina, accurate, hostile, yet a generous opponent. Hero of several Tests of the early 'sixties. Ambitious hitter with the bat: brought humour to the crease.

Neil Harvey

This dapper little left-hander was possibly Australia's best post-war batsman, if you count Bradman as being primarily a pre-war player.

Neil Harvey burst on the Test scene, as far as England was concerned, in the fourth Test of 1948 at Headingley, when he went in with the scoreboard reading 68–3, with Morris, Hassett and Bradman out. He scored 112 and featured in century partnerships with Keith Miller, then Sam Loxton, and we all knew that a new Australian star had been born.

He went on to play in 78 more Tests, hit 21 hundreds, another 24 fifties and held 62 catches. Not only was he Australia's second heaviest scorer of all time, he was possibly the best cover point fieldsman who ever played Test cricket. Certainly he was the best that I saw and everyone who saw him at Headingley on that Test debut still talks about a running catch in the deep which he picked off his boot-laces. In later years he became a most accomplished slipper and began to pile up that impressive total of 62 Test catches, but I feel sure that it is as an out-fieldsman that he is best remembered.

Watching him play the drive you got the impression that he was not imparting any particularly great power. It was only when you noticed how the field was left standing that you realized the real power of his timing and stroke-making. He was never afraid to go down the wicket to spinners and drive, even on a turner, past mid-on and mid-off.

The best Test 100 I saw him play was at Melbourne in the Second Test over New Year, 1958–59—167 out of 308. I watched amazed at the ferocity of some of his driving past the bowler and I was rather glad that I was sitting that one out, in the stands.

Only once did I ever see him ruffled, and that was when I hit him in the ribs at Lord's in 1961. He picked up the bat with a threatening gesture as though he was going to crown me with it, but I like to think that was an instinctive reaction to being hurt for a moment and that there was no real threat.

When he retired, in Australia, he got together all his kit and equipment —and gave them all away. I suppose that was his own gesture of finally accepting the fact we all have to face at some time . . . that we have come to the end of the road. It's never easy and it's never pleasant, but it has to be faced.

For myself, I shall always remember Neil Harvey as a great player and a great competitor.

Robert Neil Harvey, M.B.E. (1928–)

Victoria 1946–57; New South Wales 1958–63.
Australia in Australia 1947–48, 1950–51, 1951–52, 1952–53, 1954–55, 1958–59, 1960–61, 1962–63; in England 1948, 1953, 1956, 1961; in South Africa 1949–50, 1957–58; in West Indies 1954–55; in India 1956–57, 1959–60; in Pakistan 1956–57, 1959–60.

Test Record

	Ins	*NO*	*HS*	*Runs*	*Av.*	*100s*
Batting	137	10	205	6,149	48·41	21
Highest score	205 v. South Africa (Melbourne) 1952–53					
Matches	79					
Bowling	3 wickets at 40·00					

Career Figures

	Ins	*NO*	*HS*	*Runs*	*Av.*	*100s*
Batting	461	35	231*	21,699	50·93	67
1,000 runs in a season	8 times					

Small, compact left-hander, second to Sir Donald Bradman in Test aggregate and number of centuries. Played in more Tests than any other Australian to date. Debut at 19. Lovely footwork, crisp with his strokes, particularly the cut. Magnificent fieldsman. Now a Test selector.

Len Hutton

On *all* types of wickets Len Hutton was, I think, the greatest batsman I have ever seen; on bad wickets, he was most certainly the greatest in my lifetime.

His secret, I think, was his perfect balance. The hallmark of a class batsman is, first and foremost, the time he has to play his shots. Len seemed always to have all the time in the world. He could change his mind twice and then play his third-choice stroke perfectly. And the secret was . . . balance. You simply could not get him out of position, or (looking at it from the bowler's point of view) into a position where *you* had an advantage. A fast bowler who moves the ball in the air tries to *turn* a batsman from his side-on stance, so that his balance is, if not destroyed, affected to his disadvantage, shall we say. It was just about impossible to do this with Hutton.

The greatest innings I ever saw from him was at The Oval, on a rain-affected wicket against Laker and Lock. I think we wanted less than 100 to win but in those conditions, against those two, there seemed no way we could get them. But Leonard scored 70-odd and we won a match it was impossible for us *to* win.

One shot by him—in another game altogether—will stay in my memory as long as I live. It was a six over square cover off Les Jackson at Bradford. 'Jacko'—now there must be the most under-rated seam bowler of all time—every batsman who ever faced him was worried, and if there was the least bit of green in the wicket, more than worried. Well, Bradford Park Avenue in those days always had a bit of green, but this shot of Len's was a deliberately-executed one hitting the ball on the up. Now that was something Len didn't do very often! it was the cover drive—the classical shot along the carpet—which was the shot for which almost everyone remembers him. But this one, this six, was the stroke that this particular ball and these particular conditions, demanded and I don't suppose there have been more than half-a-dozen players in the history of cricket who would have played it. Certainly not off Les Jackson. Certainly not off Les Jackson at Park Avenue. It was a master stroke from a master batsman.

I was once hit for six over point myself, though it wasn't exactly by a master batsman. The man who nearly sent me off the deep end by doing it was Bomber Wells. He was treading on the square-leg umpire's toes at the time and he just caught it with the top edge of the very end of his bat.

Leonard didn't quite play the shot the same way, and Les Jackson didn't say to him what I said to the Bomber. But he was killing himself laughing so much at the time that I don't suppose he heard.

But to get back to Len Hutton and the orthodox cover drive, I've seen him hit a four past cover's left hand so hard (yet without any apparent effort) that the fieldsman never moved to a ball which passed within a yard of him. Then, when the captain moved the fieldsman fractionally, Len would hit one past his other hand.

The first 50 I ever made would probably never have happened but for him. They took the new ball soon after I went in and until the shine had gone I might just as well have sat in the stands. Leonard took one or three off the fifth or last ball until I was well and truly 'in'.

Len Hutton was a batsman whose bat had no edges.

Sir Leonard Hutton (1916–   )

Yorkshire 1934–55.
England in England 1937–54 (captain 1952–54); in Australia 1946–47, 1950–51, 1954–55 (captain); in South Africa 1938–39, 1948–49; in West Indies 1947–48, 1953–54 (captain); in New Zealand 1950–51, 1954–55 (captain).

Test Record

	Ins	NO	HS	Runs	Av.	100s
Batting	138	15	364	6,971	56·67	19
Highest score	364 v. Australia (Oval) 1938					
Matches	79					

Career Figures

	Ins	NO	HS	Runs	Av.	100s
Batting	814	91	364	40,140	55·51	129
1,000 runs in a season	17 times (5 overseas)					

Main pillar of England batting throughout post-war years. Left arm handicapped after accident during war made task against the likes of Lindwall and Miller no easier. Immaculate style, with the cover drive the *pièce de résistance*. His 364 has been exceeded only by Sobers in all Test cricket. His tight, attritional leadership brought England long-awaited victories. Knighted in 1956. Became Test selector in 1976.

Jim Laker

I sometimes used to wonder, in Jim's playing days, if he realized just how great a bowler he was. Certainly he didn't always look as though he believed in his own ability. Then would come one of those days—the conditions would be right, he'd *feel* right, things would be going right—and then nobody could live with him.

When that happened, and he was really spinning the ball, you could actually hear his fingers click as he delivered. He really was a prodigious finger-spinner—possibly the greatest off-spinner of my time—and, remember, that time has seen Lance Gibbs, Hugh Tayfield, Athol Rowan, Ian Johnson, Prasanna and Venkataraghavan.

Jim Laker was born a Yorkshireman and I've often wondered how he slipped through the net because he played as a young man in the Bradford League which, for so many years, has produced an endless line of great Yorkshire cricketers.

If Jim Laker had been playing for his native county, instead of for Surrey in the fifties they wouldn't have won so many championships and we would have won a few more.

I suppose everyone will remember him for all time for his 19–90 against Australia at Old Trafford in 1956. I don't particularly like to recall the match because I was 12th man and that wasn't a role I enjoyed very much. But I've heard people who like to make the right sort of noises say how much Jim owed to Tony Lock, who bowled 55 overs at the other end while Laker was taking all ten in the second innings. That's an absolute load of codswallop, for want of a better word. Lock bowled badly, which means he missed the boat completely on the sort of wicket spinners dream about when they have dined well, or else Laker bowled even more superbly than ten for 53 indicates. You can't really bowl much better than that, can you?

Jim had one or two other interesting analyses, too. Do you remember his eight for two at the so-called Test Trial at Bradford Park Avenue? Some trial. . . .

I remember it with a bit of affection because I got one of those two runs he conceded—from a cover drive, too! And that day brought one of those classic pieces of the driest Laker humour. At the end of the innings there was a bit of a Press conference and the *Daily Express* reporter asked: 'Is this your best performance?'

Jim looked at him for a minute or two, then replied: 'Well, I haven't

done it right often.'

And let's not forget that Jim Laker was a better-than-average lower order batsman and by no means the worst gully fielder of his day.

James Charles Laker (1922–   )

Surrey 1946–59; Essex 1962–65.
England in England 1948 to 1958; in Australia 1958–59; in South Africa 1956–57; in West Indies 1947–48, 1953–54.

Test Record

	Ins	NO	HS	Runs	Av.
Batting	63	15	63	676	14·08

Highest score   63 v. Australia (Trent Bridge) 1948
Matches   46
Bowling   193 wickets at 21·23
Best bowling   10 for 53 (19 for 90 in match) v. Australia (Old Trafford) 1956

Career Figures

	Ins	NO	HS	Runs	Av.	100s
Batting	546	108	113	7,298	16·66	2

Bowling   1,944 wickets at 18·40
100 wickets in a season   11 times

Probably the greatest-ever off-spin bowler, capable of abnormal degree of spin and bounce from high action. Took 8 for 2 in 1950 Test trial at Bradford (his birthplace), and all ten in an innings for Surrey against the Australians six years later. His performance in the 1956 Manchester Test is unrivalled in first-class cricket. Now a BBC television commentator.

Ray Lindwall

If J. S. Bach had seen Ray Lindwall run up to bowl he would have re-written one of his Brandenberg Concertos—or perhaps started an entirely new composition to match the perfect mathematical rhythm of that approach.

Lindwall has got to be the greatest fast bowler of them all, certainly in my time. Now I can say this without any fear of a come-back suggesting that this is part of the old pals act because I never got to know Lindwall well at all. He didn't seem to like me very much. He didn't like Len Hutton either while they were playing, though they are pretty good pals now, playing golf together when he's over here and whenever Len visits Australia.

But it was quite different when they were playing because, I suppose, Lindwall was the prototype Australian fast bowler. He hated all batsmen, and he hated English batsmen most of all.

There was no particular reason why he should dislike me. I hadn't developed my batting when I first encountered him, in 1953! But I suppose his attitude shows why the Australians are the greatest competitors on earth—at just about every game they play.

Lindwall was a great fast bowler with a medium-pacer's accuracy. The first time I saw him I marvelled at his incredibly smooth approach and the absolute control he had over his deliveries. He troubled every batsman who ever faced him, and that is the hallmark of greatness in this particular field.

He finished his Test career with 228 wickets at 23.05 each. Whether he could have achieved that if he had been bowling six days a week, 1,000 overs a season in England, we'll never know.

That was the killer—the English season as it used to be—the Daddy of them all. But we've got to judge Lindwall in the context in which he played and there's no doubt in my mind—he was the greatest.

Like all great bowlers, he was always learning, always trying to develop something new on top of the card-index of batsmen's strengths and weaknesses which he carried in his head.

He bowled a magnificent late outswinger when he came here in 1948. That was his chief weapon, along with a beautifully disguised change of pace. And when he let one go it was a very fast ball.

He took eight wickets in the Second Test of that series, at Lord's, and another five at Old Trafford and four at Headingley. But do you remember

the Final Test, at The Oval? England all out 52. Lindwall six for 20. Len Hutton, last man out for 30 of those 52 to a wonderful flying catch by Don Tallon. Then Don Bradman bowled by Eric Hollies, second ball, for nought on his final Test appearance in this country. And England all out 188 in the second innings (Lindwall 3-50) to lose by an innings and 149 runs. D'you remember?

After that Lindwall was contracted to play in the Lancashire League and in the first half of the season he took 30-odd wickets, and calculated that he had nearly 100 catches dropped in the slips. The ball came just too fast for the average League fieldsman. So he developed the in-swinger, which up to that time he didn't bowl, and in particular the in-swinging yorker.

My word—then he really was the greatest!

Raymond Russell Lindwall, M.B.E. (1921–)

New South Wales 1945–54; Queensland 1954–60 (captain 1955–60). Australia in Australia 1946–47, 1947–48, 1950–51, 1951–52, 1952–53, 1954–55, 1958–59; in England 1948, 1953, 1956; in South Africa 1949–50; in West Indies 1954–55; in New Zealand 1945–46; in India 1956–57, 1959–60; in Pakistan 1956–57, 1959–60.

Test Record

	Ins	NO	HS	Runs	Av.	100s
Batting	84	13	118	1,502	21·15	2
Highest score	118 v. West Indies (Bridgetown) 1954–55					
Matches	61					
Bowling	228 wickets at 23·05					
Best bowling	7 for 38 v. India (Adelaide) 1947–48					

Career Figures

	Ins	NO	HS	Runs	Av.	100s
Batting	268	39	134*	5,017	21·90	5
Bowling	794 wickets at 21·33					

Though less than six feet tall, the *beau ideal* of a fast bowler. Rhythmic run-up, building momentum, and smooth gyratory action with back-foot drag and comparatively low arm. Master of all the variations of swing, cut and pace. Powerful lower-order batsman.

Peter May

P. B. H. May was probably the best *amateur* captain I played under in international cricket and this may have been because he learned his trade at Surrey under Stuart Surridge, and with England under Len Hutton— the two toughest and most determined captains, amateur and professional, in the game at that time.

Peter May was a thinker about the game; he was a skipper who knew how to get the best out of his players; he could be absolutely ruthless in his determination to win. He had a kind of boyish appearance which fooled a lot of people and completely belied his real character. He was tough, really tough, and he always wanted to win. He would give you a pat on the back for doing your stuff well, but he had no qualms about handing out a public rollicking to anyone who was turning in a sub-standard performance.

But in the middle of all this he had a sense of humour. Once, on a very hot day in Jamaica, 'George' Statham for once hadn't bowled as well as he normally did and P.B.H. wanted a break-through—and he wanted it badly. He came over to me with the ball and said, 'Come on, Fred. England expects . . .' I said, 'Really, skipper. Is that why she is called "the Mother Country".' He didn't reply, but he walked away creasing himself, laughing. But I knocked out the first four wickets, and even though we didn't win—the match was drawn—I felt I had responded fairly well.

As a batsman, Peter May came nearer than any of the young, post-war batsmen to the greatness of Hutton and Hammond. The on-drive was, perhaps, the shot for which we remember him best; it is one of the most difficult shots to play well and Peter played it with power and precision— *tremendous* power and precision.

It was something of a tragedy that Peter retired so early from first-class cricket. He had scored 85 centuries and he had the quality and the class to go on to reach somewhere around the 150 mark.

He will perhaps be best-remembered for his share, with Colin Cowdrey, of the stand of 411 at Edgbaston in 1957, in which Peter scored 285 not out. We had all booked out of our hotel on the Monday morning, resigned to defeat, and we all had to book back in again as the two of them mastered Sonny Ramadhin. He had taken seven for 49 in the first innings, when we were all out for 186. West Indies scored 474, and we were 113 for three when Peter and Colin came together.

We nearly won that game.

The only time I have ever known Peter May be record-conscious was two years later in Barbados. Gary Sobers and Frankie Worrell were getting close to that 411—they had scored 399 in fact—and Peter very badly wanted them to miss it. He said as much when he gave me the ball and asked me to give it a bit extra, and I'm glad to say I obliged by knocking Gary's middle stump out.

Peter Barker Howard May (1929–   )

Cambridge University 1950–52; Surrey 1950–63 (captain 1957–62).
England in England 1951 to 1959, 1961 (captain 1955 to 1959, 1961); in Australia 1954–55, 1958–59 (captain); in South Africa 1956–57 (captain); in West Indies 1953–54, 1959–60 (captain); in New Zealand 1954–55, 1958–59 (captain).

Test Record

	Ins	*NO*	*HS*	*Runs*	*Av.*	*100s*
Batting	106	9	285*	4,537	46·77	13
Highest score	285 not out v. West Indies (Edgbaston) 1957					
Matches	66					

Career Figures

	Ins	*NO*	*HS*	*Runs*	*Av.*	*100s*
Batting	618	77	285*	27,592	51·00	85
1,000 runs in a season	14 times (3 overseas)					

Glorious driver of the ball, commanding in almost every kind of situation. Captained England in 41 Tests—a world record—35 consecutively. Successor to Hutton as England captain, with same tight approach. Led Surrey to sixth and seventh successive County Championships in 1950s.

Keith Miller

Keith Miller was another of those instinctive geniuses which cricket throws up from time to time—a player of apparently boundless natural ability.

He could look a perfectly ordinary bowler and then, for no reason which anyone else could put his finger on, suddenly, spectacularly, be transformed into one of true greatness.

Without doubt he was Australia's most colourful and flamboyant post-war cricketer and it is probable that he never really produced the figures which his unbelievable ability suggested he should have.

He was above all an entertainer. He played all his cricket in the firm belief that his job *was* to entertain and he passionately loved the limelight. He liked to be admired and he had much that was admirable. Apart from his greatness as a player he had the good looks of a film star, and he has lived his life in much the same way as one of the Hollywood stars of pre-war films.

As a bowler he had a superb action and could be distinctly quick. It has been said that he could, and did, bowl six entirely different deliveries in an over—an out-swinger, an in-swinger, off-spinner, leg-spinner, bouncer and googly. In Australia, with an eight-ball over, I am prepared to believe he would throw in two more! In an M.C.C. match at Lord's he bowled David Sheppard (now Bishop of Liverpool) with a googly using the new ball!

As a fieldsman he would stand at first slip looking as though his thoughts were twenty miles away. No doubt they were, especially if there was a race meeting in the vicinity. But the next minute, there he would be—bringing off the most blinding catch off the fastest of bowling. Remember, he would probably be fielding to Lindwall.

As a batsman he played every shot except, possibly, the hook, and it may be that the opportunity to play that didn't arise very often. After all, not many bowlers would risk pitching short to him when they weighed up his ability to retaliate.

But above all else, he harnessed and directed his abilities to being an entertainer, a showman. On his final appearance at Lord's he took five wickets in the first innings, another five in the second. Australia won by 185 runs and I can see him now, walking back to the Lord's pavilion for the last time and nonchalantly tossing the bails into the crowd of Members with a great, broad grin on his face.

It was always a pleasure to play against him because you knew that sooner or later something spectacular would happen. One way or another, he was always right in the middle of the action—as batsman, bowler or fielder.

He was always known as 'Nugget'. I never knew why but, on reflection, it must have been because he had the golden touch at just about everything he did.

Keith Ross Miller, M.B.E. (1919–   )

Victoria 1937–41; New South Wales 1946–56 (captain).
Australia in Australia 1946–47, 1947–48, 1950–51, 1951–52, 1952–53, 1954–55; in England 1948, 1953, 1956; in South Africa 1949–50; in West Indies 1954–55; in New Zealand 1945–46; in Pakistan 1956–57.

Test Record

	Ins	NO	HS	Runs	Av.	100s
Batting	87	7	147	2,958	36·97	7
Highest score	147 v. West Indies (Kingston) 1954–55					
Matches	55					
Bowling	170 wickets at 22·97					
Best bowling	7 for 60 v. England (Brisbane) 1946–47					

Career Figures

	Ins	NO	HS	Runs	Av.	100s
Batting	326	36	281*	14,183	48·90	41
1,000 runs in a season	4 times (2 overseas)					
Bowling	497 wickets at 22·29					

Dynamic and debonair cricketer, impulsive, unpredictable. Capable of classical batsmanship and bowling of astonishing variety or matchless hostility. Thrilling slip fieldsman. Always the entertainer.

John Reid

John Reid was a barrel-chested, slightly bowlegged man of immense power who *hit* the ball tremendously hard.

He first appeared in England as second wicket-keeper, in 1949, but later in his career had to develop his bowling to help out an attack which was not very often capable of bowling out the opposition, certainly not in Tests. This was as well as having to hold together the batting.

But at least this all-round development came in useful in another sphere because when John came to England to play in the Central Lancashire League he became one of the most popular and, indeed, one of the most successful, professionals the League has ever had. He accomplished the 'double' of 1,000 runs and 100 wickets and in a League season that takes some doing.

Like so many New Zealanders I have met, he was a charming man of great diplomacy and he never moaned about the inadequacies of some of the sides he skippered. I remember talking to Colin Cowdrey once in New Zealand and he said, 'I know how John feels. I've some experience of what it's like to captain a poor side.'

In 58 Tests John Reid scored 3,431 runs, with six centuries, and he took 85 Test wickets, and while he had to play many dogged, last-ditch innings for the sake of his side at international level, he was always a batsman who liked to give the ball a tremendous clout.

He is remembered with an affection and reverence bordering on awe in South-east Lancashire for his six-hitting. In New Zealand, too, he once hit 15 sixes in an innings for Wellington against Northern Districts.

He was, in fact, one of the most powerful-looking men I have played against (the first time I saw him with his shirt off I thought he had a black sheepskin rug around his chest!), but he was kindly and he was thoughtful. When I took my 100th Test wicket at Christchurch in 1959 it was John Reid who took the ball away, had it mounted, and presented it to me that evening.

John Richard Reid, O.B.E. (1928–   )

Wellington 1947–65 (captain 1951–65), apart from 1956–58 (Otago).
New Zealand in New Zealand 1950–51, 1951–52, 1952–53, 1954–55, 1955–56
(captain), 1958–59 (captain), 1962–63 (captain), 1963–64 (captain), 1964–65
(captain); in England 1949, 1958 (captain), 1965 (captain); in South Africa
1953–54, 1961–62 (captain); in India 1955–56, 1964–65 (captain); in
Pakistan 1955–56, 1964–65 (captain).

Test Record

	Ins	NO	HS	Runs	Av.	100s
Batting	108	5	142	3,431	33·31	6
Highest score	142 v. South Africa (Johannesburg) 1961–62					
Matches	58					
Bowling	85 wickets at 33·41					
Best bowling	6 for 60 v. South Africa (Dunedin) 1963–64					

Career Figures

	Ins	NO	HS	Runs	Av.	100s
Batting	418	28	296	16,128	41·35	39
Bowling	466 wickets at 22·60					

Versatile cricketer, doughty fighter, frequent saver of lost causes. Led
New Zealand to their first Test victory (1955–56). His 15 sixes in 296
(Wellington v. Northern Districts, 1962–63) was world record.

Gary Sobers

Genius. It's an over-worked word and it is too often used in talking about people who don't deserve it. But in the case of Gary Sobers there can't be any argument about it. He must be the greatest instinctive genius, with bat or ball, there has ever been.

Certainly he was the most *complete* all-rounder. Dazzling, mercurial, explosive batsman; new ball bowler with genuine pace and movement and the built-in natural advantage of being a left-armer; orthodox slow left-armer who could really spin it; purveyor of *un*orthodox SLA when the occasion demanded it; fielder extraordinary who pounced on slip catches with the speed of a panther or who streaked about the outfield like greased lightning.

On a good wicket he was one of the few batsmen who would score a century *at will*—if he wanted to. There, perhaps, is the flaw in the gem. At least it was a flaw when he played in the County Championship in this country. In English conditions and competitions you simply cannot play the sort of innings you want and when you want. There are disciplines to be observed, conventions to be followed and it was simply not in Gary's nature to do this.

I suppose (if he will forgive the analogy) it was rather like taking a magnificent, rare animal out of its natural surroundings and caging it up and still expecting it to be as fascinating and exciting.

Like so many of his countrymen, Sobers was a player of instinct. But I would have hated to be his captain at a time of crisis, when I desperately needed him to get his head down and graft. He would have wanted to do his best for me because he was that type of great sportsman. But he just wouldn't have known how.

Yet I have known his sheer brilliance draw from him an innings which for me ranks among the greatest I have seen—and it wasn't a score of 300, or 200, or even 100.

It was in the match which England won by an innings and 237 runs at The Oval in 1957. The West Indies scored 89 and 86 and of that 86 young Garfield St Aubrun Sobers made 42.

I had seen him play at home in 1953–54 when he batted at No. 9 in the last Test. He had scored 14 not out and 26, took four for 75 in our first innings and just bowled one over in the second before we won by nine wickets. He was then a slow left-arm bowler who batted a bit and—let me be quite frank about it—no one would have convinced me at that time

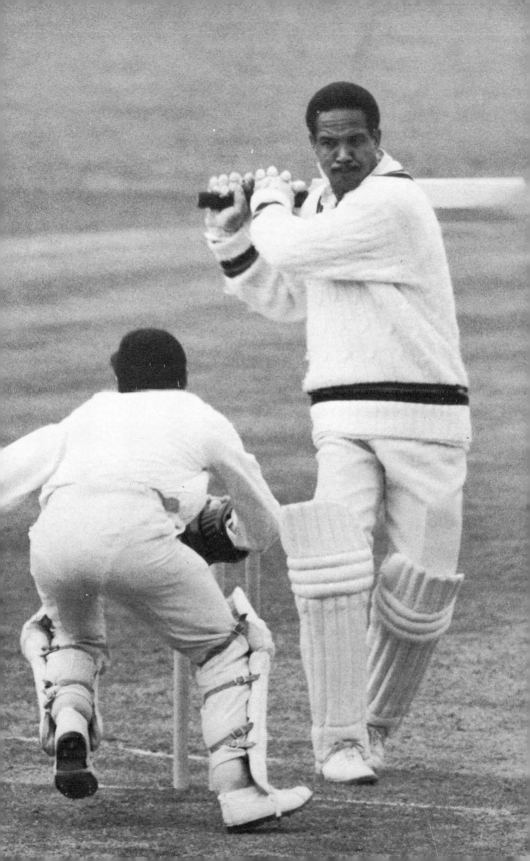

that here was a great player of the future.

That innings at The Oval three years later *did* convince me.

Sir Garfield St Aubrun Sobers (1936–   )

Barbados 1952–74; South Australia 1961–64; Nottinghamshire 1968–74.
West Indies in West Indies 1953–54, 1954–55, 1957–58, 1959–60, 1961–62,
1965–66 (captain), 1967–68 (captain), 1970–71 (captain), 1971–72 (captain),
1973–74; in England 1957, 1963, 1966 (captain), 1969 (captain), 1973; in
Australia 1960–61, 1968–69 (captain); in New Zealand 1955–56, 1968–69
(captain); in India 1958–59, 1966–67 (captain); in Pakistan 1958–59.

Test Record

	Ins	NO	HS	Runs	Av.	100s
Batting	160	21	365*	8,032	57·78	26
Highest score	365 not out v. Pakistan (Kingston) 1957–58					
Matches	93					
Bowling	235 wickets at 34·03					
Best bowling	6 for 73 v. Australia (Brisbane) 1968–69					
Catches	109					

Career Figures

	Ins	NO	HS	Runs	Av.	100s
Batting	609	93	365*	28,315	54·87	86
Bowling	1.043 wickets at 27·74					
Catches	406					

Widely regarded as the greatest all-round cricketer ever. World record
Test score; most Test runs; most consecutive appearances (85); un-
approached set of performance figures, all achieved with lithe grace and
demonstrable sportsmanship. Only player to hit all six balls of an over for
six (Notts v. Glamorgan, Swansea, 1968). Left-handed, his bowling was
fast, orthodox slow, or wrist-spin, as situation demanded. Panther-like
fieldsman. Knighted in 1975.

Brian Statham

Brian Statham is known to all cricketers as 'George', for a rather odd reason. Apparently, someone in the Lancashire side had always been called 'George' and when Winston Place, the current holder of the title, retired, Brian said, 'Right, I'm taking over the title.' And he's been George ever since. He even calls his house near Stockport, 'George's'.

He was also referred to, during his playing career, as 'The Greyhound' because of the sleek, slim build which never lost its shape and, from the look of him when we played golf recently, never will.

He was a great bowler on all wickets and was very quickly thrust into international cricket. In fact when he was flown out to Australia to join the 1950–51 tour party, he had never even seen Lord's cricket ground!

'George' relied on pin-point accuracy and an ability to make the ball come in off the seam. If the ball was swinging away in the air he couldn't control his deliveries, for some reason or other, and I have known him ask to be taken off. He didn't have no-balling troubles, because he never dragged his back foot—except when he was bowling in the nets!

We made a great pair because there was always something about the one or the other of us that most batsmen disliked. They would try to get away from one of us, to the other end, and if they then allowed themselves a feeling of complacency, we had an extra chance to strike.

'George' had a modest, diffident approach to cricket as, indeed, he has always had to life. I sometimes used to think he would have been just as happy at home having a game of tennis or football in the park as playing in a Test Match abroad. He wasn't a bad footballer either and interested Manchester United at one time.

But over the years we had a lot of fun together and sank a beer or two. I remember once, in British Guiana (as it then was) we went to the pictures with some other players and were a bit amused to find a girl walking round the cinema with the programmes-chocolates-cigarettes routine. So for a laugh we said, 'No thanks, beers would be a bit more welcome, love.'

She disappeared and we thought no more about it until she returned with a tray of bottles of ice-cold ale. Well, this was a bit of a novelty so we kept it up.

I've never come out of the pictures feeling so gay!

George now works in the trade so I've no doubt he remembers that occasion from time to time.

John Brian Statham, C.B.E. (1930–   )

Lancashire 1950–68.
England in England 1951, 1953 to 1963, 1965; in Australia 1954–55, 1958–59, 1962–63; in South Africa 1956–57; in New Zealand 1950–51, 1954–55; in West Indies 1953–54, 1959–60; in India 1951–52.

Test Record

	Ins	NO	HS	Runs	Av.
Batting	87	28	38	675	11·44
Matches	70				
Bowling	252 wickets at 24·84				
Best bowling	7 for 39 v. South Africa (Lord's) 1955				

Career Figures

	Ins	NO	HS	Runs	Av.
Batting	647	145	62	5,424	10·80
Bowling	2,260 wickets at 16·36				
100 wickets in a season	13 times				
Catches	230				

Supple, double-jointed, even-tempered fast bowler renowned for extraordinary accuracy and movement off the seam. Ideal partner for the more overtly hostile Trueman and Tyson, often taking the upwind end. Fine outfielder.

Bert Sutcliffe

The fair-haired, slightly built New Zealander was perhaps the most technically correct batsman his country has ever produced. He was also one of the nicest fellows I have ever met in world cricket.

His main asset as a run-maker was his ability to place the ball with precision through the gaps in the field, but he was a stroke-player of elegance and grace and charm.

Like all top-class openers he was nimble, with brilliant footwork, and it was perhaps unfortunate for him that he played for New Zealand when they were something of a Cinderella amongst Test-playing countries. It is never as easy to score runs in a struggling side, no matter how great one's ability, as with one which has a fair complement of class performers. One of the nicest things to happen to world cricket in the past ten years in fact has been the emergence of New Zealand, but in Bert Sutcliffe's day there just weren't enough really good players to keep him company.

Nevertheless, he contrived to score 2,727 runs in his 42 Tests, with an average of 40.96, and I never once heard him grumble about a shortage of partners to enable him to play more long innings. He just loved playing cricket.

Since I have retired, I go to New Zealand from time to time and Bert Sutcliffe is the first man I look forward to meeting and having a few beers with.

England had their first glimpse of Bert Sutcliffe on the 1949 New Zealand tour to this country. It was an interesting tour in many ways. Alan Wharton got his one and only England cap at Headingley, Brian Close became England's youngest Test player at Old Trafford—as a seam-bowler who batted—and Bert Sutcliffe charmed us for the first time with 32 and 82 at Headingley, 57 at Lord's, 9 and 101 at Old Trafford, 88 and 54 at The Oval—a pretty fair start to a Test career.

He welcomed England to New Zealand in 1951 with 116 at Christchurch, and four years later had the distinction of being the only batsman to score double figures when Appleyard, Tyson and Statham rolled over New Zealand for 26 in the Second Test at Auckland.

Well, I suppose Bert will look back on that as living through a special bit of Test cricket history.

The latter part of his career was overshadowed by injuries and I was responsible for one of them. I remember hitting him at Edgbaston, and never have I felt more sorry about anything in cricket.

Bert Sutcliffe (1923–)

Auckland 1942–49; Otago 1946–62; Northern Districts 1962–66.
New Zealand in New Zealand 1946–47, 1950–51, 1951–52 (captain), 1952–53, 1954–55, 1955–56, 1958–59; in England 1949, 1958, 1965; in South Africa 1953–54 (captain); in India 1955–56, 1965–66; in Pakistan 1955–56, 1965–66.

Test Record

	Ins	NO	HS	Runs	Av.	100s
Batting	76	8	230*	2,727	40·10	5
Highest score	230 not out v. India (New Delhi) 1955–56					
Matches	42					

Career Figures

	Ins	NO	HS	Runs	Av.	100s
Batting	405	39	385	17,283	47·22	44

Cultured strokemaker of conspicuous modesty and incalculable value to New Zealand. His 385 (Otago v. Canterbury, Christchurch, 1952–53) is highest score ever made by a left-hander and followed 355 three years before against Auckland. His 230 not out used to be the highest ever for New Zealand in Test cricket.

Hugh Tayfield

H. J. (Toey) Tayfield took 170 wickets in 37 Tests at better than 26 apiece and that straightaway established him in the front rank of international spin bowlers.

Like most top-class slow bowlers he was not so much a sharp spinner of the ball as a master of line and length. His length, in fact, was absolutely immaculate.

I saw him for the first time when he was flown to England to join the injury stricken South African tour party at Sheffield in 1951. It wasn't the most spectacularly successful initiation into English cricket, because Len Hutton hit him for five fours in an over, but, as far as one could see, he didn't let it worry him. His skipper, Dudley Nourse, kept him on and he settled down to bowl impressively, and in due course to become his country's leading Test wicket-taker.

His field was different from that of any other top off-spinner I ever saw, in that he employed two on-side men about 15 yards away, in front of the wicket. It seemed to work for him because those men took quite a few catches off mis-timed attempts to drive.

He was a thinker about the game and used flight, as well as that immaculate control of length, to out-think the opposition. He is one of the few bowlers to have taken nine wickets in an innings—in the Fourth Test at Johannesburg in 1957. Trevor Goddard nipped in to take the No. 3 batsman, Doug Insole, but 'Toey' removed the rest for 113 runs in 37 overs.

South Africa won by 17 runs after losing the first two Tests and drawing the Third, and it gave them the boost they needed to win the last one and so square the series (Tayfield 6–78 in the second innings at Port Elizabeth).

Tayfield was a great competitor who didn't like to lose, yet he later became one of the world-class players to come to England and play in Lancashire League cricket with a conspicuous lack of success. Somehow he never came to terms with the unpalatable fact that on smaller grounds, with fieldsmen not of Test class, batsmen could afford to ignore the wiles and subtleties which were his stock-in-trade.

But in the wider arenas of international cricket Hugh Tayfield ranks in the very highest echelons.

Hugh Joseph Tayfield (1928–)

Natal 1945–56; Rhodesia 1947–49; Transvaal 1956–63.
South Africa in South Africa 1949–50, 1953–54, 1956–57, 1957–58; in
England 1955, 1960; in Australia 1952–53; in New Zealand 1952–53.

Test Record

	Ins	NO	HS	Runs	Av.
Batting	60	9	75	862	16·90

Highest score   75 v. Australia (Cape Town) 1949–50
Matches   37
Bowling   170 wickets at 25·91
Best bowling   9 for 113 v. England (Johannesburg) 1956–57

Career Figures

	Ins	NO	HS	Runs	Av.
Batting	259	47	77	3,668	17·30

Bowling   864 wickets at 21·86
100 wickets in a season   2 times

With Laker, bestrode a decade as premier off-spin bowler in world. His 170
wickets are most for South Africa in Test cricket. Master of flight. Sobriquet
'Toey' for habit of stubbing toe of boot into ground.

Clyde Walcott

In some ways I suppose it is true to say that Clyde Walcott was the least famous of the three Ws.

That is not to say for one minute that he was not a great batsman.

Yet his record of big innings, the number of spectacular displays of batting, are not quite as high as those of Weekes and Worrell. But believe me, when you had finished with those two and you saw the big feller striding out you couldn't help groaning a bit, 'Oh no. Not the other one.'

Clyde Walcott was quite the hardest hitter off the back foot I have *ever* seen. He didn't stroke the ball; he didn't just belt it; he pulverized it. And when you'd had a long stint at the other two (and it quite often *was* a long one) the last thing you wanted was a mauling from the third W.

One tremendous innings I saw was one I could enjoy a bit more than usual because I was sitting this one out. It was in Barbados in 1954, the Second Test. We'd lost the First and lost the toss in the Second, so, while I *never* liked missing a Test, I thought, Well, at least my feet won't be as sore at the end of today as my room-mate's ('George' Statham).

But Jeff Stollmeyer was run out before he'd scored and Frankie Worrell was bowled by 'George' for a blodger. Everton Weekes was not in that side (he must have been injured), so Clyde Walcott came in at No. 4 with the West Indies 11 for two, and ten minutes later they were 25 for three when Holt was caught off Trevor Bailey. I was beginning to think I had missed out when Clyde got going. He hit 220 out of 383 before he was stumped off Jim Laker, and I honestly don't think I've ever seen ferocious striking of the ball like it. He absolutely mangled the bowling and, really, he had to do so, because you don't often get much of a 'tail' in any West Indies side. In that one, Sonny Ramadhin was at No. 9 so it had to be a long tail!

That innings was a masterpiece of sheer power and exquisite timing. He was an entirely different type from Weekes, yet Everton was his idol. He used to watch the little feller play, and marvel at his artistry.

Like so many great West Indians, Clyde had a spell in the Lancashire League, and while he was with Enfield a rather well-built youngster in the junior side adopted Clyde as *his* idol. That youngster was Jack Simmons, who became the Lancashire all-rounder (I refuse to call him 'off-spinner' because he plays in so much one-day stuff he rarely gets a chance to spin it, and he's played so many useful innings that he must come into the all-rounder category).

As with so many big, powerful men, Clyde was quietly-spoken and affable, qualities which made him such an immensely successful manager of the 1976 tour to England. Tours require much more than a winning, or attractive, side to be wholly successful, and Clyde managed this team with charm and dignity and great good humour.

He has always loved his cricket. He also loved winning, and he did his fair share of that in his time. But he has never forgotten that cricket is a game which commands, most of all, his affection.

Clyde Leopold Walcott, O.B.E. (1926–   )

Barbados 1941–54; British Guiana 1954–64.
West Indies in West Indies 1947–48, 1952–53, 1953–54, 1954–55, 1957–58, 1959–60; in England 1950, 1957; in Australia 1951–52; in New Zealand 1951–52; in India 1948–49.

Test Record

	Ins	NO	HS	Runs	Av.	100s
Batting	74	7	220	3,798	56·68	15

Highest score — 220 v. England (Bridgetown) 1953–54
Matches — 44
Bowling — 11 wickets at 37·09
Fielding — Ct 54, st. 11—total 65
(usually wicket-keeper)

Career Figures

	Ins	NO	HS	Runs	Av.	100s
Batting	238	29	314*	11,820	56·55	40

1,000 runs in a season — 4 times
Bowling — 35 wickets at 36·25

Big, powerful man, especially strong off back foot. Made five centuries in 1954–55 series against Australia, twice scoring a hundred in both innings of the match. His unbroken stand of 574 with Worrell for Barbados' fourth wicket against Trinidad in 1945–46 is the second-highest partnership ever in first-class cricket. Later administrator and manager of West Indies touring teams.

John Wardle

On *all* wickets, Johnny Wardle was the best slow left-arm bowler I ever played with.

He was not a prolific spinner of the ball but his command of line, length and flight won the respect of the greatest players in the world during his career of 28 Tests. These gave him 102 wickets at twenty-odd a piece.

He was a splendidly-entertaining batsman who hit the ball tremendously hard. He loved to hit sixes and most of all he loved to hit them off his arch-rival for the England SLA spot, Tony Lock. As he was a substantially better batsman than Lockie, he usually came out of these duels with a smile.

He made a lot of other people smile, too, because he entertained not only with his big hitting and accurate bowling, but also with little touches of comedy in the field. One of his pet tricks, in the gully position in which he excelled, was to pouch the ball which flashed like lightning towards him, then turn round and look as though it was on its way to the boundary. It wasn't designed to get a crafty run-out, but it used to fool thousands of spectators.

In the second half of his career he became two bowlers in one after developing the Chinaman and googly and I think at the time, especially on good wickets, he was the best bowler of that type I have ever seen. He could go weeks without feeling the necessity to bowl the 'funny stuff'— and then suddenly switch to the Chinaman, drop it straight on a length *and* spin it.

Perhaps the high-spot of his career was the 1956–57 tour of South Africa when he bagged over 100 wickets; and at Cape Town, in the New Year match, he practically won it for England on his own—five for 53 off 23 overs in the first innings, seven for 36 off 19 in the second.

As a bowler alone, I believe he should have played in many more Tests. Certainly he was a great and worthy member of that mighty Yorkshire dynasty of Peel, Rhodes and Verity. As a batsman I feel he could and should have made first-class centuries because he was far from being a slogger of sixes.

In the early and middle fifties, when England's batsmen were often being knocked over by Miller and Lindwall, Johnston and Archer, Heine and Adcock, J. H. Wardle had a pretty fair record of scores in the twenties and thirties, batting at No. 8 and 9.

He loved a laugh and he loved a joke, and though he had, in some quarters, a reputation for bad temper and awkwardness, his bark was always worse than his bite. It was a sad day for me when he left Yorkshire. It is true that he could be difficult when things were going wrong, but it is equally true that he was a magnificent cricketer and I am sure the game lost many brilliant years by his dismissal from Yorkshire when still only in his thirties.

John Henry Wardle (1923–)

Yorkshire 1946–58.
England in England 1950, 1951, 1953 to 1957; in Australia 1954–55; in South Africa 1956–57; in West Indies 1947–48, 1953–54; in New Zealand 1954–55.

Test Record

	Ins	NO	HS	Runs	Av.
Batting	41	8	66	653	19·78
Highest score	66 v. West Indies (Kingston) 1953–54				
Matches	28				
Bowling	102 wickets at 20·39				
Best bowling	7 for 36 v. South Africa (Cape Town) 1956–57				

Career Figures

	Ins	NO	HS	Runs	Av.
Batting	525	71	79	7,318	16·11
Bowling	1846 wickets at 18·97				
100 wickets in a season	10 times				

Clever slow left-arm bowler, orthodox or chinamen/googlies, as conditions and mood demanded. Bold, tail end batsman, lively fieldsman. Dispute with Yorkshire and contentious newspaper articles appearing under his name ended career summarily in 1958. Subsequently played league and minor county cricket.

Everton Weekes

Everton Weekes would *cut* the first ball he received if he felt like it. It wouldn't matter if his side were in the most desperately difficult situation; it wouldn't matter if the text-book said this is a ball you simply mustn't attempt to cut; it wouldn't matter if no other batsman, however great at that particular shot, would even have thought about it. If Everton felt like cutting, he cut.

It was far, far from being his only shot, of course. I'll remember as long as I live seeing him pick me up off the leg stump at Lord's for six. It wasn't a hook; it wasn't a pull. I'd bowled a half-volley and he just simply picked it up and put it over the boundary. Yes, fast bowlers remember cutters and in that department Everton was unforgettable.

Spinners remember them, too, of course. In that stand of 283 with Worrell at Trent Bridge in 1950, Everton showed a couple of leg-spinners what cutting was all about. In those days, when Trent Bridge was an absolute nightmare for bowlers of all kinds, Notts had a leg-spinner called Peter Harvey, and he spent hours pitching 18 inches outside the off stump with sometimes seven men in a line across the covers. Well, maybe Reg Simpson made a suggestion to the skipper, Norman Yardley, on those lines, because the off-side defensive field was so crowded it looked like a bus stop in the rush hour. But it didn't make a blind bit of difference. Everton stepped right across outside the off stump and cut and cut and cut, so that what Yardley needed, really, was nine third men! Hollies 2–134 off 43; Jenkins 1–73 off 13. And *they* certainly remember that day. Weekes actually sent the ball for four to the third man boundary from one pitched *outside his leg stump*.

Everton was a pleasant man and one of great courage. I was talking to him during the Lord's Test in the summer of 1976 about an innings he played there in 1957. The West Indies were trying to avoid an innings defeat after we had bowled them out for 127 and scored 424 ourselves. Weekes changed his gloves three or four times and on one of those occasions I saw blood seeping through. He didn't complain about anything and he didn't go off, and although West Indies lost, he scored 90 really wonderful runs out of their second-innings total of 261. At Lord's I asked him about his fingers, and he admitted that one of them had been broken. He had scored most of those 90 runs with a broken finger and no one ever knew about it.

Everton was not as correct a player as Frank Worrell, but he had an eye

like an eagle and wrists and forearms like tempered steel. He was another in that long line of instinctive geniuses that the West Indies throw at us, seemingly without end and in those splendid Tests of the 1950s you didn't really know whether it was a good thing or a bad one to get one of the Ws out . . . for after Worrell came Weekes, and after Weekes came Walcott, each a great batsman in his own right, each with an individual flair and a distinctive collection of talents.

And if you copped for two of them together on a good wicket . . . well, it became rather hard work.

Everton de Courcy Weekes, O.B.E. (1925–   )

Barbados 1944–64.
West Indies in West Indies 1947–48, 1952–53, 1953–54, 1954–55, 1957–58; in England 1950, 1957; in Australia 1951–52; in New Zealand 1951–52, 1955–56; in India 1948–49.

Test Record

	Ins	NO	HS	Runs	Av.	100s
Batting	81	5	207	4,455	58·61	15
Highest score	207 v. India (Port of Spain) 1952–53					
Matches	48					
Bowling	1 wicket for 77					

Career Figures

	Ins	NO	HS	Runs	Av.	100s
Batting	241	24	304*	12,010	55·34	36
1,000 runs in a season	3 times					
Bowling	17 wickets at 43·00					

Powerful, sprightly, agile batsman with keen eye and extraordinary reflexes. Made five successive hundreds in Tests: 141 v. England (1947–48), 128, 194, 162, 101 (followed by 90) v. India (1948–49). Popular and very successful Lancashire league professional.

Frank Worrell

If Frankie Worrell had captained that magnificent West Indian side of the fifties I believe it would have achieved even more—no, far more than it did. The three Ws, Rae and Stollmeyer, the spin-twins Ramadhin and Valentine—and coming up on the rails Sobers, Kanhai and Collie Smith (what a loss to cricket his tragic death was).

Worrell must be the best captain the West Indies have had, certainly since the war, and I can't think of many outstanding leaders *before* the war. Apart from his own natural ability, he *thought* about the game—far more than most of his countrymen who so often play simply by instinct, treating each ball on its merits at all times and never taking a wider, or a longer-term, view of the tactical state of a game.

I can't really see a West Indian opener, faced with half-an-hour's batting before the end of a day, getting out to a hook-shot and escaping a rebuke from Captain Worrell. Although it would be delivered in that quiet, courteous manner which was Frankie's way, it would still leave no doubt in the batsman's mind that he hadn't played very well *for his side*. That was very important to Frank Worrell—the performance of the team as a whole.

As a batsman he was more technically correct than Everton Weekes, and though he hit the ball hard (as all West Indies batsmen do) he did not show the same savage power in driving as Clyde Walcott. But he was a more complete cricketer than either of them, even setting aside his captaincy.

It is not easy to single out the particularly great innings he played because so much of his batting had the stamp of greatness.

At Trent Bridge, in the Third Test of 1950, he scored 261 and was involved in a stand of 283 with Weekes—and the stroke-play was sensational. But I suppose that has to be judged against its background. Trent Bridge at that time was the featherbed to end all featherbeds, and the only seam-bowling support for Alec Bedser came from Derek Shackleton and Norman Yardley—not exactly the most terrifying of opposition! And the supporting fire came from two good county leg-spinners, Eric Hollies and Roley Jenkins. Hollies bowled 43.4 overs to take two for 134—and one of those two was Alf Valentine who, as a batsman, rivalled Hollies himself!

I didn't see his 131 not out in a total of 297 on a difficult wicket at Georgetown in 1948, but they tell me it was a bit useful. I *did* see his 167

at Port of Spain in 1954, though, because I was on the receiving end of a lot of it, but I think the only man on either side who didn't make runs there was Bruce Pairaudeau who was run out for none!

Perhaps I might settle for Trent Bridge, 1957. We'd scored 619 for six with Tom Graveney getting a double century, and 'tons' for Peter Richardson and Peter May. Frank went in first for his side and carried his bat for 191 out of a total of 372, and as I got five for 63 I can tell you we didn't exactly make it easy for him.

He was a quick, athletic fielder and had a nice sense of humour. At Lords, in 1963, he raced Derek Shackleton down the pitch and won, to run him out and after knocking the bails off, he turned to Shack with a smile and complained that he was making an old 'un run about too much. Shack was pushing 40 at the time.

Sir Frank Mortimer Maglinne Worrell (1924–1967)

Barbados 1941–46; Jamaica 1947–62.
West Indies in West Indies 1947–48, 1952–53, 1953–54, 1954–55, 1959–60, 1961–62 (captain); in England 1950, 1957, 1963 (captain); in Australia 1951–52, 1960–61 (captain); in New Zealand 1951–52.

Test Record

	Ins	NO	HS	Runs	Av.	100s
Batting	87	9	261	3,860	49·48	9
Highest score	261 v. England (Trent Bridge) 1950					
Matches	51					
Bowling	69 wickets at 38·73					
Best bowling	7 for 70 v. England (Trent Bridge) 1957					

Career Figures

	Ins	NO	HS	Runs	Av.	100s
Batting	325	49	308*	15,025	54·43	39
1,000 runs in a season	4 times					
Bowling	349 wickets at 29·00					

Graceful batsman, languid style; left-arm medium-pace bowler; West Indies' first black captain. A leader of magnanimity and inspiration, concentrating the talents of ten others into a powerful team force, something new for Caribbean teams. Knighted in 1964. Universal grief at his early loss through leukemia.

Acknowledgment is due to the following for permission to reproduce photographs:

AUSTRALIAN INFORMATION SERVICE Davidson, page 221; BODLEIAN LIBRARY, OXFORD St Cuthbert, page 15; CAMERA PRESS Trueman, page 103, Statham, page 104; CENTRAL PRESS Benaud, page 212, Grout, page 230, Harvey, page 236, Lindwall, page 245, Sobers, page 257, Sutcliffe, page 263, Everton, page 275, Worrell, page 278; COOPER-BRIDGEMAN LIBRARY Moulseyhurst, page 129, Jubilee match, page 130, Eton, page 131, Lords, page 132–3; PATRICK EAGAR Richards, page 111, Thomson, page 115, Roberts, page 136; GEORGE HARRAP & CO. LTD England team, from 'The Noblest Game' by Neville Cardus and John Arlott, page 132; MCC 'Cricket in the Artillery Ground', page 23, Australian team, page 57, Giffen, page 59, Gloucestershire team, page 62, Trumper in action, page 81, Australian team, page 88, Bradman, page 93, ticket, page 121, cricket 1740, page 123, Shepheard's sketchbook, page 125, Beldham, page 126, Bedser, page 209; PRESS ASSOCIATION Rhodes & Hirst, page 79, McDonald, page 86, Gregory, page 87, Miller, page 99, Evans, page 224, Graveney, page 227, Hutton, page 239, Laker, page 242, Wardle, page 272; RADIO TIMES HULTON PICTURE LIBRARY Clarke, page 36, Brighton match, page 46–7, Maclaren, page 64, Stoddart, page 70, Jackson, page 77, Trumper (portrait), page 80, Hobbs, page 89, Hobbs & Sutcliffe, page 91, Grace, page 134, Spofforth, page 135, 'Pickwick' cricket, page 142, Arctic cricket, page 148, score book, page 150, Lancashire team, page 168, Barrington, page 206, Miller, page 251, Reid, page 254, Tayfield, page 266; SPORT & GENERAL PRESS AGENCY Lindwall, page 99, village cricket, page 190, Trueman, page 199, Bailey, page 203, Compton, page 215, Cowdrey, page 218, Hall, page 233, May, page 248, Statham, page 260, Walcott, page 269.

The photographs on the covers and pages 9, 130 (Rowlandson), 133 (four cricketers), 136 (Bradman) and 201 were photographed for the BBC by courtesy of John Arlott.

Acknowledgment is also due to the following:

AUTHOR for 'The Song of the Pitch' by Daniel Pettiward; J. M. DENT & SONS LTD for 'Village Cricket' by Gerald Bullett from *Collected Poems* (1959); LESLIE FREWIN for an extract from 'The Hill Down Under' by Jack Pollard, for 'The Honest Batsman' by Cardew Robinson, for an extract from 'Some Cricketing Yarns' from 'Three of the Best' by Brian Johnston, for 'Willow the King' by Herbert Farjeon and for cartoon by Artie on page 158 all from *The Boundary Book*; WILLIAM HEINEMANN LTD for 'A Time will come' by Arnold Wall from *The Pioneers* (1930); LADY HERBERT for 'Ninth Wicket' by A. P. Herbert from *Mild and Bitter* (published by Methuen 1936); DAVID HIGHAM ASSOCIATES LTD for 'Cricket in Cumberland' by Norman Nicholson; MISS MARGARET HUGHES for an extract from 'Lancashire Cricket' by Neville Cardus from *Second Innings* and an extract from *English Cricket* by Neville Cardus; MACMILLAN, LONDON AND BASINGSTOKE for an extract from *England, their England* by A. G. Macdonnel; OXFORD UNIVERSITY PRESS for 'The air is hushed' by R. W. Moore from *Trophy for an Unknown Soldier* (1952); A. D. PETERS & CO. for 'Pride of the Village' by Edmund Blunden; THE TIMES NEWSPAPERS LTD for an extract from 'Implements of Cricket' by H. J. Henley (The Times Supplement—MCC number, May 25, 1937); MELODISC RECORDS LTD for an extract from 'Calypso' by Egbert Moore from *Lord Beginner* (1950); PITMAN PUBLISHING LTD for an extract from 'Some Eccentric Matches' in *Odd Men In* by A. A. Thomson (published by Museum Press, 1958).